HOBBES AND CHRISTIANITY

HOBBES AND CHRISTIANITY

Reassessing the Bible in Leviathan

Paul D. Cooke

ROWMAN & LITTLEFIELD PUBLISHERS, INC.
Lanham • Boulder • New York • London

ROWMAN & LITTLEFIELD PUBLISHERS, INC.

Published in the United States of America
by Rowman & Littlefield Publishers, Inc.
4720 Boston Way, Lanham, Maryland 20706

3 Henrietta Street
London WC2E 8LU, England

British Cataloging in Publication Information Available

Library of Congress Cataloging-in-Publication Data

Cooke, Paul D.
Hobbes and Christianity : reassessing the Bible in Leviathan /
Paul D. Cooke.
p. cm.
Includes bibliographical references and index.
1. Hobbes, Thomas, 1588–1679. Leviathan. 2. Hobbes, Thomas,
1588–1679—Religion. 5. Philosophy and religion.
I. Title
JC153.H659C66 1996 320.1—dc20 96-12031 CIP

ISBN 0-8476-8196-3 (cloth : alk. paper)
ISBN 0-8476-8197-1 (pbk. : alk. paper)

Printed in the United States of America

⊚ ™ The paper used in this publication meets the minimum requirements
of American National Standard for Information Sciences—Permanence of
Paper for Printed Library Materials, ANSI Z39.48-1984.

For Ruth

That subjects owe to sovereigns, simple obedience, in all things, wherein their obedience is not repugnant to the laws of God, I have sufficiently proved, in that which I have already written. There wants only, for the entire knowledge of civil duty, to know what are those laws of God. For without that, a man knows not, when he is commanded any thing by the civil power, whether it be contrary to the law of God, or not; and so, either by too much civil obedience, offends the Divine Majesty, or through fear of offending God, transgresses the commandments of the commonwealth. To avoid both these rocks, it is necessary to know what are the laws divine.

—*Leviathan*, chapter 31

If one prophet deceive another, what certainty is there of knowing the will of God, by other way than that of reason?

—*Leviathan*, chapter 32

Contents

Preface

Hobbes's *Leviathan* may be said to be a work of great beneficence, of well-wishing, and, indeed, of hope, for humanity. This consideration is paradoxical, for Hobbes's hopes for mankind are paired with his understanding that human beings are burdened and troubled with incorrigible inclinations out of which they forge the instruments of their own destruction and unhappiness. In this pairing of hope with full awareness of burden, Hobbes seems to assume a biblical dimension, for like Scripture, he finds a way to build something good out of the most discordant matter and, as with Scripture, the building is done on nothing, if not on the profoundest acceptance of human limitations.

In America, Hobbes's beneficence, based on the acceptance of the incorrigible limitations of men and women and on the notion that these same men and women possess natural rights, has found good soil and produced good fruit. His hopes, by means of the political reasoning he created, for cultivating enduring peace and safety for the harvesting of the goods of the earth, for reaping the products of arts and letters, for finding knowledge of nature, and for guaranteeing the liberty of the individual human being, have been to a great extent realized in America because the American founders, following Hobbes by way of John Locke, took human beings as they are, not as many said they ought to be. Hobbes, one of the great modern apostles of "taking men as they are," fashioned out of those bare bones a kind of salvation based on the natural rights of man whereby human beings can be the best they are capable of being, given what they are; that kind of salvation is best exemplified by the liberal polity founded on the American Constitution.

In taking human beings as they are, Hobbes also knew what good

Calvinists know, what the great Jewish prophet Jeremiah knew, and, indeed, what the New Testament teaches, that the human heart is deceitful above all things and that out of it proceed murders, adulteries, thefts, false witness, and so on. Thomas Hobbes is a rude awakener concerning sweet dreams of who and what human beings can be. He shows us we are all potential blackguards, to use an old-fashioned word—we just may not all know it. If we think we could be no such thing, perhaps it is only because we have not found ourselves in the state of nature, or because we have been too cowardly to act on our impulses; the protection of civilization makes it easier to preserve one's innocence.

Though the Scriptures and Hobbes are in agreement about the nature of what St. Paul calls "the old man," "the carnal man," and "the natural man"—our blackguard selves—it has become clear to me that, unlike the Scriptures, Hobbes is concerned above all to make this world a place that is safe for this natural, carnal, old man, once his natural tendencies have been safely checked. My study of Hobbes's treatment of the Bible has led me to the conviction that, in order to set forth principles that will establish peace and safety in this world on a new foundation to make it safe for human beings as they are, Hobbes finally limits the Bible to supporting and justifying this goal. While the Christian gospel does seem to represent an interest in saving all human beings from the war of all against all Hobbes describes in the famous thirteenth chapter of *Leviathan*, the aim of authentic Christianity, I believe, extends finally beyond a teaching about what men *are* to one about what they *ought to be*. This teaching involves the supplanting of the "old, natural, carnal" man by the "new man," who is Christ.

The Christian teaching concerning supplanting the natural man with a "new man" is not infrequently described as a mystery—something Hobbes has almost no use for—and it certainly is not a natural solution to the problem of who this natural man is. Hobbes, however, has a natural solution: it is called "the science of natural justice," it is found out by "political reasoning," it is based on the natural rights of man, and it was first discovered by Hobbes in a place called "the state of nature." While the biblical solution, the unnatural, or supernatural solution, *begins* with the notion that human beings are, even as Hobbes and St. Paul might say of them, blackguards, it *ends* by teaching that people may be something else, indeed, they *ought* to be something else. If one compares carefully *Leviathan*, chapter 13, with Romans 3:9–19 and 7:15–25, this understanding of the differences between Hobbes's teaching and that of Scripture may begin to emerge. This study reveals more fully the distinction we introduce here.

Hobbes is concerned finally to make the world safe for human beings as they are fundamentally in the state of nature, though he does this by appreciably limiting their natural liberty so that he might maximize the exercise of the largest possible degree of that liberty *in safety*. His aim is not to change what men and women are but to understand and order civil association so as to channel and check human inclinations to make their own blackguard nature less dangerous and, even, less apparent.

Hobbes will not accept the proposition that human beings "ought" to be fundamentally something other than he finds them in the state of nature of *Leviathan*, chapter 13. He is convinced that too many violations of the natural man's liberty are perpetrated by lovers of power over others in the name of what men ought to be. Those who think they know the answer, once given political power, are for Hobbes precisely the problem. Hobbes would rather accept men as they are; it is safer that way, at least regarding this world's peace and safety.

The question then, if one accepts human beings as they are, is, how can the world be made safe for such beings? The answer Hobbes suggests is presented in his teaching concerning the generation of the commonwealth on the basis of the principles of natural rights outlined in the first half of *Leviathan*. But once he has given this answer, he adds a corollary: "pay attention to religion." The second half of *Leviathan* may be understood as Hobbes's teaching and warning that religion is the one great thing necessary to guarantee the success of the project he inaugurates in the first half of *Leviathan*. This study of the Bible and Christianity in Hobbes's *Leviathan* considers the importance of religion to Hobbes's "science" for making the world safe for human beings as they are.

My exploration of *Leviathan* also will show Hobbes to be a teacher of the autonomy or masterlessness of man. I believe that in *Leviathan*, Hobbes disguises a tension between Christianity and human autonomy or masterlessness in order to preserve religion for its utility to his "science of natural justice." Religion for Hobbes, then, is a tool; it is not fundamental to his thought. But why does Hobbes find religion so important when his political reasoning is founded on human masterlessness? I seek to answer this question is the ten chapters ahead.

Understanding Hobbes concerning human beings and religion is important because the liberal society of which men and women today are beneficiaries is founded on ideas concerning rights and the purposes of government that were first established by Hobbes. If Hobbes inaugurated the teaching from which our understanding of human rights developed—a teaching that forms the basis for what is often termed classical liberalism—then we do well to study the kind of religion he betrothed to it in order to understand the nature and foundation of liberal principles more fully. But what kind of religion *did* Hobbes marry to the project of his science of natural justice? Is it authentic Christianity?

The late Judith Shklar, after reading this study in its original form, told me, "Bishop Bramhall would have been proud of you." Professor Shklar, I think, was right: Hobbes's great seventeenth-century adversary at least would have approved of this because it reaffirms what he argued almost 350 years ago: that the religion Hobbes teaches does not constitute Christianity and that, indeed, Hobbes's theology aims at something else entirely.

It is true that a growing number of contemporary Hobbes scholars believe that Hobbes was a Christian—and even an orthodox one— and that *Leviathan* reflects this. It is evident by now that such a view is rejected here. Part of the purpose of this study is to show that Hobbes authored a kind of conspiracy against authentic Christianity in the name of his science of natural justice and the rights of man, and that those who accept Hobbes's treatment of religion as ingenuous have been taken in by his deception. I wish to show that, indeed, this was as Hobbes intended.

It is a pleasure to acknowledge the assistance of institutions, teachers, colleagues, friends, and family who helped me as I wrote this book. The National Graduate Fellowship created by the U. S. government, later known as the Jacob Javits Fellowship, provided generous funding for four years of graduate study at Harvard during which I did the research necessary for this study. I am grateful for the support provided by friends and colleagues at the University of Houston over the past three years. I appreciate especially the assistance of Professor Ted Estess, dean of the Honors College, and Professor Kent Tedin, chairman of the Political Science Department.

The Reverend Joseph Wall first showed me the Bible was a book of the greatest depth. The Reverend Samuel Abbott reminded me of that depth. Edward and Laura Banfield's friendship gave me a kind of assistance that had nothing to do with Hobbes. John Danford, through his teaching and friendship, first interested me in reading Hobbes and in the study of political philosophy. Harvey Mansfield, Jr., encouraged my studies and advised this project when it was a doctoral thesis. His careful comments gave me indispensable guidance. Samuel Beer's hearty advice helped get me started, while Judith Shklar made thoughtful challenges to my argument, which encouraged me to make this a more solid study. I also wish to acknowledge an anonymous reader engaged by Rowman and Littlefield whose written remarks were very helpful. These scholars and friends helped me and, directly or indirectly, strengthened my work; its weaknessess are all my own.

My mother and father, Patricia and Ezra Cooke, unfailingly supported my scholarly endeavors with love and encouragement. Henry and Barbara Delfiner have shown me heartfelt kindness again and again. Finally, to my wife, Ruth Delfiner, whose love sustains me, and to our daughter Emma, I owe more than I can say.

Chapter One

Introduction: Human Rights and Biblical Religion in *Leviathan*

The Tension Between Human Rights and Biblical Religion

In the first half of Thomas Hobbes's *Leviathan*, the rights of man form the basis for his argument concerning how and why civil society comes into being. But in the second half he seems to make a second beginning to his work as he turns to the subjects of God, religion, Christianity, and the Bible. He treats these themes for another 350 pages, virtually doubling the length of his masterpiece.

The meaning of the second half and its relation to the first half has been the subject of vigorous discussion among students of Hobbes's work in recent years. So far, no one in the debate has considered the relationship between the two halves as a disputation between the subjects they treat—the rights of man, which I claim to be the theme of the first half, and the teachings of Christianity, which all agree is the principal subject of the second. This is not to say that the second half and the first are in tension, but rather that their subjects are. Hobbes's treatment of the subject of the second half—the Bible—does away with this tension by reinterpreting the teachings of Christianity to make them support the idea implicitly set forth in the first half of *Leviathan*, that human beings are endowed by God with rights and that they possess naturally an astonishing degree of freedom.

This study does not treat principally the issue of rights, but rather Hobbes's treatment of religion, specifically his treatment of the Bible in *Leviathan*. Hobbes's treatment of rights enters in only as it elucidates his representation of religion and the Bible. This work advances three claims, the first being that Hobbes presents a reinter-

1

pretation of the Bible in *Leviathan*. Hobbes suggests that human beings should be understood in a new way, as endowed by God with natural rights. Natural rights, in Hobbes's order, occupy the highest possible rank, providing the justification for all moral and political life. Secondly, while Hobbes elevates rights, he implicitly, if not explicitly, dethrones God and the Bible from any positions of supreme authority. Finally, in making natural rights, and not responsibility to God, the foundation for thinking about the human situation and civil association, Hobbes reveals the true character of his teaching about man and his rights: that his work is in tension with revealed religion. By exposing the tension between Hobbes's rights teaching and his treatment of revealed religion, we may understand the magnitude of the challenge religion presented to Hobbes in his political thought—and presents to all forms of political association.

The Appropriation of the Bible to Serve Human Rights

In Thomas Hobbes's *Leviathan*, civil associations are to be ruled by a natural reason that discovers natural laws that Hobbes equates with the word of God. Hobbes bases the actions taken by natural reason, finally, on the natural right of each human individual to preserve himself above all. Though Hobbes teaches that God does not make demands on human beings that are contrary to these laws of nature and to the natural rights they serve, if we examine Hobbes's laws of nature and the principle of natural rights they serve, we find them in great tension with the biblical view that there are higher principles than self-preservation and the right to self. Though Christianity does not disallow the legitimacy of self-defense, it does not place it at the heart, or as the basis, of man's civil life as does Hobbes. The Christian faith teaches that the right to oneself is the principal thing a person must give up to be a disciple of Christ. The stamp of true faith is the capacity to waive one's own rights; indeed, the life of faith ends up in the annihilation of the *right* to oneself: "If any man will come after me, let him deny himself, and take up his cross daily, and follow me. For whosoever will save his life shall lose it; but whosoever will lose his life for my sake, the same shall save it" (Luke 9:23–24). The Bible views insisting on what Hobbes would call one's rights as *natural*, but it calls on human beings to do the *unnatural* thing.

But in Hobbes's hands the Bible is transformed. It covers the coarse and stark truth of the foundations of his political thought to make the law of self-preservation holy and transcendent; it hallows it. By means of his explanation of the Bible, Hobbes elevates the meaning of self-preservation, which is central to human rights, thus placing rights at the center of what God does for man, and hallowing the freedom of the individual in a new way.

There is nothing very noble or glorious about this seed from which modern liberalism first grew, based on the naked law of self-preservation. There is nothing to sacrifice for, no higher meaning to live for. But by clothing this bare body with the vestments of the Bible, making the Scriptures fit it, Hobbes lends to these principles a sense of the glory that once was reserved for the biblical kingdom of God alone. To be stirring, to be beautiful, to be loveable, the teaching of the rights of man must be clothed in something that hints at the glorious, the beautiful, the lovely. The Bible provides transcendence and inspires human beings to do what the laws of self-preservation do not do very well—to love one's neighbor, to see beauty in selflessness, to see loveliness in sacrifice.

But Hobbes's basing man's political life in the fear of violent death at the hands of men and the passion for safety and for self-preservation has the effect of calling attention more to the common and basic instincts than to the more elevated and distinctly human characteristics. The law of self-preservation is not easily made into the basis for a view dedicated to beauty, glory, honor, truth, or virtue. With the fear of violent death at the hands of human beings placed as the basis of political association, it seems probable that the people who participate in such a society will tend to lead lives characterized by a respect for such a principle and the consequent demotion of other principles that might rival it.

Hobbes understood that building on this low but solid foundation was not enough either to mitigate the fears of the individual facing natural death or to entirely safeguard against the behavior that leads to violent, unnatural death; for this mitigation of fears and the further safeguarding of civil society, a religion was needed. Hobbes supplies this religion—a new understanding of God, nature's God, to bless a new view of man.[1]

I will show that Hobbes reinterprets the teachings of Christianity to demonstrate that biblical teachings and the biblical God are not in tension with natural rights and that, inasmuch as human beings are therefore hindered by no impediments from God, they are endowed with an astonishing freedom. It is important to be more explicit about what freedom and natural rights mean for Hobbes as

part of the effort to eventually make clear the meaning of the
second half of *Leviathan*.

On Freedom and Natural Rights in *Leviathan*

Freedom (or liberty) in the state of nature of Hobbes's *Leviathan*
means a natural freedom of the human passions from duties to any
higher authority than the self-interest of the individual.[2] This would
mean not only a natural freedom for self-defense, but also a natural
freedom to attack and subjugate others. For Hobbes, human beings
in the state of nature only lay down some degree of natural freedom
in order to maximize the safe exercise of rights, that is, to advance
the safe exercise of defense of ourselves and the safe exercise of
competition whereby we triumph and glory over others. Natural
rights in Hobbes's *Leviathan* mean a complete freedom from
thoughts of duty that might interfere with the satisfaction of the
demands of the passions; in fact, thought is to be employed principally to find the best way to satisfy the passions (EW III, 61–62
[139], 197 [262–63]). Conceiving of ourselves in thoughts that limit
our freedom to satisfy our passions for any other reason than
maximizing the safe exercise of that freedom is, finally, nothing
more than a violation of our natural rights. This view of human
freedom constitutes the key element of Hobbes's view of man.

In considering Hobbes's establishment of human freedom, the
first and most considerable feature to take account of must be that
such freedom can only exist if there is no one "There" who might
represent a restraint on such liberty. As one commentator has put
it, "Once he realizes his true situation, his 'natural condition
concerning his felicity and misery,' he becomes filled with fear
indeed, but with a kind of fear which points the way toward its
overcoming: the stupendous whole which oppresses him lacks
intelligence" (Strauss 1959, 181). Once the "God who is There"—
the biblical God—is discovered to be no master over human beings
at all (and is, indeed, the hoax used for the perpetuation of the
power of those who use human fear of invisible spirits to secure
themselves), man's "rights" appear, by default of the former established object of human responsibility and duty.

If there is no natural master, indeed, no master at all over human
beings, then men and women are by nature free. Rights only appear
when God is gone, if not dead, and man is alone. These remarks

indicate what this writer understands to be the implicit content of *Leviathan;* the task of this study is to substantiate these conclusions, but we shall outline our view further before proceeding to our explanation.

By what knowledge could Hobbes have come to the conclusion that man is alone in the universe? Hobbes's study of human psychology teaches him and reveals to us, first of all, that by reason human beings can know nothing of God and, second, that religion and God are the inventions of human anxiety.[3] Finally, a careful study of the third part of *Leviathan* reveals that Hobbes believed he had knowledge that the religion taught by biblical revelation is so subject to doubt for so many reasons that the wise cannot believe it. Though these three reasons supporting the claim that Hobbes teaches that human beings are alone in the cosmos are set forth in *Leviathan,* each is, as soon and as often as it is expressed, quickly obfuscated by Hobbes's deft hand, lest the foundation of his understanding of man and nature be too plainly seen, and thus the utility of his project, not to mention its author's safety, be lost. Together, these three reasons teach us of the natural freedom and masterlessness of man. Here, in a few words, is the essence of Hobbes's humanism; without God, man is alone and free. Apart from this "theological fact," the word freedom may finally have only little importance for Hobbes's thought. We may be bound by the passions that drive us, but we are left free—very free—to find the best way to their satisfaction; no authority naturally or divinely limits our choices.

Human beings are thus left without a master to hinder them and they are thus left quite alone to confront all of nature. This means that man's chief interest is no longer to know God. Thus we may say the fear of God and the knowledge of the holy are no longer the beginning of wisdom for man; knowledge of what human beings owe God and knowledge of what they owe each other *under* God is no longer the beginning of what constitutes a wise man or woman (Prov. 1:7, 9:10). When human beings leave the biblical universe where men and women in the first place have duties, and enter the Hobbesian universe in which human beings in the first instance have rights, we take a gigantic step and knowledge now has a new end. Formerly, the fear of God was the beginning of wisdom, which suggests the mastery of self for the purpose of pleasing God. But now fear of death at the hands of men and the understanding of human beings concomitant with this realization suggest that wisdom is not mastery of self but a kind of necessary egoism that is satisfied only by mastering other men. Now, human beings are understood to be estranged fundamentally from notions of duty to man and conceive of themselves as possessors of rights, which is to say, as possessors of a natural freedom to use power without any responsibility to anyone. Men and women who see themselves in this way also understand that other human beings view the world in the same way. Human beings who conceive of themselves as possessors of rights are thus estranged from the world around them, which was only a home for them because God, as a parent, presided over it and gave them a place in it. They are also estranged from other human beings, having no way of conceiving of duties to men except through an understanding that obligations to others are constituted solely through self-interest. The end of wisdom for such human beings is no longer knowledge of the holy; it is, rather, knowledge of how to triumph over others, or find safety from them.

When the lawyer in the Gospel of St. Matthew asked Jesus what the great commandment was, he answered, "Love God with all your heart. This is the first and great commandment. And the second is like unto it, Thou shalt love thy neighbor as thyself" (Matt. 22:37–40). The great end of knowledge in the biblical view is love. Mastery of the self was for the end of love—the love of both God and man. But Hobbes teaches that love can no longer be part of the equation. Knowledge is no longer ruled by a duty to love, but by the need for human beings to remain secure in their masterlessness. No doubt the biblical view values safety, too, but the end of knowledge in this view is mastery of self for the sake of wisdom, a wisdom that begins with "the fear of the Lord." The essence of Hobbes's humanism may be said to be that knowledge of the state of nature, and not of the holy, is the beginning of wisdom.

In the state of nature then, human appetites and aversions operate unhindered by any moral restraints; human passions know no law but their own satisfaction. Natural rights refer to the freedom the passions know when there are no impediments to their exercise whatever. But there is something other than law made by God that can restrain the passions; there is the entire gamut of external impediments in the form, among other things, of the bodies and wills of other passionate human beings. Any study of these by men and women conceived as finding themselves in the state of nature will teach human beings a set of rules, which Hobbes calls articles of peace or natural laws. These will restrain the passions and teach human beings to limit their natural rights to actions understood as only self-defense. But Hobbes's beginning place is before the chief meaning of natural rights becomes the right to self-defense.

Before natural rights becomes a term to describe the right to self-defense, we should be able to see that the term indicates the right to exercise power for the purpose of self-satisfaction. The term "natural rights" indicates not only the liberty each human being has to use his or her power for the preservation of life, but also the liberty a person has for doing *anything* he or she judges will satisfy him or her. This is why in chapter 13, while Hobbes observes that in desiring something, most men's end is "principally their own conservation," he adds that sometimes it is "their delectation only" (EW III, 111 [184]). In either case, human beings may endeavor to destroy or subdue others to obtain their ends, and in either case, they are doing nothing more than exercising their natural rights. Natural rights in both cases mean the liberty a person has to use his own power. The end or aim of life is simply to keep on exercising one's power because there is pleasure in self-satisfaction. The experience of impediments in the pursuit of satisfaction, however, teaches human beings fear, and so self-preservation, and not "delectation," tends to become the chief concern of the exercise of natural rights.

Hobbes wrote that men become inclined to civil obedience not only because they fear death and seek safety, but also because they "desire . . . ease, and sensual delight" (EW III, 86 [161]). In fact, Hobbes speaks of desire for ease and sensual delight *before* he speaks in the same paragraph of "fear of death, and wounds," and he says that men enter into civil society to escape the latter *because* they want the former. This is so for Hobbes in spite of the fact that he considers the most powerful passion to be fear of violent death at the hands of human beings. Thus, rights are to be understood, first of all, as the freedom to exercise power for the satisfaction of desires, and next, for the sake of self-defense.

Hobbes says right is to be understood in contradistinction to law. The relation of right to law, he says, is like that of liberty to obligation; right, then, is like liberty. Law binds; to have a right is to be unbound, to be free of obligation, and Hobbes's natural-rights teaching indicates just how unbound, how free, human passions are.

Rights, then, for Hobbes, are what human beings have when they have nothing else, or, to put it another way, they are what human beings begin with or have first; and knowing one's rights is the beginning of wisdom. Though everything else may render men and women unequal, human beings lose all distinguishing characteristics and are understood as all the same when viewed through Hobbes's concept of rights. Human beings once might have been considered fundamentally equal because God created them as living souls having equal value to Him, but Hobbes introduces a new basis for equality: all human beings are equal because each has equal freedom to use his or her power as each will.

On the State of Nature

We may say all these things are so because Hobbes teaches us of a place, a new world, where his observations of equality and his perception of natural rights became so clear that he could postulate them as the first axioms of all political life—indeed, as self-evident. In the title of the thirteenth chapter of *Leviathan*, Hobbes called the place where he discovered these truths "the Natural Condition of Mankind"; we have shortened this, with John Locke's encouragement, to "the state of nature." In Hobbes's state of nature, all differences between men and women were abrogated and human beings revealed naked and free in such a way as had not been celebrated in literature before, with the exception, based on a different vision, of the images originally found in the earliest chapters of Genesis. We can begin to see the evidence for all that we have suggested above concerning the meaning of freedom and natural rights for Hobbes by looking closely at this state of nature. Men and women are free there because there is no obligation at all to obey any law. Men and women are naked there because there are no vestments of law, no shadow of sin, no anxiety of guilt; human beings are there able to give natural freedom full reign.

Hobbes writes, "Where there is no common power, there is no law" (EW III, 115 [188]). But, as we have indicated, freedom from obligation to a lawmaking power does not mean there are no limits to freedom, no limits to the liberty of human behavior; on the contrary, because of the initial freedom each person possesses there, if any two persons come into competition for the same things that they cannot both enjoy, they "endeavor to destroy or subdue one another," since there is no person nor power, no government nor god to prevent this (EW III, 111 [184]). The liberty of one person inevitably clashes with that of another where there is complete liberty from law; in such a state, ultimately, human beings compete among themselves on every side for possessions, glory, and honor and, finding the power of other persons at least as great as their own in that each is subject to the secret machinations of others who may wish to do them harm, each learns to fear all.

In this state of nature, freedom leads to quarrel and fear and finally to war, "and such a war, as is of every man against every man" (EW III, 112–13 [185]). Viewing Hobbes's state of nature, we see that the greatest hindrance to each person's freedom is the freedom of every other human being. We see there is great danger in freedom; Hobbes shows it to be so dangerous that the most important thing in each person's heart is to escape it, and this, Hobbes teaches, is how civil association originates.

Hobbes claimed to have discovered the full and true extent of natural freedom, the maximization of which, coexisting with the greatest possible safety, was the reason why human beings are united into political societies. Thus, for Hobbes the passions of human beings are unrestrained by any law, but are restrainable by the fact that all human beings are equally free. Out of this freedom and equality, Hobbes fashions peace and safety.

In a poem celebrating Hobbes, his contemporary Abraham Cowley called him "Thou great Columbus of the Golden Lands of New Philosophies" (*True Effigies* 1680, 4).[4] The golden land Hobbes discovered was no new geographical place, but, as Hobbes called it, an "inference, made from the passions" (EW III, 113–14 [186]). He admits such a "locale" may seem strange to his readers, but he asks them to consider their own behavior as a kind of proof of its existence. Hobbes offers the argument that men's own actions suggest that the freedom and equality of the state of nature truly exists and that the character of human beings to be viewed in the state of nature can also be viewed all around them in the civil society in which they live if they will only consider the change that would occur in the quality of their lives if fear of the highest legislative power and its police arm and the gravity of the order such power has established, were removed. "Read thyself," Hobbes again advises:

> Let him therefore consider with himself, when taking a journey, he arms himself, and seeks to go well accompanied; when going to sleep, he locks his doors; when even in his house he locks his chests; and this when he knows there be lawes, and public officers, armed, to

revenge all injuries shall be done him; what opinion he has of his fellow subjects, when he rides armed; of his fellow citizens, when he locks his doors; and of his children, and servants, when he locks his chests. Does he not there as much accuse mankind by his actions, as I do by my words? (EW III, 114 [186–87])

By these words, Hobbes shows human beings are ultimately unprejudiced in regarding others with fear—all are equally suspect. At the same time, he shows that all human beings regard all others as potentially astonishingly free—capable of actions that conform to no other law than that of their own interests. We all believe in an astonishing human freedom and equality, Hobbes indicates, only we do not realize it because our natural state is hidden from us by the power that legislates law and enforces it, a power that cultivates additionally the cultural habits that also hide our natural state from us.

The state of nature is a "golden land" and Hobbes a new "Columbus" to the praising poet because in this uncomely discovery Hobbes finds something of great value: an understanding of the human heart leading to the only sure foundation upon which peace and safety can be guaranteed. Thus, Cowley's poem celebrates Hobbes's work of discovery as far greater than that of Columbus:

> *Thy task was harder much than his;*
> *For thy learn'd America is*
> *Not only found out first by Thee,*
> *And rudely left to future Industry;*
> *But thy Eloquence, and thy Wit*
> *Has planted, people, built and civilized it.*
> *(True Effigies* 1680, 4)

Hobbes has discovered a new land and from it brought back something golden, more valuable than all the gold those following after Columbus brought back from their new world. Hobbes discovered a more sure foundation for human society, something human beings had not formerly thought could possibly form the sole basis for civil association, since it was something so common, simple, and low: the appetites and aversions that all share most of all—fear of violence and death at the hands of human beings and the desire for peace and safety. In demonstrating this new basis for civil life, Hobbes turned away from considerations of what human beings ought to be; his foundation is on what they are. Hobbes's foundation in what all share is itself based on the propositions that all human beings are equal and are by nature free. Since human beings who are by nature free and equal will always want to avoid the natural consequence—the state of nature—of this equality and freedom, out of passionate desire for self-preservation a true science of politics may be born. This suggests how much Hobbes expects from politics, and perhaps this expectation is so great because he asks very little of it. He wishes to exploit the fear of violent death only to cultivate a political realm that aims above all for peace and safety. Thus, self-preservation, a fallback position taken by human freedom aware of the dangers of its own extensiveness, is the new basis for civil association announced by Hobbes.

Politics are no longer to be based on a foundation in religion or in images of honor that human beings should uphold; these old standards are replaced by a new basis, one far more egalitarian, one that invites more individuals than ever before to agree upon it—nearly all individuals, in fact, for who can fail to agree that staying alive is a good thing? But let us not fail to understand the ultimate implication of Hobbes's innovation: the matter of what staying alive is *for* is now no longer to be of principal importance. All standards other than peace and safety have been demoted, obfuscated, made light of, and subordinated. We shall return to this implication, for a study of Hobbes's treatment of religion will reveal that this new implicit standard must be hidden for the sake of a prosperous civil association.

Hobbes builds his argument for a new basis for civil association on a lowest common denominator, reckoning that most human beings most of the time fear violent death at the hands of man more than anything else. In *Leviathan* (1651) this reckoning is stated in chapter 13, but it was the very first chapter of *De Cive* (1642), the preceding version of Hobbes's political philosophy, indicating the primacy of the state of nature for Hobbes's thought. In *Leviathan*, the state of nature remains the foundation of his political philosophy as it was in *De Cive*. Only, in *Leviathan*, Hobbes added an important "preface"—the first twelve chapters—attempting to show that his discovery about human liberty and human passions, especially the fear of death, is actually substantiated by the very laws of physics, the most fundamental natural laws of all.

Hobbes's argument from physics is intended to prove the truth of his discovery about the passions (or human psychology), and hence of the worth of this discovery as a foundation for politics. The edifice Hobbes builds on top of the state of nature thus finds support in a human psychology built upon the laws governing all matter. The state of nature in this sense appears to be substantiated by natural science and is to be seen as a scientific discovery, since it seems ultimately to be supported by the laws of physics Hobbes introduced in the very first chapter of *Leviathan*. Hobbes makes the state of nature appear to explain the origin of human government on the evidence of human nature, which is itself explained by a mechanical materialism expressed through the most fundamental physical laws.[5] The first twelve chapters of *Leviathan*, by supplying a new account of the inner workings of man, only underscore the pivotal importance of the place Cowley celebrates. The state of nature becomes a "golden land" because it places Hobbes's new understanding of man in a social context, revealing his further discovery within it: a promise for a new way to peace and safety.

We have stressed the meaning of rights and freedom here because Hobbes's natural-rights teaching, at the heart of the first half of *Leviathan*, is of great importance for understanding the meaning of the treatment of the Bible in the second half of the work. We come now to the principal theme of this study: in light of the understanding of natural rights and freedom that we have traced above, what is the meaning and purpose of Hobbes's treatment of the Bible in *Leviathan*?

"To Avoid Both These Rocks": Hobbes's Treatment of the Bible

Building on the foundation of the state of nature in chapter 13, Hobbes erected the great system of his political thought over the next eighteen chapters of *Leviathan*. In these chapters, he shows how, beginning from natural rights, government is generated from human freedom and fear, partly by means of passion and partly by means of reason. Yet after chapter 31, the last chapter of the part of his work entitled "Of Commonwealth," his work apparently complete, he does not finally conclude but rather embarks on a new part entitled "Of a Christian Commonwealth." Here he begins a treatment of the Bible and Christianity that continues for sixteen more chapters, doubling the size of the book. Why does he seem to begin again? Or, more to our point, why must human freedom, why must human rights and the generation of human government, be joined to a complicated and very lengthy study of the Bible?

Hobbes seems to have recognized that provision for an account of the whole of being constituted under the rubric of religion is essential to the success of his project. Hobbes taught that human fear and anxiety about death, which he called the "seed of religion," are inescapable, and thus the public demand for religion—for some "story" that accounts for the political realm and the purpose and meaning of life—is inescapable. For Hobbes, no political association can afford to ignore or discount the need for an account of the whole, that is, religion, which most human beings, when fearful, will always turn to. Hobbes considers man to possess an incorrigibly religious nature; this is made most clear in the twelfth chapter of *Leviathan*. While there are exceptions to this in particular individuals, even as there are exceptions to the predominance of fear of violent death at the hands of men in some individuals, Hobbes clearly seems to believe that most human beings will be as faithful to the principle of religious inclination as they are to the principle of fear of violent death. If political association does not harness religion for its own preservation, Hobbes suggests, political association will become the target of dangerous passions religion inevitably attracts to itself. These passions potentially generate divisions of loyalty among citizens that then threaten public peace and safety, and ultimately can lead to the dissolution of society into a state of nature. Unwisely governed religion can be fatal to civil association.

Hobbes thus connected a reinterpretation of the Bible (*Leviathan*, parts 3 and 4) to his teaching about human rights (*Leviathan*, parts 1 and 2) so that religion may be wisely governed and human beings may clearly know where their duties lie. In joining together in civil association, human beings take on obligations—duties—by laying down rights in order to maximize their safe exercise of natural rights. Civil duties or obligations, then, are for the sake of maximizing natural rights or the freedom of the individual. The effectiveness of civil association as a guarantor of peace and safety depends upon citizens knowing and performing their civil duties. The last half of *Leviathan* is evidence that Hobbes thinks the greatest threat to citizens' performance of the duties necessary for the preservation of civil association comes from the susceptibility of men to persuasion that their duties to God have priority over any other responsibility. Hobbes treats religion with such care in order to make it clear where human loyalties must finally lie. This task requires great

delicacy, for Hobbes knows that to tread in any other way concerning human belief in invisible worlds is neither safe nor wise. He
speaks of this vital issue in the concluding chapter of the first half
of *Leviathan* with a metaphor that has Homeric tones, indicating
the ship of commonwealth must sail between two great threats.

Hobbes writes that if human beings think the civil power commands them to break divine laws, they will think their civil obedience "offends the Divine Majesty." Hobbes indicates that human
beings must not be made to feel *that*. On the other hand, they may
disobey the civil power for fear of offending God, and this is the
source of the very greatest danger to civil peace and safety and must
be avoided with the greatest diligence. Hobbes writes, "To avoid
both these rocks it is necessary to know what are the lawes divine"
(EW III, 343 [395]).[6] Hobbes's concern with reinterpreting the Bible
may thus be said to reflect his conviction that political association
must be properly connected to the religious needs of human beings,
but that above all, these teachings must be made consistent with
his teaching about the human situation summarized in his discussion of the state of nature and the human rights he found there.

Throughout *Leviathan*, Hobbes teaches a pattern in his treatment
of the Bible for the correct relationship between rights and religion.
In the second half of *Leviathan*, he established the procedure for the
safe channeling of the passions most susceptible to religion in order
to "avoid both these rocks." Hobbes's teaching is that religion must
not be allowed to challenge the standard set by politics while at the
same time teaching how seriously religion must be taken. Hobbes's
Leviathan is based on an awareness of a fundamental tension
between biblical religion and natural rights; the great purpose of his
reinterpretation of the Bible in the second half of *Leviathan* is to
hide this tension for the sake of the political project he hoped to
inaugurate. Understanding this disguise is also part of our aim in
this study.

In chapter 2, we will introduce the growing controversy concerning Hobbes's treatment of religion (this subject is an increasingly
popular and contentious one in Hobbes studies). It will prove worthwhile to discuss this controversy in order to establish the context
and relevance of our own exploration of the issue. In chapter 3, we
will then study Hobbes's state of nature to argue that deity plays no
role in establishing the obligations that get human beings out of
that state and into civil association. In chapter 4, we shall show,
inasmuch as Hobbes does speak of God in the context of the state

of nature and the laws of nature, that he does so with intentionally deceptive ambiguity. After discussing these things, we shall then begin our examination of Hobbes's treatment of the Bible in the second half of *Leviathan* in order to show the tension between that treatment and the tenets of authentic Christianity. In all these explorations we shall explain further why Hobbes's antipathy to biblical religion is disguised to appear as genuinely religious.

The original tension between the teaching of natural rights—which teaching Hobbes inaugurated—and revealed religion is still not plain to see today, in part because Hobbes treated this tension with such care. In contemporary America, the polity *par excellence* founded on the natural rights Hobbes discovered, men and women still take the statement of the Declaration of Independence regarding natural rights as an expression of self-evident truth—rights come from God; among such persons this rights-endowing deity is almost universally associated, though in a loose sort of way, with the deity of the Bible. The original tension between biblical religion and human rights is not plain to see to this vaster audience, even today, in part because of a reinterpretation of the Bible inaugurated by Thomas Hobbes nearly four hundred years ago, which was later taken over by the more broadly recognized founders of liberalism. But it was Hobbes who originally and skillfully appropriated Scripture to hide the antagonism between the two views of the world represented by Christian faith and natural—or human—rights, making that antipathy far harder to apprehend. The one thing, above all, that our study seeks to do is to make this antipathy between Hobbes's thought and biblical religion easier to apprehend.

Chapter Two

The Controversy Concerning Hobbes and Christianity

An Introduction to the Controversy:
Leviathan and Three Kinds of Readers

This book explores a specific problem in Hobbes's thought and its significance, a problem that was born among his nineteenth-century readers and has now become one of the major areas of contemporary Hobbes studies: the role of religion in his political thought, and, more specifically, the meaning of the entire second half of *Leviathan*, which deals exclusively with the Bible.

Hobbes extensively incorporated the Bible in his work principally because he was very much aware of the tension between natural rights and biblical revelation and understood the great importance of easing it. In order to ease this tension Hobbes engaged in a kind of "conspiracy" against orthodox Christianity. He reinterpreted the Bible to ally it with the human freedom represented by natural rights, deliberately disguising the original tension between Christianity and his new teaching.

I hope to reveal this disguise anew, for it was originally understood as only a disguise in Hobbes's own time by many professional religious men of both Anglican and Puritan churches, who were appalled by Hobbes's exegesis of Scripture and who thought it barely disguised atheism. I also suggest that at least some of his most philosophically inclined contemporaries may have appreciated Hobbes's treatment of the Bible two ways: as a prudently ambiguous but effective demonstration of the questionableness of biblical faith as it was widely understood by most men and women who called themselves Christians, and as an implicit declaration of new liberty from the strictures of Christianity.

While this disguising of the original tension between Christianity and Hobbes's political teaching based on natural rights was readily penetrated by the astute defenders of Christian faith, perhaps the most philosophically attuned readers were not so much shocked as instructed by Hobbes's exegesis of the Bible. They would not have been blind to the deeper implications of his teaching—such as that religious accounts of the human situation were created out of human fear, as Hobbes wrote in the twelfth chapter of *Leviathan*, and that Christianity was therefore implicitly indicted by such descriptions. This kind of reader may have seen in Hobbes's work the tension between the claims of reason and the claims of revelation decided in favor of a solvent reason capable of dissolving Christianity into myth. The most philosophically thoughtful reader would be pushed in this direction if such a person were prepared to be skeptical about biblical religion. These might view Hobbes's treatment of the Bible as rhetorical, ironic, and prudent. To this audience, Hobbes's treatment of the Bible may also have revealed that religion has a political utility, that it is necessary for the successful management of human passions and the ordering of the civil society.[1] Thus two sets of readers, the sincerely religious and the philosophically "enlightened," saw more deeply into Hobbes's work and detected further meanings disguised by a surface argument (cf. Lange 1881, I: 253–68).

But for others, though they themselves were not of the philosophers who favored Hobbes, nor of the theologians who opposed him, Hobbes's treatment of the Bible actually did not appear to involve a disguise. Hobbes's intention in treating the Bible as he did, I believe, was to sustain the form of Christianity while changing its actual substance for such readers, and this intention required the greatest care, manifested as a kind of duplicity, or, as I call it, a conspiracy against Christianity.[2] Hobbes's picture of Christianity may well have instructed the knowing few who would penetrate his intentionally obfuscating ambiguity to seek greater understanding of the truths underlying the human situation, but his work is chiefly addressed to a broader audience, including those who were looking into ways to reconcile genuine Christian hope with the new findings of science. For Hobbes, the new thinking presented an opportunity: among Christians a genuine need existed to adjust to these new ideas, and in the need to adjust could be found the chance to guide.

It was of the highest importance to the fulfillment of Hobbes's aims to speak to a broad, educated audience, though these readers did not understand him as did either the earliest *philosophes* or his most vehement critics among the devout Christian leadership. These latter understood Hobbes only too well and saw Hobbes's teaching as darkness and not as the light the followers of the new philosophers perceived it to be.

To a great degree, then, Hobbes's main goal was not to help the most knowing to know more fully; he wanted instead to change the world by guiding a wider, more traditional, and religiously inclined audience. Thus, in "Review and Conclusion" at the end of *Leviathan*, Hobbes advised that that work be adopted by the universities of England so that the gentry and clergy who were trained there might benefit from its teaching and then, in turn, employ it in teaching the broader populace their civic duties (EW III, 712–13 [728]).

While we may assume he wanted to communicate knowledge of the true foundations of civil life to those he believed able to receive his teaching, he desired most of all to establish those foundations as the basis for civil association. Hobbes's goals were not only knowledge and the honor of discovering the formula for the establishment of political power on a new and more lasting basis of what man *is*, rather than what he ought to be, but also the honor of advancing the practical application of his discovery. For Hobbes, philosophy was not therefore about knowing chiefly, but about establishing political power on the surest foundation, the new foundation of political *science*, a science based on the discovery of that state of nature and the natural rights human beings possess there. To do this, the former foundation had to be altered. Thus, as Hobbes put it, again in "Review and Conclusion," the leaders of the people themselves have to be led away from principles founded upon "the venom of heathen politicians" (and particularly the teachings of men like Aristotle and Cicero), and from "the incantation of deceiving spirits"—those whose Christianity leads other men and women away from loyalty to the kingdom of this world, which kingdom Hobbes teaches should be founded on the rational principles of a "science of natural justice" (EW III, 712–13 [728], 357 [407]).

To make rights-based civil association safe, Hobbes did not wish to make the antipathy between natural freedom, that is, natural rights, and revealed religion explicit. His work thus required him to employ duplicitous ambiguity in diverging from traditional biblical interpretations: he was, in short, involved in a conspiracy against the old faith, which only he and his greatest allies and foes perceived. He was fully persuaded that religion based on revelation would always have an intractable hold on enough people to dangerously destabilize society if they were sufficiently aroused against civil authority. It was thus vitally important that the fundamental antagonism between his discovery of a new world of human freedom and equality—his natural-rights teaching—and biblical religion be kept hidden, at least from the largest element of his potential readership.

We may summarize our understanding in this way: Hobbes's treatment of the Bible seems to allow for three views that readers may take: first—one of the outraged indignation of traditional faith; second—a sense of skepticism shared with Hobbes about traditional Christian faith, and an awareness of the extent of human freedom and isolation from anything above man in the universe; and third, the view he made most room for, that which provided for those who required a religious footing upon which to stand before their full commitment to any new understanding of justice and the moral order could be expected.

An increasing number of scholars today take Hobbes's treatment of the Bible to be a manifestation of Hobbes's genuine belief, thus placing these scholars in the third group of readers—the group Hobbes seems to have intended most to influence. These scholars read Hobbes's biblical exegesis with a credulous eye and a trusting heart, as Hobbes intended, which means they would discount the critical reactions of Hobbes's religious contemporaries, as well as the viewpoint of this study.

By advancing the thesis that Hobbes's thought is in great tension with the tenets of Christianity, I challenge the conclusions of this growing body of modern scholarship and enter into a controversy concerning Hobbes's treatment of God, the Bible, and Christianity. A claim such as mine about Hobbes's religiosity made one hundred and twenty-five years ago would have found little opposition. However, beginning in the last few decades of the nineteenth century, interpretations claiming that Hobbes was a believer began to appear, exciting what has now become a substantial controversy concerning the man, his Christian faith, and the meaning of his political philosophy. Today Hobbes is regarded by an increasing number of scholars to be a sincere theist or an orthodox Christian. The older tradition affirming Hobbes's insincerity and unbelief, which dates back to the opinion of his contemporaries, has continued in our time and is increasingly on the defensive, but by now it must be clear that in this study I take the side of the older tradition.

The distinction between the view taken here and much of the modern scholarly explanation of Hobbes's religion may be illustrated by a metaphor. It is my argument—and I will offer ample evidence to support my claim in subsequent chapters—that Hobbes's treatment of the Bible and his portrait of Christian doctrine may be likened to one of those three-dimensional postcards one may find on sale in drugstores or gift shops. I have before me one such postcard of an underwater scene. In the background are rock formations, sea plants fastened to the ocean bottom, and a bit of wreckage from a sunken ship. In the foreground colorful fish are pictured, swimming. Viewed from the edge or from a certain angle, the image is flat, apparently only two-dimensional. Yet if I tilt the card, the entire surface seems to become alive, as though there were real space with real depth between the fish and the ocean-bottom background, as though I could reach my finger into it; there's an illusion of three-dimensionality. Then if I tip it again, a flat, two-dimensional scene reappears.

If one looks at Hobbes's treatment of the Bible presuming his genuine religiosity, a seemingly profound Christian "depth" appears. If the picture, however, is tilted ever so slightly, we see the Bible presented without genuine depth and a secularist, materialist, utilitarian picture of the Scripture emerges. But the postcard, our metaphor for the role of the Bible in *Leviathan*, is actually *flat*. Those who read Hobbes and think his treatment of the Bible indicates genuine faith do not "tilt" the postcard: they do not see his biblical exegesis from the angle of a more thorough study of Christianity, or the angle of Hobbes's earliest critics, or even from the context that I will argue the first half of *Leviathan* should allow. They do not rightly understand Hobbes's treatment of the Bible because Hobbes, the conspirator against Christianity in the name of human freedom, is the master of counterfeiting depth, or, to put it another way, of counterfeiting "height"—of counterfeiting the fastening of his thought to something higher than unassisted human reason.

The survey of the controversy over Hobbes's treatment of deity in the section that follows will describe the chief lines of argument and suggest underlying causes of the conflicting opinions concerning Hobbes's treatment of Christianity, God, and the Bible. After presenting this overview, I will begin a new assessment of Hobbes's treatment of God and Christianity in *Leviathan*. Such an assessment is warranted, for an antidote for the current regard for Hobbes as theist or orthodox Christian is now overdue.

A Survey of the Controversy

One of the earliest published studies of Hobbes as a theist and orthodox Anglican Christian is contained in John Hunt's *Religious Thought in England*, first published in 1870. In a volume of 470 pages, more space is given to Hobbes than to either Hooker, Laud, or Milton—a total of 28 pages (Hunt 1973).[3] Hunt begins with the declaration that "Hobbes has been a name of terror to the religious world," called "atheist, infidel, monster." But Hunt wonders how anyone who speaks of faith in God and the Bible as Hobbes does could ever be accused of unbelief. He declares, "not only is Hobbes a professed believer in Christianity, but in the most orthodox form of it" (Hunt 1973, 383).

Though Hunt affirms Hobbes's religiosity, at the end of his survey he cannot deny that Hobbes seems to belie Christian faith by making the sovereign the originator of both religion and morality. Hunt cannot help seeing that the authority Hobbes gives the sovereign in his political theory makes this creation of human will and reason the real foundation of religion and virtue. Since this does not jibe with Hunt's conviction about Hobbes's piety, he writes that Hobbes does not mean what he seems to mean, and then adds, revealing his own uncertainty, "It is difficult on this subject to reconcile Hobbes with himself" (Hunt 1973, 410). Hunt then goes further, unable to escape one conclusion while still holding to his claim that Hobbes is an orthodox Anglican: "it is certain that he did ascribe to his grotesque monster a power to make right and wrong, and to dictate both religion and laws to the people. This position, even as laid down by Hobbes himself, seemed to leave no other foundation for either religion or morality than the will of the sovereign" (410). Believing Hobbes is a sincere Christian, Hunt cannot understand why Hobbes seems to make the will of the sovereign superior to all things.

Hunt nevertheless reads Hobbes's text without any inclination to suspect him of duplicity. He declares untenable the supposition "that under pretense of defending revelation he took every opportunity of raising doubts concerning it," and adds, "we do not know what any man believed if we do not know what Thomas Hobbes believed. If we doubt *his* sincerity, we may as well doubt the sincerity of any man who ever professed to be a Christian" (384).

This propensity in Hunt to take Hobbes as utterly sincere seems to arise chiefly from the form of Hobbes's work, for it presents itself as a seamless whole, an integrated system complete and comprehensive, and as such it assumes a very persuasive gravity. The component of religion in this system is compellingly and thoroughly joined to the whole. As Hunt says, "All his ideas depend on each other" (389). The structure of *Leviathan*, then, makes each aspect of the work appear indispensable. The "mathematics fit into his physics, his physics into his politics, his politics into his religion," suggesting the inseparable unity of the whole. Thus, though Hobbes may, in Hunt's words, exhibit "extravagant or eccentric" notions in passing or appear at times to be "irreconcilable with himself," this may be because he is "not always understood." Yet, "there is no reason for supposing him insincere" (384).

Certainly many readers of *Leviathan*, even when they repeat their efforts several times, might find Hobbes's treatment of Christianity odd, but acceptable, as they are pulled along by the centripetal logic of the mass. Hobbes's apparent comprehensiveness seems to constitute an argument for regarding him as a sincere theist. Hunt's susceptibility to the coherence and comprehensiveness of the work is understandable. Such an argument is appealing, however, only so long as the apparent seamlessness of *Leviathan* is sustained.

Views such as Hunt's did not represent the common attitude of scholars at the time. Frederick Lange, in Germany, regarded Hobbes as a crafty manipulator of religion. In his 1881 *History of Materialism*, he described an aspect of the early modern effort employed by philosophers to free themselves from the authority of Scholasticism—of Aristotle and the medieval ideas that dominated Europe for centuries: the development of "the doctrine of the twofold truth, philosophical and theological, which may exist side by side in spite of their entire inconsistency" (218).

Lange concludes that this twofold strategy among philosophers explains the equivocal nature of their writing at times—so that they only rarely showed their true loyalty was to philosophy, as opposed to theology. He says this relationship between faith and knowledge was "characteristic of the period of transition to the modern freedom of thought. . . . In connection with it appears the tendency to an equivocal defense of Christianity . . . which loves to turn the darker side outwards" (225).

Lange adds that Hobbes's real view of religion

> is so trenchantly expressed in a single sentence, that we cannot but be surprised at the unnecessary breath that has been spent upon the theology of Hobbes. He lays down the following definition: "Fear of power invisible, feigned by the mind or imagined from tales publickly allowed, Religion: not allowed, superstition." (283)

As far as I have been able to determine, Lange and Hunt represent the general lines of published argument marking the beginning of the modern divergence of opinion concerning Hobbes and religion. It should be noted that in marking his surprise "at the unnecessary breath that has been spent upon the theology of Hobbes," Lange testifies that there already existed some division of opinion on this matter in his own day. It is difficult to determine who he refers to. This divergence of opinion grows more complex with A. E. Taylor's "Ethical Doctrine of Hobbes," which appeared in the journal *Philosophy* in 1938 (Taylor 1965, 31–55).[4]

Taylor, whose work later inspired Howard Warrender's book-length defense of Hobbes's theism, heralded the maturation of a new argument for the importance of God and religion in Hobbes's work. Taylor, too, may be compared with contemporary scholarship that takes the traditional view, Basil Willey's *Seventeenth Century Background* (1934) and Leo Strauss's *Political Philosophy of Hobbes* (1936).

Taylor argued that the obligation to obey the laws of nature described by Hobbes in *Leviathan* chapters 14 and 15 "is antecedent to the existence of the Legislator and the civil society; even in the 'state of nature' the law obliges *in foro interno*" that is, it "bind[s] to a desire they should take place" (41). He writes that the law of nature must be understood as "a *command*, and a command the reason for obedience whereto is that it is the precept of a 'person' with the right to command" (49). Taylor asks, "What 'person', then, is this, whose commands are binding on princes?" He concludes, "I can only make Hobbes's statements consistent with one another by supposing that he meant quite seriously what he so often says, that the 'natural law' is the command of God, and to be obeyed *because* it is God's command" (49).

And so for Taylor it is clear that "a certain kind of theism is absolutely necessary to make the theory work," and he adds, "the reasons which used to be given for supposing these theistic utterances to be insincere verbiage are really not creditable" (50). He goes even further, saying that Hobbes's insistence on the incomprehensibility of God and the impossibility of having a conception of God are not to be taken as expressions of atheism; rather, they have much in common with orthodox Christian Scholasticism. Hobbes's sayings, in Taylor's view, are only repetitions of things we can find in St. Thomas Aquinas. Though F. D. Maurice considered Hobbes's natural-law teaching and declared Hobbes to be a traditional natural-law theorist whose views represented an orthodox religious position (Maurice 1862), Taylor focused exclusively on Hobbes's statements about natural law, treating them as the key to understanding Hobbes's treatment of the divine and the linchpin that made his entire political theory workable. Thus, as Kenneth Minogue (1974) says,

> Taylor's article was . . . an extremely radical change of interpretation. It not only brought the ethical theory to the forefront of attention, but replaced Hobbes the cynical atheist with Hobbes the believing Christian. Taylor's Hobbes was a natural law philosopher working in a tradition that came directly from the middle ages; his scandalous reputation was now attributed to the superficiality of readers who had mistaken such trimmings as the scientific idiom and the slightly eccentric theology for the substance of the argument. (93)

Taylor (1965) concluded his article with a rather personal declaration, refreshing for its candor:

> My own belief, for whatever it may be worth, is that Hobbes simply meant what he said about the natural law as a command of God . . . his religion does impress me as a genuine thing, and it is not very different from that of many worthy persons of to-day who would be sincerely shocked if they were to be accused of "atheism." (53–54)

We note that Taylor's claim for Hobbes's theism is made entirely on the basis of the first half of *Leviathan*, indeed, from the arguments about natural law found chiefly in chapters 14 and 15. He does not speak at all of the second half of the work. This new tack in interpreting Hobbes did not address Hobbes's treatment of the Bible at all—except in a footnote:

> I certainly do not myself think that the feats of Biblical interpretation in the *Leviathan* are, in the main, a mere game. Hobbes's exegeses, where they are opposed to those generally current in his time, are often manifestly sound, and even where to our better informed age they are not sound, they may well have seemed to their seventeenth century author. (54)

While Taylor put forward his new view, Basil Willey and Leo Strauss read Hobbes in the older vein, supporting a completely different picture. Willey perceives a "radical incompatibility" between Hobbes's philosophical principles and Christianity, but explains that "in his biblical criticism, Hobbes employs his usual indirect tactics, so that it is not immediately manifest how little he is really leaving to the supernatural authority of holy writ" (Willey 1934, 111–12, 116–17).

Leo Strauss (1952) agreed with Willey, adding his doubts about Hobbes's belief in any sort of natural religion:

> He considered any natural knowledge of God which is more than the knowledge of a First Cause exists, completely impossible. . . . In order to hide the dangerous nature of this scepticism, to keep up an appearance that he attacked only scholastic theology and not the religion of the Scripture itself, Hobbes fought his battle against natural theology in the name of a strict belief in Scripture. (74, 76)[5]

But the writings of those who viewed Hobbes as an unbeliever did not dissuade others from championing arguments such as Taylor's and Hunt's. Thus, twenty years after Taylor, Strauss, and Willey, we come to Howard Warrender, the best known of all the controversialists in support of Hobbes-the-theist, whose work turned Taylor's argument into what is now called the Taylor-Warrender thesis.

In *The Political Philosophy of Hobbes*, Warrender's argument has much in common with Taylor's, but he develops it with greater care over some 350 pages, as compared to Taylor's briefer journal article, making it a more thorough and thus significant defense of the position (Warrender 1957). Warrender, whose work will occupy us in chapter 3, argues that the laws of nature in Hobbes's state of nature are to be considered the commands of God. If these natural laws are God's commands, they are true laws, and thus have an obligatory character. They oblige human beings because God is "entitled to obedience," as Warrender says. Just as Taylor had argued, God becomes the essential factor in making Hobbes's political theory work and so Hobbes's religious expressions must be taken as sincere.

With this book, the proposition of Hobbes as theist came into the mainstream of modern Hobbes studies, virtually establishing the theme of religion as one of the chief areas of Hobbes studies today. At the same time, Warrender's book claimed to repudiate the long series of critical arguments describing Hobbes as anti-Christian, if not atheistic, that had been produced since the middle of the seventeenth century. The controversy Warrender stimulated may be stated in a question: what is the meaning of Hobbes's religious expression? or, what is the role of religion in his political thought—above all in *Leviathan*? Warrender sought to answer this question through a study of the first half of *Leviathan*; he does not touch chapter 32 through the end. In fact, he concentrates on chapters 13 through 15. But his argument is meant to refute all those who read the second half of *Leviathan* as the work of an atheist.

Through Warrender's initiative, the support for the viewpoint of Hobbes as sincere theist, devout religious Bible exegete, and orthodox Christian is very much alive at present. Most of the support for this viewpoint is now being developed not through studies of the first half of the work, but in examinations of Hobbes's theology in the second half of *Leviathan*. Some of the works published in the wake of Warrender have gone much further in their claims than he did, for example F. C. Hood's extreme view found in *The Divine Politics of Thomas Hobbes* (Hood 1964).

Hood wrote in the preface to his work that he had always regarded Hobbes as a mechanist who used the Bible ironically to discredit those clergymen who would use it for political ends. But he could not make sense of it in this way: "I could not make sense of his civil philosophy by itself. . . . He freely expressed moral convictions for which I could see no ground in his moral theory." He began to reread *Leviathan*, ultimately resigning his university chair to study only Hobbes. After ten years he came to consider Hobbes "as a Christian thinker." Hood claimed that Hobbes's thought made no sense unless the whole work was seen to be in the service of a Christian orthodoxy. Warrender had shied away from arguing that Hobbes's theism was specifically Christian and specifically based on the Bible, but Hood argued that Hobbes's deity was the God of the Bible. It was that God who obliged human beings to obey the laws of nature and not some less-specific natural God of the "deist" understanding.

Hood saw Hobbes's work as an attempt by a very sincere Christian to make Protestant Christianity speak to the modern era of scientific revolution and new political realities that was the seventeenth century. Thus, the first half of *Leviathan* was actually written in the service of the second half, and problems of consistency between the two parts were due to difficulties Hobbes had in reconciling his faith with the world of natural science. For Hood, then, doubts about the second half of *Leviathan* were to be completely overthrown and the argument that Hobbes cynically used religion to support his fundamentally atheistic philosophy, as his seventeenth-century critics believed, was turned around: Hobbes used his political philosophy to support his fundamentally religious position.

Though Hood's argument was extreme, his contention that Hobbes was a Christian was finally not so different from Hunt's response of a hundred years earlier, nor do some of the most contemporary evaluations vary greatly from it. George Wright, for example, in a very recent article wrote that he could not agree that Hobbes "reinterprets Christianity cynically so as to make it more conformable to his political designs than any orthodox interpretation would otherwise permit" (Wright 1991, 344n57). Wright is inclined to count Hobbes's work as a variant of orthodox seventeenth-century Protestant theology. He writes, "critics have failed to appreciate the full radicalness of the Protestant tradition of which Hobbes was a trenchant proponent" (Wright 1991, 327).[6]

Two more figures in this controversy, scholars who represent still another approach to Hobbes's work, enable those who accept it to argue for the sincerity of Hobbes's religious expression. Bernard Willms, in a survey of recent Hobbes studies, viewed as one of the main thrusts of current Hobbes scholarship the new appreciation of Hobbes as a contributor to seventeenth-century theology and named Paul J. Johnson and Herbert W. Schneider as among "the most important contributors" to this significant trend (Willms 1982, 148). Willms also named an anthology, *Thomas Hobbes in His Time*, which included the contributions of Johnson and Schneider, as representing the very best tendencies in contemporaray Hobbes research (Ross, Schneider, and Waldman 1974).

In Johnson's contribution to this collection, he suggests we do not know what *all* of Hobbes's contemporaries thought, arguing that some Christian readers approved of *Leviathan*, or would have approved of it had they read it. He states that Hobbes shared with his contemporary, William Chillingworth, the conviction that men find the way to Christ "by following our reason to the Scripture." Johnson (1974) argues that Chillingworth and Hobbes had similar concepts of reason; he quotes Chillingworth to prove his similarity to Hobbes: " 'Right reason grounded on Divine revelation and common notions, written by God in the hearts of all men, and deducing according to never failing rules of Logick . . .' will discover the necessary foundations of faith. The man who follows Scripture and reason 'in all his opinions and actions . . . followes alwaies God' " (109).

Yet Johnson brings only Chillingworth—and no others whom he claims to be like-minded—to the defense of his claims for Hobbes. The argument of my study, however, is that contrary to Johnson's view, Hobbes never grounded reason on divine revelation but rather on the human passion for self-preservation and therefore Hobbes's sense of reason cannot be equated to that of Chillingworth.

Johnson associated Hobbes's work with the latitudinarian openness present in some quarters of the Anglican Church in the early seventeenth century; and he argued that Hobbes was not an atheist, but rather an orthodox Anglican. But he himself admits, contrary to the advantage he wishes to draw from citing Chillingworth "if Hobbes was not an atheist then, one might very well wonder why his contemporaries so uniformly took him to be one" (124).

Johnson's answer is that Hobbes's brand of Christianity "sharply separated faith from reason and isolated piety from theology." This separation created two independent realms, leaving Hobbes free to develop a political theory "in which the idea of God played no functional role and in which traditional religious issues could be subjected to the severest criticism and finally left in the hands of the secular ruler." Johnson wrote that to Hobbes's religious contemporaries, "Hobbes's system would seem to be the product of an atheistic mind. But that was their mistake; we needn't repeat it."

Johnson suggests Hobbes's contemporary critics were mistaken in accusing Hobbes of atheism, but he does not indicate why Hobbes's critics from his own day do not represent valuable testimony of the meaning of Christian faith in the historical context in which Hobbes wrote. He does not explain why their reactions to

Hobbes should not supply fairly accurate notions about the substance of orthodoxy in his day and thus comprise important indications of the nature of Hobbes's religious expression. Beyond his problematic appropriation of Chillingworth, Johnson gives no reason to think we are better prepared to judge the orthodoxy of Hobbes's religious expression than were his contemporaries.

But by means of a sharp separation of faith and reason, making reason independent of faith, Johnson would save Hobbes from the varied and numerous published arguments of his many contemporary accusers. Finally, Johnson looks to Bacon, of all people, to defend his proposition that Hobbes was a man of faith, since Bacon wrote clearly of this twofold truth that Johnson wishes to apply to Hobbes in order to favor his argument for Hobbes's sincere theism. But calling on Francis Bacon's faith to establish grounds for Hobbes as a believer is also very problematic.

Herbert Schneider, a second scholar singled out by Willms as an important contributor to the trend for seeing Hobbes as a theologian, in a 1974 essay entitled "The Piety of Hobbes," also argues for Hobbes as a biblical theist and also looks to Bacon for support. Schneider, sounding much like Hunt from one hundred years earlier, cites long passages from *Leviathan* in which Hobbes speaks of God, faith, and the Bible, and argues that no atheist could say such things. Schneider's argument culminates with his declaration that Hobbes's *Leviathan* is "a passionate sermon to a warring world" and adds that "beneath the sermon lay the philosopher's patient hope in the eventual coming on earth of the Kingdom of Christ, when peace and security will be enthroned by 'natural justice' " (97–99, 101, 122).

Was Bacon a man of faith whose teachings provide the basis for establishing Hobbes as essentially the same? Johnson suggests that Hobbes follows Bacon's "maxim of rendering unto faith what was faith's," which, he argues, characterized the compartmentalization of faith and reason typical of both philosophers and did not preclude piety in both men. But how much is rendered to faith by Bacon? For Bacon, though the truth was understood as consisting of two separate realms, the inequality of these realms in his thought should not be overlooked. Basil Willey speaks of this, and while agreeing with the implication of Johnson's remark that for Bacon the truth is twofold, he goes on to offer the qualification that Bacon's use of the concept of the twofold truth is duplicitous.

I agree with Willey's evaluation; the implications of the extent of

Bacon's materialist philosophy, manifested, for example, in the relationship of science to religion in his *New Atlantis*, supplies grounds for serious doubt about Bacon's piety (White 1972, 340–59; Willey 1934, 27–30; Lange 1881, 218, 225; Faulkner 1993, 96, 179–80, 238, 244–46). While Bacon indicates, in Willey's words, that there is "a truth of religion and a truth of science," Bacon kept the two realms separate. He did so, Willey explains, in order to keep religion from contaminating science. The purpose of the two spheres was not in the mutual interest of religion and philosophy, but above all in the interest of philosophy. Willey summarizes Bacon's view: "Religious truth, then, must be . . . elevated far out of reach, not . . . in order that so it may be more devoutly approached, but in order to keep it out of mischief" (29).

Bacon, Willey goes on to say, furnished men with a technique of reconciling philosophy with religion, "by arguing that God has revealed himself to man by means of two scriptures: first, of course, through the written word, but also, secondly, through his handiwork, the created universe." But if the two teachings are ever in conflict, as, for example, when analysis of the universe leads to the conclusion that all that is is matter and there is nothing else, as the Democritean-Epicurean school argued and to whose thought Bacon was devoted, does this not have an effect on our understanding of the written word of God? How are we to account for such sayings in Scripture as "God is a Spirit" (John 4:24)? But the twofold truth concept allows such tension to be made less apparent. The use of Bacon's thought by Johnson and Schneider, then, is a problematic tactic for the defense of their position, since Hobbes's similarity to Bacon may readily be called to illustrate Hobbes's *break* with the divine.

A Most Recent Study

The survey concludes by addressing the most recent study to argue that Hobbes's treatment of the Bible demonstrates his Christian orthodoxy and genuine religious inclination. This voluminous 1992 work, *The Two Gods of Leviathan: Thomas Hobbes on Religion and Politics* by A. P. Martinich, represents the culmination of much, if not all, of the work supporting this argument that comes before it.

As A. E. Taylor suggested the idea that led to Warrender's grand study arguing for Hobbes's religiosity, so Martinich seems to have been prompted by Paul Johnson, whose article, "Hobbes's Anglican Doctrine of Salvation," was considered above. Martinich acknowledges Johnson in the beginning of his book, a work that amplifies and "fleshes" out the barer bones presented in Johnson's article.

On the first page of *The Two Gods of Leviathan*, Martinich writes, "the consensus of scholarly opinion now counts him [Hobbes] as a tepid theist. My view, in contrast, is that Hobbes was a sincere and relatively orthodox Christian." On the third page of the book, he distinguishes between "orthodox" and "standard" religious views and thus sets up a basis upon which to say Hobbes was orthodox, but *not* standard. He then argues that Hobbes was motivated by the desire "to answer the challenges the new science of Copernicus and Galileo posed for religion and to prevent the abuse of religion for political purposes." He goes on to say that Hobbes's goals were, first, "to show that the distinctly religious content of the Bible could be reconciled with the new science," and second, "to prove that religion could not be used legitimately to destabilize government" (Martinich 1992, 5).

I agree with Martinich concerning this first goal, for Hobbes *does* very much aim toward reconciling the Bible with the findings of unassisted human reason, with the findings, that is, of modern science (Martinich's concerns here also are reminiscent of the work of F. C. Hood). But I must disagree with Martinich concerning what this reconciliation means for Christianity, for in his consideration of Hobbes's effort to reconcile the two—science and Christian faith—Martinich does not believe Christianity is done any harm, while I believe that Hobbes aims to place it in permanent eclipse.

I also agree with what Martinich calls Hobbes's second goal—to prove that religion could not legitimately be used to destabilize government. But again, Martinich does not think Hobbes's biblical exegesis undertaken to establish religion as nonthreatening to government constitutes any damage to the tenets of authentic Christian faith, while this is precisely what I do think.

In spite of my disagreement with him, I cannot help feeling a certain comradeship with Martinich, for in reading his book I see that we both have been looking at the same books these last several years, looking at the same "postcard," as it were, to refer to the metaphor I suggested earlier, the surface of which can be tilted to produce different effects. Martinich has been absorbed in Hobbes's apparent depth while I have argued that the entire treatment of

Christianity constitutes an exceedingly clever illusion manufactured by Hobbes.

In a passage on the theme of Christian salvation, Martinich uses Augustine and Anselm to describe two variants of the meaning of this concept and he argues that Hobbes genuinely speaks to the differences he, Martinich, identifies. But he leaves these aside briefly to say that he does not deny "there is another side to Hobbes's views about redemption. He transmuted the religious paradigm and applied it to the secular issue" (Martinich 1992, 271). He then describes Hobbes's secularization of Christian salvation, seemingly "tilting the postcard" for himself and plainly demonstrating that he is able to view Hobbes's work from a different "angle." But he does not see from the ambiguous properties he can plainly demonstrate for himself that the religious depth he finds in Hobbes is in any way disingenuous. He writes, "it is possible to see Hobbes's transmutation of theological theories of redemption as a subversion of religion," and yet he never gives this possibility any further consideration and instead immediately declares, "rather than trying to subvert religion through his transmutation of the idea of redemption . . . I believe that he was trying to show how religious ideas pervade all aspects of human experience and how theology can be made relevant to securing peace and happiness in the present world" (272). Though he acknowledges "it is possible" to see evidence in Hobbes that runs contrary to this belief, in his comments on page 272, it is evident that Martinich has no regard for the possibility that Hobbes's affections may be turned fully to this world.

But even this last statement from Martinich is not wrong, since Hobbes's incorporation of religion was made necessary because he understood religion to be attached to passions that made it such a pervasive force in all human affairs and without attending to these passions upon which religion is grounded, peace and the happiness that comes from security cannot be attained. But Martinich does not see that Hobbes "transmutes" religion—that is, transforms it—for the very purpose of promoting peace and security over other ends, and that both prudence and the aims of Hobbes's "political reasoning" required he carry out this transmutation under the shelter of seeming religiousness.

Hobbes's religious argument required a masterful knowledge of theological disputes and dogma, a knowledge that Hobbes weaves with great artfulness throughout *Leviathan*. It is this artfulness and masterful knowledge that dazzles so wonderfully, leading a scholar

such as Martinich to declare, after surveying Hobbes's knowledge
of the theological concept of the covenant,

> [Hobbes] cares about the correct theological doctrine of salvation.
> There is no other explanation for his attempt to understand these
> terms other than a deep intellectual commitment to theology. I would
> be willing to rest my entire thesis on the fact that he weaves these
> theological concepts [to do with grace and faith] into his discussion of
> a covenant, if there were not so much other evidence for his commit-
> ment to the Christian religion. (142)

Martinich is not mistaken about Hobbes's commitment to theology
and to the most thorough understanding of the Christian religion,
but there *is* another explanation concerning the reason for Hobbes's
great commitment to theological questions. Hobbes was aware that
his readers were persons with deep intellectual commitments to
theology, and, indeed, that they were persons whose commitments
were even deeper than those characterized by the term Martinich
described in Hobbes as "deeply intellectual." To persuade such
readers, Hobbes had to be persuasive, but Hobbes's capacity to be
persuasive does not necessitate the genuineness of his commitment
to those things he understood so well.

Though Martinich presents many arguments in support of
Hobbes's sincere religiosity and Christian orthodoxy, these arguments ultimately testify that for him the presence of deeply intellectual and eloquent discussions of Christian doctrines constitutes
sufficient proof of Hobbes's ingenuousness. Yet deep knowledge of
Scripture and doctrine is not always equivalent to the acceptance of
the intent or spirit of Scripture and doctrine. It is, perhaps, worth
noting that in the New Testament even Christ's chief adversary
quotes Scripture with the greatest skill and understanding (Matthew
4:1–11). I hope to show that there is sufficient evidence of non-
Christian, indeed, anti-Christian spirit and intent in Hobbes's work
to belie the appearance of Hobbes's skillful threading of biblical
quotations and presentation of dogmatic positions that might constitute sincere faith. These elements, I believe, were placed in
Leviathan to sway a larger audience that Hobbes hoped to influence.

However, my purpose here is not principally to engage each
scholar with whom I disagree, but to place this study in the context
of the debate concerning Hobbes, the Bible, and Christianity and
allow the alternative it presents to stand as a critique of the

arguments posed by the theists. Nevertheless, I do engage in great detail one of the principal holders of the Hobbes-as-theist position: in the next two chapters I discuss the work of Howard Warrender, who, as one of the foremost among these modern scholars, may stand in part for almost all of them, including Martinich. I recommend Martinich's book as the most thorough explication of the opposing view; his is an exhaustive study and gives the best defense available for that position. However, see Curley 1996 for a detailed critique of this work.

A Summary of the Hobbes-As-Theist School of Arguments

The Hobbes-as-theist school of scholarship may be divided into three groups, though these are by no means mutually exclusive. The first group, represented chronologically first by interpreters such as Hunt, but including even the latest scholars, such as Martinich, reads the second half of *Leviathan* and impressed by the mass of biblical argument there comes away convinced that Hobbes's religious expression must be sincere. They carry this conviction back to their reading of the first half of the work and, propelled by their attitude regarding the biblical exegesis that comprises the second half, recognize the God of the Bible in Hobbes's references to deity in the first parts of *Leviathan*, as well. This manner of reading is helped particularly by the apparently seamless unity of the entire work, as Hunt's reading attests, and by Hobbes's brilliant capacity to handle Scripture, as Martinich bears witness to. To counter the "Hunt view," it would be necessary to demonstrate that that exegesis is not what it appears to be. This may be done both by an exploration of that exegesis and by demonstrating the tension between Hobbes's secularly based arguments about the nature of man in the first half of *Leviathan* and the religious harmonization of the Bible with those arguments which Hobbes appears to establish in the second half of the book.

The second group reads the first half of *Leviathan* and finds, as does A. E. Taylor, who inaugurated this view, that God is necessary for the first half of *Leviathan to work*; the divine is needed to make obligation possible. Thus, Howard Warrender, successor to Taylor in this point of view, subtitled his book on Hobbes, "His Theory of Obligation." How else can human beings honor their covenants to escape the state of nature by mutually laying down their rights in order to create civil associations unless they are obliged by a greater power? And what greater power is there than God? This view, a reading of Hobbes that relies on traditional natural law and that connects Hobbes to the Thomistic tradition positing a divine judge who stands behind the laws of nature, then informs these readers' reading of the second half of *Leviathan* engendering an attitude free of doubt about the sincerity of Hobbes's religious expression, despite the surprising theological innovations found there. This view's partisans included partisans of the first category, as well.

A third group is composed of those who subscribe to the twofold truth teaching instituted by Bacon and described above by Lange, who noted it in his argument *against* the claims of Hobbes's piety (see pages 23–24, above). With this interpretation, the areas in Hobbes's text seeming to represent irreligious skepticism or the irrelevance of deity are overcome by segregating matters of faith from the workings of reason and holding that neither need be diminished by the tenets or findings of the other. Such a view is employed to overcome tensions between what appears as religious and seemingly anti-Christian aspects of *Leviathan*; matters of faith are simply matters of a realm beyond the physical world and need not be impugned by the findings of unassisted human reason regarding the physical dimension.

Having surveyed the arguments for the sincerity of Hobbes's religious expression, the challenge now is to prove that Hobbes's treatment of the Bible is antagonistic to authentic Christian belief and then to show the meaning and purpose of Hobbes's writing about God and the Bible at such length in the second half of *Leviathan*.

Hobbes's Diaphanous Veil

There has been a failure among many contemporary scholars to appreciate fully the antipathy between Hobbes and Christianity and yet Hobbes intentionally did much to assure their failure. The interpretations of these scholars have served to obscure the meaning of the role religion plays in *Leviathan* and the view of man upon which Hobbes's political philosophy—and modern liberalism—is based, but Hobbes disguised the full meaning of his work with a diaphanous veil that both reveals and hides.

These modern commentators who claim Hobbes's theism is genuine help cover what Hobbes intended to remain covered: that the formerly highest authorities—the Bible and God—have been dethroned and replaced by the sovereignty of man. By arguing for Hobbes's genuine Christian faith they hide what might otherwise be more easily revealed: that human beings are not only free to establish their own moral authorities, they are also alone in the universe and have no choice—they must create their own moral order with no other guide than their own needs. Hobbes did not intend to teach a broad audience that in the liberation of human beings from all authorities they do not themselves create, there is no longer to be any higher support for human lives than the foundation called natural rights. But this is precisely what his teaching indicates, once his treatment of the Bible is revealed for what it is.

Hobbes did not want to emphasize his conviction that lives built on foundations of biblical faith tend to stand in opposition to lives built upon the basis of peace and safety. He did not want to reveal that placing fear of violent death at the hands of man *first* in the concerns of human beings ultimately meant that the fear of God cannot be foremost among human interests. This study will indicate the religion Hobbes did wish to reveal and propagate: it is one clothed in biblical texts, but which justifies human freedom from all authorities men do not set up themselves.[7]

Hobbes meant the idea that human beings possess inalienable rights to become the great and central protection from complete loss of coherence and traditional order in societies governed by what Hobbes terms "the science of natural justice" (EW III, 357 [407]). But for Hobbes, the enormous burden thus placed on the notion of rights, on this new understanding of human freedom in the world, was not to be starkly proclaimed. Its inauguration demanded a great disguise to cover it, which also served to support and to sustain it. Thus Hobbes joined a "domesticated" or "corrected" Christianity to his teaching of the natural rights of man to cover up the nakedness of human beings in the universe. He did not want to reveal—for the sake of the stability of rights-based society—that moral order was unsupported by anything higher than man. Thus Hobbes's teaching, founded in the drive for self-preservation that ultimately became the substance of liberalism, has a religious "vestment," a sort of "Christian" covering that was tailored with great care, requiring a "conspiracy" against genuine Christianity. This covering of religiosity clothing the rights of man suggests that the polity based on rights, which today we call the liberal polity, itself needs such a garment. The need for a "garment" in turn suggests that for Hobbes "nakedness"—human solitude as the only reasoning power in the cosmos, or as the only power that will care for man—was a problem for politics.

In order to understand more plainly the meaning of Hobbes's interpretation of the Bible and thus begin to reestablish the view that Hobbes is hostile toward Christianity as it has been traditionally understood by the greatest number of human beings who have called themselves by that name, it is important to further elucidate the meaning of his original human-rights teaching. Thus, we shall turn to the subjects of the state of nature and the laws of nature in Hobbes's *Leviathan* and to Howard Warrender's work. Warrender's argument provides us with the opportunity to clarify fully both Hobbes's natural-rights teaching as it is given in the first half of *Leviathan,* and the tension between that teaching and the teaching of authentic Christianity. This argument will then serve as the context necessary for our analysis of Hobbes's exegesis of the Bible in the second half of *Leviathan.* The study of Warrender will also serve as the first refutation of the arguments for Hobbes as a genuine theist, for these arguments must be refuted to make plain the full meaning of Hobbes's teaching.

Chapter Three

The Nontheistic Foundation of the First Half of *Leviathan*

One of the clearest of declarations for Hobbes as sincere believer came in 1960 with W. B. Glover's dramatic article declaring that "the legend of Hobbes the atheist is doomed" (Glover 1965, 168). His article concluded with this challenge:

> In view of the fact that Hobbes devoted more than a third of his political writings to discussion of religion and wrote several polemical books to combat a charge of atheism and show himself, not only a theist, but a sound Anglican Christian, it is incumbent on any who think he did not mean what he said to provide some principle of interpretation that will show what he did mean or at least to explain why he should write insincerely at such length. (148)

This is part of the challenge before us as we now turn to Hobbes's argument concerning obligation, natural rights, and natural law.

A leading scholar supporting the sincerity of Hobbes's theism— Howard Warrender—argued that in the state of nature in *Leviathan* there is not complete freedom from all obligation to law, but rather God obliges human beings to behave in certain ways by means of natural law, and punishes them when they fail to do so. This scholar supports his argument in a way that will allow us, upon examining it, to begin to show how Hobbes misled not only this interpreter, but many other like-minded readers, by writing in a manner that allowed his audience to think his work part of the authentic religious and, or, natural law tradition. But I will show that Hobbes's human-rights teaching is built instead on the understanding that there is both no God concerned with the affairs of human beings and that therefore, in the state of nature, there is complete freedom from law.

In this chapter, also, I will show Hobbes's antipathy toward any authority not made by man that would limit human freedom. I will also display plainly the extent of the freedom Hobbes revealed and how this freedom is the foundation of his teaching concerning the rights of man.

Warrender's Importance

What authority is behind the obligations that bind human beings in Hobbes's thought, both before they enter civil associations, in their decisions to enter civil society, and in their lives as citizens or subjects? Does the presence of natural law in Hobbes's political theory signify his project's dependence on the existence of a divine power behind such law, thus connecting Hobbes's work with a religious tradition that relies on the presence of a God whose sanctions give that law authority?

The principal contemporary rejuvenator of interest in Hobbes's treatment of religion, Howard Warrender, argued that Hobbes's political philosophy very much depended on a belief in God, even though such belief might not be termed Christian. Warrender, in fact, argued that Hobbes's Christianity was irrelevant to the fundamental importance of God to his thought. Warrender was convinced that behind Hobbes's understanding of the laws of nature stood a God of nature who obliged human beings to obey these laws and this is the deity he claims Hobbes's political theory fully depends on.

Warrender situates his discussion of Hobbes and God in part 1 of *Leviathan* and not in the extensive treatment of the Bible in parts 3 and 4. More specifically, he invites us to situate discussion about the sincerity of Hobbes's religious expression around the state of nature and the laws of nature that Hobbes treats in *Leviathan*, chapters 13 to 15. This is useful because it makes it possible to examine the relationship between Hobbes's political thought and any natural and nonbiblical theology before we proceed to speak of Hobbes's authentic Christianity or his Christian orthodoxy.

The principal concern of Warrender's book *The Political Philosophy of Hobbes: His Theory of Obligation* was to defend the proposition that Hobbes's work is based genuinely on the existence of a

God who obliges human beings to obey the laws of nature both before and after they have entered civil society. Since Warrender's work poses a well-developed argument for Hobbes's genuine theism and the vital importance of that theism to Hobbes's political theory, his view represents a significant challenge to my own argument and it is therefore appropriate that I show how his notion of Hobbes's theism is mistaken.[1] My response to Warrender also lays the groundwork for refuting other interpretations of Hobbes that are based in the sincerity of his religious expression. The task of this chapter will be to explore fully the question of obligation in Hobbes and to show that in Hobbes's work God is not the vital basis of obligation to law.

Warrender's primary assumption is that Hobbes's theism is plausible because it is *necessary* to support his notion of obligation. His argument is based on the conviction that in Hobbes's political philosophy the reason men leave the state of nature and the reason they obey civil authority *after* leaving that state is because God obliges them to. Warrender presumes a theory of obligation in Hobbes that is dependent upon the existence of God, but independent of any biblical account of that God—a natural theology. The substance of this theory of obligation is that God, by *natural* rewards and punishments, and by a further unexplained force of divine power, obliges human beings to obey his natural law.

My analysis of Warrender begins with his argument that in the state of nature described by Hobbes in *Leviathan*, chapter 13, an obligation to God rests on all human beings. My first aim is to examine what Hobbes says about the state of nature to see if such an obligation can be found.

The State of Nature Characterized by Complete Natural Freedom

Hobbes begins his description of the state of nature with paragraphs on the equality of human beings, showing how this equality leads to competition that quickly has fatal consequences. He concludes that human beings are physically equal because the weakest is able to kill even the strongest with the help of "secret machinations." Concerning mental faculties, Hobbes says he finds "yet a greater equality amongst men, than that of strength." The mental capacities he calls prudence, which he says "is but experience: which equal time, equally bestows on all men, in those things they equally apply themselves unto." He adds that if this seems incredible, it "is but a vain conceit of one's own wisdom, which all men think they have in a greater degree, than the vulgar, that is, than all men but themselves, and a few others, whom by fame, or for concurring with themselves, they approve" (EW III, 110–11 [183–84]).

This equality gives rise to "equality of hope in the attaining of our ends," and to occasions where two or more individuals desire the same thing that, as Hobbes puts it, "they cannot both enjoy" and so they become enemies (EW III, 111 [183–84]). Hobbes speaks of what then follows: "and in the way to their end, which is principally their own preservation, and sometimes their own delectation only, endeavor to destroy, or subdue one another." Enmity exists not only through competition for physical benefits that make life more secure, but also through competition for honor and glory. Thus enmity prompted by what Hobbes terms the passion for survival is exacerbated by the passion of pride.

In chapter 13, Hobbes says that fear arises from this competition; and due to the absence of any natural power to restrain human beings, the fear is very great. Such competition arises out of the natural freedom of man, a freedom often characterized by pride; thus fear surrounding man in the state of nature arises due to freedom and pride. Because they are naturally free of any authority that might restrain them, human beings find that there is no better way to secure themselves from the fear arising from competition than to *anticipate* what others may do and so use "force of wiles to master the person of all men he can." Such an attitude of taking anticipatory action also takes into consideration that some persons, because *they* are also naturally free, out of "pleasure in contemplating their own power in the acts of conquest" persist in the use of force and wiles beyond what their security requires. This, in turn, makes those who might be content "to be at ease within modest grounds" anticipate further than they might in order to provide for their own self-defense.

The social milieu created by this natural freedom is the very dangerous place we call the state of nature, where human beings compete not only for security due to fear, but also for honor due to pride:

> where there is no power able to over-awe them all . . . every man
> looketh that his companion should value him, at the same rate he sets

upon himself: and upon all signs of contempt or undervaluing, naturally endeavors, as far as he dares, (which amongst them that have no common power to keep them in quiet, is far enough to make them destroy each other), to extort a greater value from his contemner, by damage; and from others, by example. (EW III, 112 [185])

Thus Hobbes explains why this state of affairs, "during which time men live without a common power to keep them all in awe . . . is called war."

It is worthwhile to recall that Hobbes's title, *Leviathan*, indicates the resolution or solution of this war of the state of nature. The term "leviathan" is taken from the Bible, where the entire forty-first chapter of Job describes this creature as an almost omnipotent force as hard as stone who "esteemeth iron as straw." Hobbes's choice of the term for his title is an indication of the extent to which he associates human freedom with pride. The importance of maximizing that freedom in the peace and safety of civil society through the restraining of the passion of pride is indicated by the epigraph on the frontispiece, taken from the penultimate verse of Job chapter 41: "Upon earth there is not his like, who is made without fear." Hobbes says there is no rising up against this powerful being; as the final verse of the chapter states, "he is king over all the children of pride." Hobbes thus seems to be saying that pride is the human passion that is most actively threatening to peace and safety and the passion that ultimately makes Leviathan necessary. The passion of fear thus seems to be the natural reaction to the primary passion of pride. Thus, in a way, the notion of natural right is a depiction of the extent or compass of pride in man.

Hobbes says that no human behavior—the competition for rare goods, the appetite for glory that will kill another human being over a smile, the willingness to destroy for the delight in contemplating one's own power in the act of conquest, and anticipatory preemptive acts, including homicide—is sin in the state of nature, for no law limits such behavior. Thus, pride in the state of nature is no sin. As Hobbes puts it, "The desires, and other passions of man, are in themselves no sin. No more are the actions, that proceed from those passions, till they know a law that forbids them" (EW III, 114 [187]). Men "do not know a law that forbids them," because no such laws have been made. They have not been made because human beings in the state of nature have not agreed upon the person that shall make them. Thus Hobbes says in *Leviathan*, chapter 13, that in the state of nature whatsoever conduces to the satisfaction of a person's desires and hopes and the allaying of his fears, is legitimate. This is so because men and women in that state are *completely* free of all law, as law is properly defined by Hobbes (EW III, 118 [190–91], 343 [399]).

Warrender, however, argues that there is a law-making authority in the state of nature that obliges men and women independently of their agreement on who shall make law. He believes that Hobbes teaches that obligations come to human beings via laws of nature that are the commands of God. We shall see how he arrives at this conclusion as we proceed (Warrender 1957, 97–100).[2]

The Problem of Complete Natural Freedom

While human beings have complete liberty from all law in the state of nature, they do not have unrestrained, unlimited liberty in other senses. Law limits liberty by binding a person to refrain from its exercise, but liberty can be limited in ways besides by law—it can be limited by what Hobbes calls external impediments—including the power of other human beings. Let us briefly jump forward to chapter 14 to see how liberty is limited by what Hobbes calls "impediments."

At the beginning of chapter 14, Hobbes writes that the "Right of Nature," is "the liberty each man hath to use his own power." He says that "according to the proper signification of the word," we should understand liberty to mean "the absence of external impediments." He further says that by impediments he means that which "may oft take away part of a man's power to do what he would" (EW III, 116 [189]).

In our reading from chapter 13, one can see that men are posited as beginning with an initial liberty but that they then find themselves competing and becoming the enemies of other men in the state of nature and in doing so, they come up against the power of other men, which power, matched against their own, becomes an impediment to their liberty, taking away part of their power to do what they would. These impediments are limitations to the actions, but they are not bonds to the will—to the desiring hearts of human beings; that is, they are not the stuff of obligation in Hobbes's thought.

At the beginning of chapter 14 is Hobbes's definition of liberty:

"By liberty, is understood, according to the proper signification of the word, the absence of external impediments: which impediments, may oft take away part of a man's power to do what he would." To this Hobbes adds, "but cannot hinder him from using the power left him, according as his judgment, and reason shall dictate to him." Impediments may *limit* actions but they do not *bind* the will of the agent himself. His desires may be frustrated in their courses, but he will seek other routes to their satisfaction. According to this passage, and to the definition of the right of nature ("the liberty each man hath to use his own power"), while impediments do often "take away part of a man's power to do what he would," they cannot be said to bind a man's will. In other words, only when, by his own volition, he gives up his power to use his own power as he will, is a man then said to be bound or obliged.

Hobbes is here making an important distinction between being at liberty and being obliged. It becomes explicit in the third paragraph of chapter 14, where he distinguishes between natural law and natural right. A law of nature, he writes, "is a precept or general rule, found out by reason, by which a man is forbidden to do that which is destructive of his life, or taketh away the means of preserving the same; and to omit that, by which he thinketh it may be preserved" (EW III, 117 [189]).

Natural law is not the same as natural right ("the liberty each man hath to use his own power, as he will himself, for the preservation . . . of his own life") because "right, consisteth in liberty to do, or to forbear" while "law, determineth, and bindeth to one of them." So "law and right differ," he says, "as much as obligation, and liberty; which in one and the same matter are inconsistent" (EW III, 117 [189]).

Impediments do not oblige because human beings are only obliged by *binding themselves* to some choice presented to them according to a precept or general rule, found out by reason. Impediments limit *power*, but the human *will* is only limited by the desires. Thus the desires and a person's power to satisfy these desires are distinguished: a human being is *not* bound so long as he has not yielded his desires, and a person cannot be both bound to give up his desire to do something and free not to give up his desire to do it at the same moment.

In speaking of being obliged here, Hobbes speaks of law as being what determines or binds a person to a course—and he speaks of law in the context of *natural* law—thus implying the notion of the *obligatory* character of natural law—and yet we shall see that this sort of obligation is not what Hobbes considers true and proper obligation. Here is an early manifestation in *Leviathan* of what one can consider his second sense of obligation, for I shall argue that Hobbes speaks of obligation in two ways. The important point for the moment, however, is that we have established that the freedom of the state of nature is freedom from obligation to proper law—law whose author human beings have agreed upon and who can be known and whose power is available to keep all persons in awe.

When human beings are in such a state of liberty from law, that liberty leads to a situation so dangerous that they realize they must seek above all to escape it. Hobbes describes the means of escape: "And thus much for the ill condition, which man by mere nature is actually placed in; though with a possibility to come out of it, consisting partly in the passions and partly in his reason" (EW III, 115–16 [188]). He says the passions that "encline men to peace" are the fear of death and desire "of such things as are necessary to commodious living."

Passions, then, particularly fear of violent death in the war of all against all, make for the possibility of coming out of the ill condition of the state of nature, but passions are not enough; the way out is "partly in the passions, partly in his reason" (EW III, 114 [187]). These two, however, are not equal partners. Hobbes has said that the thoughts, which comprise a man's reason, serve the passions, acting as their scouts. "For the thoughts are to the desires as scouts, and spies, to range abroad, and find the way to the things desired: all steadiness of the mind's motion, and all quickness of the same, proceeding from thence" (EW III, 61 [139]). Thus, the passions "encline men to peace" by prompting reason to suggest "convenient articles of peace." Reason's part is that it "suggesteth convenient articles of peace, upon which men may be drawn to agreement." These are the articles, Hobbes says, which otherwise are called the "Laws of Nature."

Man's natural liberty comes first. Human beings find such liberty extremely dangerous—that is the problem with natural liberty—and the treatment for this problem lies in these "articles of peace" that human beings, under the pressure of the problem of natural liberty, find for themselves. Under the heading, "Laws of Nature," they *appear* to take on another stature, though their substance actually does not change. They are essentially the conclusion Hobbes leads us to through his treatment of human psychology in chapters 1 through 13 of *Leviathan*. They are the rules human beings find to satisfy their most fundamental appetite—staying alive. It is their change of heading—from articles of peace found out by reason to "laws of nature"—which seems to open the door for Warrender's associating them with the commands of God, which association he thinks sufficient to make them obligatory for human beings.

In chapter 14, "On the First and Second Laws of Nature, and of Contracts," we see that Hobbes's "articles of peace" have taken on a new name and have been given a place in the chapter title; they will now be known as "natural laws." Warrender seems to assume that Hobbes's natural law is the traditional one that bears that name, a natural law associated with Thomas Aquinas, for example, and with Christian theology, but we suggest here—and we shall treat this subject more thoroughly in the next chapter—that something has changed. In his book *The Hunting of Leviathan*, Samuel Mintz observes what has taken place:

> What Hobbes has done is to secularize the traditional concept of natural law; he has removed it from the sphere of absolute morality; he has deduced it, not from the idea of man's perfection, not from what man ought to be, but from what man is, or at any rate from what Hobbes thought man is. (Mintz 1962, 27; see also Gauthier 1969, 70)

This mistaking of Hobbes's laws of nature for their nominal predecessors going back to Thomas Aquinas has a good deal to do with Warrender's persistence against so much evidence that contradicts his thesis in Hobbes's work. Warrender is operating here on two assumptions: first, that Hobbes believes power alone can oblige, and that God's absolute power obliges absolutely, and second, that Hobbes's work is founded on the understanding that God is present in the state of nature and that human beings can know that God is watching over them and is concerned with their actions. In the rest of this chapter, I shall demonstrate that for Hobbes neither of these is the case.

The Will to Limit Natural Liberty to Self-Defense and to an Obligation to God

Hobbes begins chapter 14 with a definition of the "Right of Nature," which at first seems to contradict our conclusion of the preceding sections of this chapter that there are no true legal limitations to natural liberty. Hobbes says the right of nature is "the liberty each man hath, to use his own power, as he will himself, *for the preservation of his own nature;* that is to say, of his own life; and consequently, of doing any thing, which in his own judgment, and reason, he shall conceive to be the aptest means thereunto" (EW III, 116 [189], emphasis added). In this definition, Hobbes is *apparently* altering the complete liberty from law, this legally unrestrained freedom of the passions and actions that we saw in chapter 13, to a reduced version: "the liberty each man hath, to use his own power, as he will himself, for *the preservation of his own . . . life"* (ibid., emphasis added).

The freedom from law in the state of nature *now appears* to be limited to the "right of nature," which from the definition above seems to constitute the right of self-defense. That right does not extend to the actions that Hobbes mentions as occurring when human beings may desire something not only for their own conservation but sometimes for "their delectation only"—that is, for some other reason than their own conservation. For Hobbes says there are some human beings who pursue conquests because they take pleasure in contemplating their own power in the act of doing so, and Hobbes observes they may pursue these acts of conquest "farther than their security requires" (EW III, 111–12 [184–85]). We had concluded in our review of chapter 13 that there is no law against these actions in the state of nature; but now it seems that since such acts are not for self-preservation, by Hobbes's own admission, they appear to be violations of the right of nature.

To reiterate, the right of nature *appears* to be a qualification of the liberty human beings have in the state of nature as it is depicted in chapter 13, limiting the total freedom from law to the freedom of self-defense (even if such limits leave it still an exceedingly broad liberty). But if human freedom from law in the state of nature *is* limited to self-preservation, *how* is it limited? What limits it?

The text of chapter 14 will resolve the problem and show that the initial human liberty of the state of nature is total and that these apparent qualifications only develop upon discovering the power of other persons. Hobbes writes,

And because the condition of man, as hath been declared in the precedent chapter, is a condition of war of every one against every one: in which case every one is governed by his own reason; and there is nothing he can make use of, that may not be a help unto him, in preserving his life against his enemies; it followeth, that in such a condition, every man has a right to every thing; even to one another's body. (EW III, 117 [189–90])

In this passage we see that the war of all against all explains the right of nature—of self-defense—("and because the condition of man . . . is a condition of war"). This is to say that because of man's condition (his natural freedom), he is, at the same time, thrust into a condition of war; such freedom for the passionate nature of human beings means that they will war among themselves. The self-defensive right of nature is made necessary by an initial liberty to all things due to the absence of all law. Thus, an initial liberty appears as the engine or cause of war, and so the state of war is the necessary corollary of our natural liberty. Then war gives occasion for the right of nature, that is, the right of self-defense. Human beings may do whatever they can and use all manner of force and fraud due to a principle of self-defense, because, theoretically *prior to that*, they are naturally in a state of total liberty from all obligation; the right of self-defense is simply a statement of the prudent "retrenching" of that liberty in the face of the threat to a person's safety.

In the picture Hobbes draws in these chapters, both the complete liberty from law in the state of nature *and* the right of nature (that is, the right of self-defense) signify a person's liberty to use his or her own power as he or she will, free of any obligation to any other authority, including any notion of a deity to which human beings might be responsible. As human beings try to satisfy their desires and find themselves thwarted and hurt by impediments, they first experience fear, which teaches them that they had better not go about using their natural liberty simply and straightforwardly in trying to satisfy themselves; they must learn that the sword—the offensive quality of taking—must be converted, for the sake of their own preservation, into the shield—the quality of defending and protecting. This conversion is guided by the profound realization that their entire orientation must be to restrict the exercise of their natural liberty to this latter stance, which means that the sword now can only be used in the name of the shield.

The liberty of the right of nature thus consists in the self-defensive "anticipation" Hobbes spoke of in chapter 13, though the state of affairs that is the state of nature becomes such that, as human beings all fear for their lives and must take anticipatory steps to secure themselves, liberty becomes exceedingly broad. Thus, the guiding principle in the state of nature that limits natural freedom to the right of nature is the self-interest of the subject. God does not oblige men and women to make this restriction; it is made, rather, due to their own passion for self-preservation.

Warrender, however, insists that the guiding principle consists in the obligatory character of the laws of nature, which are obligatory because they are the command of one entitled to obedience—God. But where is a divine legal check on the freedom of man in the state of nature? As far as human beings are concerned, God is not there—nor is any law men know is God's law; as Hobbes says, there can be no natural knowledge of God since human beings cannot know anything of God by natural reason alone, except that there must be some First Mover.[3] The absence of restrictions, the postulate of an unbridled human nature—so that man in the state of nature *means* man without limits, except for what Hobbes calls "impediments," physical limits to his power—is what makes the state of nature a state of war and gives rise to the rules of reason that help human beings escape it. These impediments convert human beings from potentially roaming freebooters to caution-bound plotters peering out from behind shields. The liberty of the state of nature is qualified by a rule of self-defense because, through encounters with impediments composed of the self-interested actions of other human beings, men and women see the importance of seeking peace for the purpose of self-preservation. Human beings are compelled by self-interest alone in the state of nature to minimize their freedom in order to maximize it. This is the least dangerous, least offensive manner in which to possess one's liberty, for it gives the least possible cause for others to resent and quarrel with a person. No divine legislating power obliges human beings to restrict their natural freedom to self-defense in Hobbes's *Leviathan*; the right of nature—self-defense—becomes a limit to natural liberty for reasons derived from human nature as it is understood through the state of nature—and from no other cause.

Confirmation of Complete Liberty from Law in the State of Nature

Hobbes divides the first law of nature in the beginning of chapter 14 into two parts, "the first branch of which rule containeth the first, and the fundamental law of nature; which is, to seek peace and follow it." Hobbes says the second branch of this first rule is "the sum of the right of nature," which he renders succinctly as "by all means we can, to defend ourselves." Hobbes then writes of his second law of nature:

> That a man be willing, when others are so too, as far-forth, as for peace, and defense of himself he shall think it necessary, to lay down this *right to all things*; and be contented with so much liberty against other men, as he would allow other men against himself. (EW III, 118 [190], emphasis mine)

These laws of nature are derived from the same experience that teaches human beings to convert their total natural freedom to the right of self-defense. Hobbes speaks here of a "right to all things" in a completely unqualified way, suggesting that the motive for a person to lay down this right is not some responsiblity to a higher power, but to see other human beings do as he is doing—the purpose being the mutual advancement of the respective personal safety of all individuals concerned. Implicit in this passage is the notion that natural liberty is a right to all things, with no qualifications, and that human beings are led to limit themselves not because God commands it, but because their own self-interest dictates it.

Hobbes also says, "For as long as every man holdeth this right, of doing any thing he liketh; so long are all men in the condition of war." Here we note the words "holdeth the right of doing any thing he liketh," a description of natural liberty, are associated with what they *cause*, the condition of war. The clear implication is that the liberty is the *cause* of the war, for it is antecedent. This is an unequivocal description of the liberty of the state of nature—a liberty not limited to the necessity of self-defense, but of "doing anything" a person "liketh." Thus, we conclude that in Hobbes's state of nature there are no laws that can bind human beings, that can oblige them, seeing there is no overarching power to make them obey. God is not involved fundamentally in Hobbes's teaching concerning obligation.

But in a natural sense there is another sort of law—not a positive law of God—and Hobbes calls it a "precept found out by reason." This precept is "brought home," as it were, to each human being by his or her cognizance of impediments, especially those taking the form of the liberty of all other human beings. Such a "precept found out by reason" is but the conclusion drawn from observing other persons or even inanimate nature: when bodies of equal power and size seek to occupy the same space or to possess the same object, they collide and may damage one another. Self-interested, reasoning human beings are thus aware that they ought to avoid such damage to themselves.

In this sense there *is* a *sort* of obligation in Hobbes's state of nature—a kind of compulsion based on man's situation in nature. Human beings are, in a sense, *obliged* by the nature of things to fall back on a line called self-defense. But this is not how Hobbes first broaches the subject of obligation, and this is not what Hobbes *formally* means by it. It is, however, a *sense* of obligation employed in Hobbes's political philosophy.

Hobbes's Definition of Obligation

In the text of *Leviathan* from its beginning up to chapter 14, including this understanding we have garnered about the state of nature, there is no discussion of the notion of obligation, though the term "oblige" is mentioned in one passage in chapter 11 in a sense that will be taken into account as we proceed. It is in chapter 14, following Hobbes's treatment of the right of nature, that the term is formally introduced in the discussion of the laws of nature. When fearful human beings seek to escape death, they use their faculty of reason to find this precept: they ought to seek peace while being ever ready to defend themselves. From this first precept they derive a second, that, holding the first precept as their guide, they should be willing, when others are, too, to "lay down their right to all things."

Hobbes says that when a person lays down a right to anything, he "divest[s] himself of the liberty of hindering another of the benefit of his own right to the same." Hobbes explains that a person who renounces or "passeth away his right" does not, in so doing, give any other person a right that the other person did not already have before, since "there is nothing to which every man had not right by nature" in the first place. Thus the person who renounces a right only "standeth out of [the other person's] way, that the other "may enjoy his own original right, without hindrance from him; not without hindrance from another. So that the effect which redoundeth to one man, by another man's defect of right, is but so much diminution of impediments to the use of his own right original" (EW III, 118 [190–91]).

Hobbes goes on to explain in a passage that includes the only formal definition of "obligation" in *Leviathan*, that when a person has "either abandoned, or granted away his right; *then* is he said to be OBLIGED, or BOUND, not to hinder the~ ~, to whom such right is granted, or abandoned, from the benefit of it" (EW III, 119 [191], emphasis mine). Hobbes marks his formal definition by rendering it entirely in capital letters. This is the only occasion in *Leviathan* where the word is so treated. Here we see obligations identified by the laying aside of a right, something that happens only when human beings *divest themselves* of rights. To reiterate, obligations only occur when men and women give up some liberty or right themselves. They are self-assumed and not set over human beings by any other means.

For Hobbes obligation is a formal act prompted first of all by the desire to stay alive, a desire Hobbes traces back for us through his treatment of human psychology to a mechanistic, materialistic foundation.[4] There is no necessity to bring the God of traditional natural law into the bargain. I have contended that human beings confronted by the dilemma of their natural state find themselves obliged in an informal or natural sense by that condition—which then leads them to formally oblige themselves.

Warrender, however, argues that Hobbes has another notion of obligation that necessitates a role for a higher law in Hobbes's political thought. Though Warrender insisted in an essay written after his book was published (Warrender 1960) that he was not actually saying that God was vital to Hobbes's theory, but only that an obligatory natural law was, he clearly admits in *The Political Philosophy of Hobbes* that natural law must be understood as the command of an agent who obliges. He plainly tells us that this agent can only be God:

> If it is asked with regard to the State of Nature, for example, "why ought I to keep my covenants or to refrain from cruel actions?", the immediate answer is, "because the laws of nature prescribe such behaviour". If it is then further inquired, "why ought I to obey the laws of nature?", the reply may be made, "because these laws are the commands of God, who is entitled to obedience". . . . It is sufficient for our immediate purpose to accept the formula that granted the laws of nature are God's commands, they do oblige. (Warrender 1957, 98–101)

Warrender, then, explicitly connects his argument for a higher law to a God who makes it.[5]

Another Definition of Obligation

In *Leviathan*, chapter 15, Hobbes writes, "The laws of nature oblige *in foro interno*; that is to say, they bind to a desire they should take place: but *in foro externo*; that is, to the putting them to act, not always" (EW III, 145 [215]). Here we see the word "oblige" used in a way that is distinct from Hobbes's formal definition (EW III, 118–19 [191]). From that definition in chapter 14, it seemed that obligation occurred only when a person either renounced or transferred a right, but in implicit ways in that chapter and explicitly in chapter 15 we find Hobbes saying there is *another* kind of obligation and that in some respect the law of nature *obliges*. He speaks of this other sense not only in regard to the notion of *in foro interno*, but also refers to it at the outset of chapter 15: of "that law of nature, by which we are *obliged* [my emphasis] to transfer to another, such rights, as being retained, hinder the peace of mankind." Here Hobbes refers to an obligation that precedes the laying down of a right. But have we not already established that in *Leviathan* men have no obligations *before* such a transfer or renunciation of right?

Among the laws of nature, for example, is this rule: "That a man be willing, when others are so too, as far-forth, as for peace, and defense of himself he shall think it necessary, to lay down this right to all things" (EW III, 118 [190]). Hobbes is now saying that men are *obliged* to perform laws of nature such as this, but he has not given us any preparation, he has not explicitly told us the grounds for any such form of obligation. What does he mean when he speaks, in the first sentence of chapter 15, of being *obliged* to a law of nature?

Hobbes's Two Senses of Obligation

Hobbes uses the term "oblige" in *two* senses, a formal and an informal or natural sense (Raymond 1962, 345–48). Although the formal sense has its straightforward and explicit definition, the *natural* or informal meaning is not made explicit. Human beings are formally obliged when they lay down a right; we have seen this in chapter 14 where Hobbes gives his only formal definition. In this sense, when a person grants away a right, he or she is said to be obliged not to hinder those to whom such a right is granted (Barry 1968, 117–18). There are stated beneficiaries of the words and actions of the person who is obliged. Hobbes tells us that the strength of the bonds by which a human being is thus obliged lies not in words, that is, in the making of promises themselves, since "nothing is more easily broken than a man's word"; rather they are from "fear of some evil consequences upon their rupture" (EW III, 119 [191]). In formal obligation, fear based in the desire for self-preservation guarantees that human beings will abide by their commitments. We may presume that the evil consequences human beings would fear would be from those to whom they had renounced or transferred their right, if they should fail to allow them to benefit from this act. Formal obligation then, is guaranteed through fear—and it has this in common with the other sense of obligation, which we are calling *natural obligation*.

Natural obligation in Hobbes is obligation in the way natural law in Hobbes is law—in neither case are they properly so, but in both cases they represent the meeting of human desires and nature as mediated by human reason. Reason mediates in the case of natural law by means of precepts that show the desiring subject the way to peace; natural obligation represents the human will yielding to the precepts that reason has revealed to it.

This second use of obligation—that which we have seen in chapter 15—shows human beings being obliged in a way that predates the formal sense of obligation outlined above (EW III, 130 [201], 145 [215]). Here persons are not indicated as having, by words and actions, specifically laid down any right, and yet they are said to be obliged (S. Brown, Jr. 1965, 64–71).

Near the end of chapter 15, Hobbes speaks of the laws of nature *obliging in foro interno* (EW III, 145 [215]). He explains that this means the laws of nature "bind to a desire they should take place." In this sense, there is no one from whom a person would expect evil consequences should he fail in his obligations. In the formal sense of obligation, however, there *are* such sources from which to expect consequences. The laws of nature instead oblige in the sense that failure to observe them in the state of nature leaves a person more subject to the general fear of all human beings. This is why they bind to a desire they should take place—for human beings desire to live without such fear. It is the passion of fear that has the effect, in the state of nature, of making human beings find the laws of nature, and once they find them, self-interest persuades each person to yield his or her will to them. Fear acts to bind persons to what self-interest teaches them and in this sense it *obliges*.

The Role of Fear in Obligation

Fear is a common thread between both senses of obligation we have seen. The laws of nature oblige because human beings, by nature, always seek their own good, the primary good being maintenance of life itself, or, putting it another way, the avoidance of death. The laws of nature oblige in that they prompt human beings to choose the surest means they can to obtain some good for themselves—especially as such goods protect their lives and well-being. For Hobbes, obligation always involves human beings choosing to align their wills to a course of action that best serves their particular interests: it is thus self-assumed. Fear of death obliges human beings by prompting them to use their reason to find a way of escape that Hobbes calls "the laws of nature." When persons see these laws are in their interest as contributing to their survival, they naturally are inclined to follow these dictates of reason; this is Hobbes's sense of natural obligation. They are bound to choose these laws of nature because, as Hobbes puts it, human beings naturally always seek their own good, or at least seek to avoid what they consider an evil to themselves, "for man by nature chooseth the lesser evil" (EW III, 127 [199]).

Fear starts the ball rolling and keeps it rolling—since it remains there all the time to remind men and women of the original reason for their choices. The same fear ultimately leads them to enter *formally* into covenants and take upon themselves formal obligations through the process of forming commonwealths, whether these concern commonwealths of institution or of acquisition (*Leviathan*, chapters 18 and 19). Fear leads human beings to bind themselves and is the strength of the bonds of obligation once they do so.[6]

Fear itself, however, does not oblige, but rather human beings are obliged by their own desire to live and thus take the best possible course for life when confronted by fear, especially fear of violent death at the hands of human beings. Fear is then the strength of obligation, but obligation itself is the binding of the will to a course of action, which Hobbes reserves to the volition of the individual. The final desire of the individual, since each person desires escape from death, will be that the laws of nature should take place. Human beings are bound by self-interest, each by his or her own will, which is his or her own desire to escape fear and death (EW III, 126–27 [198–99], 185 [251–52]).

In *Leviathan*, in both formal and natural senses of obligation, human beings take obligations upon themselves by their own volition. They choose to bind themselves formally and they choose to follow the laws of nature—in both cases the choice is theirs, according to Hobbes. The first beneficiary of assuming the obligation to obey the laws of nature or of formally renouncing a right would thus be the obligation-assuming individual himself (Barry 1968, 125–27, 129–30). Hobbes writes, "Whensoever a man transferreth his right, or renounceth it; it is either in consideration of some right reciprocally transferred to himself; or for some other good he hopeth for thereby. For it is a voluntary act: and of the voluntary acts of every man, the object is some good to himself" (EW III, 119–20 [192]). This specifically refers to formal obligation, but it applies equally to natural obligation.

Obligation in *Leviathan* is Based in Laws of Human Nature and Not in God

At the outset of chapter 13, concerning man in the state of nature, Hobbes outlined the tendency of human beings to be grieved by the company of others when there is no power able to overawe them all. In such a state, persons look out for signs of their being undervalued, they resent signs of contempt, and they are willing even to destroy one another when they find or imagine themselves so treated. The power of such characteristics is at its greatest when there is no law, for law represents the product of an agreement to "tame" such behavior through setting up a power that will be present to overawe these and any other behaviors antagonistic to peace. Such agreements to set up this power cannot come about until human beings lay down their right to treat others with such liberty as Hobbes describes in chapter 13. Thus Hobbes indicates the fear of the liberty of man in the state of nature turns human beings against injustice, ingratitude, arrogance, and pride. In Hobbes's argument, this is a situation attributable to human nature and fully explained by it and does not require a notion of God.

Hobbes's view of man is grounded in the state of nature, and such a view allows us to see human beings as unchangeably who they are—no prior state, no golden age, no Eden is presumed.[7] The state of nature represents Hobbes's demonstration of what he has determined most human beings will always do in a given circumstance. Thus, the laws of nature are the eternal rules of escape from the state of nature because human nature can be depended upon to act in a uniform and predictable manner where self-preservation is concerned. They do not seek peace because of a divine injunction for they have no natural knowledge of God, but they seek it in order to save themselves from the death that is so close in their natural state. Thus Hobbes concludes, "The laws of nature are immutable and eternal; for injustice, ingratitude, arrogance, pride, iniquity, acception of persons, and the rest, can never be lawful. For it can never be that war shall preserve life, and peace destroy it" (EW III, 145 [215]).

It ought to be clear, then, that the laws of nature will always oblige as long as human beings see them as the truth about their situation and as the principles of their own safety. Hobbes builds them strictly from human nature and they are based on the human desire to stay alive. The laws of nature founded on human nature as Hobbes's teaching explains it, are planted firmly in the substance of this world. They are as sure as any physical law—they are always true principles for survival, for the conditions that produce them are unchangeable. To ignore them is to encourage war and to ignore one's own good. In Hobbes's political philosophy, then, a person's own good, and not God, obliges him.

Warrender's "Validating Conditions"

Warrender separates the question of what constitutes obligation for human beings in Hobbes's thought into two parts: the "ground of obligation" and "validating conditions" that make such a "ground" a justifiable basis for acting. There is no clear reason why Hobbes's text should be made to suggest these two terms and they are found nowhere in the text; they are Warrender's inventions, though there are passages in the text that allow him this view. By noting Warrender's view here, it is possible to understand something of the motivation behind his position and the source of this motivation.

Warrender's "validating conditions" are conditions, he says, that must be met *before* persons in the state of nature are obliged to obey the laws of nature. This term allows Warrender to bypass the possibility that self-preservation alone is the basis for all motivation in Hobbes's treatment of obligation. Warrender's discussion of validating conditions for obligation is, as he says, "based throughout upon the assumption that the ground or true source of obligation is present" (Warrender 1957, 97). We learn that that ground is God and that the laws of nature must be understood, therefore, as God's commands. From Warrender we also learn that for those who are insecure or unbelieving in the state of nature, the laws of nature do not oblige because the validating conditions that would make them obligatory—safety and belief—have not been met.

By his separation of obligation into "ground" and "validating conditions," Warrender preserves a traditional notion of moral obligation based in divine will for those for whom the requisite conditions have been met. But if Warrender is correct, one must wonder what becomes the basis of obligation for all those who are insecure and unbelieving, that is, for all those for whom the validating conditions have not been met? Warrender leaves such persons unable to escape the state of nature unless, of course, they adopt the laws of nature as we have argued here Hobbes intended they should be adopted: as principles of prudence that they are obliged to follow for no other reason than self-interest. Warrender, however, making self-preservation a validating condition of obligation, writes, "The reason why I *can* do my duty is that I am able . . . to see it as a means to my preservation; but the reason why I *ought* to do my duty is that God commands it. The ground of my obligation is therefore God's command" (1957, 213).[8] Warrender wants to preserve Hobbes as a teacher of old-fashioned morality and to escape the conclusion that human beings are ultimately motivated only by self-interest; the invention of the notion of "validating conditions" enables him to do these things.

I have argued that for Hobbes, self-preservation is the ground of obligation and that what human beings ought to do is determined by nothing else than self-interest. For Hobbes, there is no higher moral authority. The view of man described in *Leviathan*, chapter 6, the view that human beings are ultimately only self-interested beings free from all authority that would hinder the exercise of their passionate natures, is carried over to the state of nature in chapter 13 and is in no way changed in the process of getting human beings from that state into civil society. The natural laws that enable human beings to escape the state of nature are founded, too, on the drive for self-preservation. The only "ought" involved that touches the issue of obligation is based on the notion that human beings are, in a way, obliged by their own nature.

Warrender, it seems, believes the *only* sense of obligation Hobbes ever employs is the formal sort introduced in *Leviathan*, chapter 14—the voluntary laying aside of a right, which means to contract a duty, not to hinder those to whom such a right is abandoned or granted. But in chapter 15, Hobbes says, "the laws of nature *oblige* in foro interno [emphasis mine]; that is to say, they bind to a desire that they should take place (EW III, 145 [215]). In this latter case, as Brian Barry puts it, "a new, noncontractual, sense of obligation" is being introduced, a sense that we discussed earlier in this chapter under the rubric of "natural obligation." Barry explains that in this employment of the term, Hobbes is "using the term 'oblige' where he has previously been using 'dictate' " (1968, 129–30). Thus Hobbes's text might read, "The laws of nature *dictate* in foro interno." Here we join with Barry in calling this kind of impulsion or dictation of nature "natural obligation." A "dictate" in this sense comes not from God, but from the natural human desire for self-preservation. A dictate of the laws of nature does not constitute true, formal obligation for Hobbes. Hobbes's use of the term "oblige" in these two ways, therefore, is certainly confusing—and misleading—and helps explain how Warrender was misled. The next chapter of this study deals with Hobbes's intention in writing ambiguously as he does concerning obligation here.

My purpose in this chapter has been simply this: to show that God is not necessary to establish a basis of obligation upon which Hobbes's political philosophy may operate. I have shown this by demonstrating that Warrender is mistaken; Hobbes's placement of God in his argument in *Leviathan*, chapters 13 through 15, does not prove the ingenuousness or candidness of Hobbes's treatment of deity, despite Warrender's claims. If Hobbes's treatment of deity represents a genuinely held theological view and evidence of real belief, some other argument must be made than one constituted by the issue of obligation in *Leviathan*.

Hobbes's Law of Nature is Distinct from Traditional Natural Law

As much as human beings fear the evil consequences of war—which is principally violent death—so much are they obliged to desire that these precepts of reason, these laws of nature, should take place. Thus Hobbes can conclude that "the chiefest of natural evils . . . is Death," which man shuns "by a certain impulsion of nature, no less than that whereby a Stone moves downward" (EW II, 8). The fear of death and the desire for life push human beings to act, almost as gravity impels a stone to fall downward. This is why the "articles of peace" found out by reason in *Leviathan*, chapter 13, are said by Hobbes to be "laws of nature," but they are not natural laws in the classical or medieval sense of the natural law generated by some higher being or some ideal, but in the modern sense—generated by an impersonal nature.

Through the discussion above of Hobbes's teaching of natural liberty and natural right in *Leviathan*, chapters 13 and 14, we see that Hobbes understands human beings to possess a freedom unlike anything natural religionists envisage for man—and certainly unlike anything portrayed in the Bible or believed by almost anyone who called himself a Christian in Hobbes's time. Hobbes's teaching is that the natural world is divorced from any "higher" purpose or teleology. The law of nature in Hobbes has a deflated status in that it is no longer tied in any meaningful way to the law of a God who cares for human beings. But at the same time it has an elevated status, since it has, as it were, "moved up" to fill the place formerly held by God's commandments. They are now nature's commands, found out by human reason.

Chapter Four

A Curious Ambiguity: Hobbes's Departure from the Christian Natural Law Tradition

Hobbes sought to persuade the largest group of his readers that the Bible and Christian theology supported his political teaching based on the human freedom outlined in the first part of *Leviathan*; these readers were the object of his great effort to reinterpret the Bible (EW III, 713 [728]). To succeed in his endeavor, Hobbes had to transform the meaning of the Bible, appropriating the Scriptures to justify a moral order based on the self-interest and self-preservation of the individual. He sought to accomplish his goal, furthermore, by means of much duplicitous ambiguity, which allowed him to seem not to depart from the tenets of Christian faith; his ambiguity has allowed Hobbes "converts" today among a number of his scholarly readers.

The purpose of this chapter will be to examine the means by which a reader concerned with Hobbes's religious expression, such as the subject of much of the preceding chapter, Howard Warrender, could fail to perceive Hobbes's departure from the tenets of Christian faith. It is my argument that Hobbes is interested in appealing to religious passions in a manner that will channel them toward supporting his teaching. In order to do this, Hobbes had to appeal to these religious passions to persuade—and avoid offending—his intended audience; this, I contend, involved a certain lack of candor. This chapter deals with only one aspect of Hobbes's disingenuousness, that is, with the manner in which he disguised his departure from the Christian natural law tradition. Subsequent chapters will reveal more completely Hobbes's intentions in his ambiguous treatment not only of Christian natural law, but of the Bible, and orthodox Christian theology, generally.

The Hobbesian and Thomistic
Conceptions of Natural Law

In the conclusion of *Leviathan*, chapter 15, Hobbes equates conclusions of human reason, which he calls natural law, with the revealed word of God found in the Bible. The association of the Bible with natural law has precedents, going back, for example, to Richard Hooker, and, most powerfully, to Thomas Aquinas. Howard Warrender in his *Political Philosophy of Hobbes* does not consider Hobbes to have moved away from what we may call the Christian or Thomistic natural law tradition and accepts Hobbes's equation of the law of nature and the word of God. That equation has provided the grounds for esteeming Hobbes a sincere Christian, or at least a genuine theist or deist participating in the Christian natural law tradition, but I contend this equation is a tactic, a part of Hobbes's ambiguous style directed at disguising his fundamental departure from Christianity. This tactic is part of Hobbes's plan to advance his teaching based on natural human freedom, a plan that ultimately required the appearance of the support of revealed religion. To establish this, I begin by comparing Hobbesian and Thomistic treatments of natural law in order to make plain Hobbes's leave-taking from this traditional Christian position.

Thomas Aquinas speaks not only of a natural law and a divine law, that is, of a natural law and the Bible, as Hobbes does, but also of an "eternal law," which he treats before ever discussing these other laws. For Aquinas, "the entire universe is ruled by divine reason, and this 'ratio gubernationis' has the character of law; the end of the divine government is God Himself, and His law is no other than Himself" (Carlyle and Carlyle 1928, 38; Thomas Aquinas n.d., 12–13 [*Summa Theologica*, 91:1]).

Hobbes equates natural law and the revealed or "divine" law of the Bible, but a higher divine reason, the higher law, or *telos*, which Aquinas's eternal law proclaims and that the Bible makes explicit, is neglected in Hobbes's natural law teaching where self-preservation is the chief end. In *Leviathan*, natural law does not point to an end in God as it does for Aquinas (for which purpose an "eternal law" is posited above all other law). For Aquinas, natural law is the way God helps " 'provide' . . . for the rational creature" in helping it partake of the eternal law, and it assists the Bible—the revealed or divine law—in this task. In fact, Aquinas terms natural law "participation of the rational creature in the eternal law." He wrote, "The light of natural reason, by which we discern what is good and what is evil, belongs to the natural law; it is nothing else than the impression of the divine light in us" (Carlyle and Carlyle 1928, 38-39; Thomas Aquinas n.d., 14–16 [*Summa Theologica* 91:2]).

Hobbes contrariwise argues there is no eternal good or evil to discern outside of precepts based on satisfying the passions (EW III, 41 [120]). Good and evil are completely subjective except for this primary tenet: each reasonable creature would agree that its own violent destruction as a desiring being is an evil. Thus reason, which Hobbes also calls "the law of nature," might be said to see a natural "law" that could be called good: the "law" of self-preservation.

Such a view of natural reason does not "participate" in any higher law. It has, that is, no association with a notion of what self-preservation might be *for*, which association might enable a person to say that self-preservation is for the sake of something higher, such as loving, serving, or enjoying God. The notion of law implies a lawgiver, and in the Thomistic understanding, the law represents the intention of this legislator to instruct those who lack full understanding. This instruction serves some end the legislator has in view, be it wisdom or righteousness or some other sense of completeness. For Hobbes, the natural law is not the work of a lawgiver but rather a precept found out by reason that, when followed, conduces to the peace and safety, and thus the self-preservation of the rational being; no higher purpose is involved (Thomas Aquinas n.d., 59–61 [*Summa Theologica* 94:2]; *Leviathan*, chapter 13, especially EW III, 115–17 [188–89]).

The divine law—the revealed law of God found in Scripture—was added to the natural law according to Aquinas,

> because the final end of man is beyond reason, because of the uncer-tainty of men's judgments, because human law can only deal with the external actions of men. . . . The divine law . . . was added that men might participate in the eternal law in a higher manner. (Carlyle and Carlyle 1928, 40; Thomas Aquinas n.d., 21–22 [*Summa Theologica* 91:4])

Hobbes departs from this by making the divine law conform to (and thus confirm) his notion of natural law rather than pointing to a higher end in God, that is, in eternal law.

We find in Richard Hooker, the great theological authority of the Anglican Church from the sixteenth century, that the Thomistic tradition is carried forward by the established English Church. In *The Laws of Ecclesiastical Polity*, Hooker writes of the eternal law, the natural law (which he also calls the law of reason), and the divine law in the same manner as does Aquinas (Hooker 1970, 1:198–212 [Bk. I, i–iii]; 1:226–36 [Bk. I, viii.3–11]; 1:278–82 [Bk. I, xvi.2–5]). Hooker states the first principle of natural law in a manner that at first seems similar to the way Hobbes puts it, but on examination we see their views are quite different. Hooker quotes the Bible, "No man hateth his own flesh, but doth love and cherish it" (Eph. 5:29) and calls this quotation an axiom "of that law whereby natural agents are guided." He adds that this principle has its use also "in the moral, yea, even . . . the spiritual actions of men, and consequently in all laws belonging to men howsoever."

The distinction between Hooker and Hobbes here is that for the former the law of self-preservation is stated in the context of an end—what self-preservation is *for*. Hooker writes that Christ has provided this natural law of loving and cherishing one's life for the protection of the church—the body of believers who love God—and for all other human beings as well, that they might live a long life and thereby have ample opportunity to be persuaded of the verity of divine love (Hooker 1970, 1:279 [Bk. I, xvi.3]). Thus Hobbes's teaching departs not only from St. Thomas, but also from Richard Hooker in his understanding of natural law.

Two years after Hobbes's death, a work appeared written specifically against Hobbes's natural law teaching. Samuel Parker wrote his *Demonstration of the Divine Authority of the Laws of Nature and the Christian Religion* (1681) to show "the evident obligation of the Law of Nature." Parker "attack[ed] Hobbes for asserting the existence of a right of nature antecedent of the laws of nature," that is, for suggesting the autonomy of man from all higher authority (Hinnant 1980, 5–6). His chief argument was that natural law can only oblige human beings through the "supposition of a Deity," a supposition he declared Hobbes denies.

Another of Hobbes's contemporaries, bishop of St. David's William Lucy, saw Hobbes's statement in *Leviathan*, chapter 13—"to this war of every man against every man this also is consequent that nothing can be unjust"—as the denial of the existence of natural law. Lucy wrote that when Hobbes said "where there is no common power, there is no law, where no law, no injustice," he further denied the existence of such a law of nature. He declared against Hobbes,

> There is no man born in the world without a law and a common power over him and others; the law is that writ in their hearts, and this is it which St. Paul speaks, Ro.2.15. which shews the law written in their hearts, that law of Nature which is writ in the heart of every man, and this common power is God; and therefore as St. Paul speaks there, their consciences also bearing witness, and their thoughts the meanwhile, accusing or excusing. (Lucy 1663, 158)

All these writers—Aquinas, Hooker, Parker, and Lucy—represent the traditional Christian understanding of natural law and the antagonism between that view and Hobbes's new rendering of it. As one modern student of Hobbes's contemporaries put it, Hobbes's "doctrine of ethics grounded in positive law conveyed irresistibly the notion of atheism. Hobbes, it was felt, had cut the laws of nature off from their divine source" (Mintz 1962, 27).

Hobbes appears to have been the inaugurator of the idea of a natural law unattached to God, an idea marking a great departure from the medieval Christian tradition. This new view of natural law launched a new school of thinking on this subject that emphasized human reason set free from the authority of Christianity, instead even subjecting "the Church to natural law, rather than natural law to the Church" (Barker 1934, xli; see also Troeltsch 1934, 207). The new view of natural law only became clear as Hobbes explained it in the context of his great discovery—the state of nature. The only law existent there was actually not true and proper law but precepts gleaned by human reason from the very nature of things— the "law" of self-preservation. But of Hobbes's law of nature, the great German scholar of natural law Otto Gierke wrote: "Such Natural Law was no law at all: it only sailed under the name of law like a ship under false colours, to conceal the bare piratical idea of power" (Gierke 1934, 97). Gierke concluded that Hobbes's treatment of natural law was "laying an axe to the roots" of the old tradition.

The purpose of this brief survey of natural law is to emphasize that Hobbes's new natural law teaching based on his discovery of the state of nature, is ultimately separated from any real reliance on deity and yet also to stress that Hobbes nonetheless associates his treatment of natural law with the divine, and, indeed, with the God of the Bible. Our question is, what is the specific manner of this association and why does Hobbes make it? To answer this question, we turn to Warrender and his reading of *Leviathan* because Warrender is representative of a kind of audience I spoke of earlier in the second chapter—those readers open to new understandings whom Hobbes wished to meet on grounds that would not be disruptive to their most fundamental and fixed moral and religious ideas.

Warrender's Acceptance of Hobbes's Equation of the Word of God and the Laws of Nature

In order to support his conviction that there is a genuine linkage of Hobbesian and Thomistic natural law, Warrender's treatment of obligation in *The Political Philosophy of Hobbes* focuses on the end of *Leviathan*, chapter 15, where Hobbes finishes his two-chapter discussion of natural law. The final paragraph of the chapter reads:

> These dictates of reason, men used to call by the name of laws, but improperly: for they are but conclusions, or theorums concerning what conduceth to the conservation and defense of themselves; whereas law, properly, is the word of him, that by right hath command over others. But yet if we consider the same theorems, as delivered in the word of God, that by right commandeth all things; then are they properly called laws. (EW III, 147 [217])

Warrender fastens on this passage, but because he does not interpret it with careful reference to its context and to qualifiers even within the passage itself, he follows a path leading to a critical misunderstanding of Hobbes's thought. A careful reading of the last sentence of chapter 15 will show how Warrender reached his conclusion, further confirm Hobbes's break with the Christian tradition of natural law and, finally, begin to indicate how Hobbes may have purposefully tried to mislead readers like Warrender.

Hobbes begins this paragraph by saying these precepts are not laws, but dictates of reason. Laws, he has said, can only be made when human beings have agreed upon persons who shall make them (EW III, 114 [187]). No person can make laws unless each one in any number of human beings lays aside his or her right of command over others, which Hobbes calls each person's natural right to command all things, thus leaving at least one beneficiary of that laying aside of right with an undiminished natural right to make law—the position to be held in civil association by Leviathan, which Hobbes introduces in the sixteenth chapter (EW III, 114–15 [187–88]).

When Hobbes writes in the second sentence of the paragraph quoted above, "But yet *if* we consider the same theorems, as delivered in the word of God, that by right commandeth all things; *then* are they properly called laws [my emphasis]," he is *suggesting* these theorems can be considered proper law *if* they are understood to be *the same as* the principles in the prophetic, positive law, revealed to human beings miraculously by God. If this were the case God would then fulfill the stipulation required for true law-makers, that is, "him that by right hath command over others." Hobbes allows us to presume here that the principles of his laws of nature are the same as those of God's prophetic written word. In doing this, he is suggesting that God is a legitimate lawmaker after the fashion of proper lawmakers described in all of chapters 14 and 15 that precedes this final paragraph of chapter 15. Here he also introduces God as the possessor of rights. God now appears as a lawmaker, one that human beings have not set up and one that is not their equal by nature.

It is curious that Hobbes employs this qualification at the end of chapter 15 so contradictory to what he has said throughout chapters 13, 14, and 15. He wishes in one short and ambiguous paragraph at the end of these three chapters to equate his radical new understanding of natural law with the old natural law. We shall examine this final sentence of chapter 15 because Warrender makes it a cornerstone of his thesis and because by examining it we shall discover the root of his mistaken understanding of the role of God in *Leviathan*.

A Problem with Hobbes's Equation

Hobbes's equation of the laws of nature and the word of God in the first phrase of the last sentence of chapter 15 was actually first attempted in a statement made a few pages earlier in chapter 15 where he stated that all these laws of nature "*have been* contracted into one sum" (EW III, 144 [214], emphasis added). If we notice the verb tense (it is past-perfect), we see Hobbes's indication that this "summation" of the laws of nature was completed at some time prior to the present discussion. The words "have been contracted" suggest the work of summation was done *before* the composition of Hobbes's work, so that Hobbes is suggesting that his laws of nature are merely confirming what human beings already knew from another source. Hobbes tells us what this "contraction" is, revealing its source: "Do not that to another, which thou wouldest not have done to thyself." We immediately recognize this as language resembling the Golden Rule of the Bible, taken from the words of Jesus himself (Matt. 7:12 and Luke 6:31).

By this "summation" Hobbes associates the Bible with the laws of nature. But Hobbes's rendition of Scripture is not quite identical to the biblical passage; it is a negative statement introduced by "do not" and not the original positive, "*Do* unto others." This is no small change. This passage of Scripture is known as the "Golden Rule" because it represents a summary of all the laws God has revealed to man (as opposed to all the laws of nature found out by unassisted reason in Hobbes's work). The Bible even indicates that if this rule is fulfilled, all the other laws will thus be fulfilled. A further insight into the importance of this "summary" passage may be obtained by juxtaposing it to one other summary expression in Scripture: "Thou shalt love the Lord thy God with all thy heart, soul and might and Thou shalt love thy neighbor as thyself" (Matt. 22:35–40, Deut. 6:4–5, Lev. 19:18, Gal. 5:14). The New Testament equates these two summaries: "Love worketh no ill to his neighbor, therefore love is the fulfilling of the law" and "This commandment have we from him [God], that he who loveth God love his brother also" (Rom. 13:1–10, I John 4:7–21).

Hobbes turns this imperative around from the positive injunction "Love God and love thy neighbor" into an implicit "right to privacy"—"Leave others alone as you want them to leave you alone"—so that Hobbes's summary of the laws of nature, not to mention the particular laws themselves, says nothing of *loving* either God or man.[1] The sense here is not only that self-concern has priority over the command to love others, but that love nowhere enters into the picture (I John 4:8; EW II, 5). It is this law of nature that allows human beings to gratify self-love in civil society—and this is the law Hobbes wishes to equate with the law of God. When he suggests that we consider the laws of nature as the word of God,

Hobbes is speaking ultimately of a God who has been crowded out by nature, yet he appears to be suggesting that we consider the "laws of nature" as equivalent to the laws of the God of the Bible.

We must not fail to see here that the duty to love God is replaced by the right to be left alone, but this "replacement" is not obvious; it is disguised by the work of equation Hobbes is carrying forward in the last sentence of *Leviathan*, chapter 15. Making God's law equivalent to the law of nature hides what is actually taking place: the transformation of the Bible into a defense of human autonomy or the right to oneself.

The Notion of God's Right

The second phrase of the last sentence of chapter 15—"If we consider the laws of nature the same as the word of God, *that by right commandeth all things*" (my emphasis)—represents an addition to what Hobbes has said up to this point about the notion of *right*, and Warrender understands it as a key to Hobbes's notion of obligation. Previously, right was defined as the "right of nature," the right or liberty all men have to all things by nature in order to defend themselves.[2] Hobbes here seems to be introducing God as the one who would naturally have the greatest liberty of all. This is a radical addition because formerly right was seen in the context of a state of nature in which no one was finally more powerful than anyone else.

Formerly, right in *Leviathan* had been posited on the equality of all human beings (Barry 1968, 118–19; EW IV, 295). But in the last sentence of chapter 15, we see what appears to be a new notion of right, for here is God, a being who is superior to everyone else, and the possibility arises, since now all beings are not equal, that the inferior ones, that is, all human beings, might have some natural obligation to yield to the superior one—God—by virtue of his infinitely superior power.

The theater in which this discussion has been set—the state of nature—remains unchanged from chapter 13, and yet Hobbes at the end of chapter 15 now seems to introduce God into it. The moment he does, he gives God the kind of position he will later give the sovereign, once human beings have renounced or laid aside their rights. Hobbes, if he is applying rights to God as rights are understood by his former description of the state of nature—"the liberty each man hath, to use his own power, as he will himself, for the preservation of his own nature" (EW III, 116 [189])—makes God the power that can overawe everyone else, the effect of which is to instantly transform the state of nature into God's commonwealth by acquisition as outlined by Hobbes in *Leviathan*, chapter 20. God has total freedom to do what he will—for what law binds him? In fact, God creates laws and thus legislates what is good or evil. Warrender concludes that God, by this notion of right, obliges men to obey in Hobbes's thought.

If God were present in the state of nature—as Hobbes's statement at the end of chapter 15 could be taken to suggest—could he not transform the state of nature into his commonwealth by his power? Would human beings be obligated to obey God, then—since he would be so superior to them? This is the case Warrender wants to make, that Hobbes believes power alone can oblige and that God's absolute power obliges absolutely. But will Hobbes's text permit it? Hobbes does write, "The right of nature, whereby God reigneth over men, and punisheth those that break his laws, is to be derived, not from his creating them, as if he required obedience as gratitude for his benefits, but from his *irresistible power*" (EW III, 345 [397]). Hobbes goes on to say that if, by nature, there had been any person of irresistible power, there would be no reason why that person could not have ruled all men. Hobbes says, "To those therefore whose power is irresistible, the dominion of all men adhereth naturally by their excellence of power" (EW III, 346 [397]). The principle of God's *right* is his irresistible power.

But even if God were present to men in the state of nature (and nothing in *Leviathan* should be construed to indicate Hobbes believes God would be present to men there), and though God's power would overawe the inferior power of all human beings because he holds the "right of afflicting men at his pleasure" by virtue of his power (EW III, 345–46 [397]), yet *if* men have not put aside their own natural right, in the terms of Hobbes's *Leviathan*, they cannot be said to be *obliged* to obey God's commands. We say this because in *Leviathan* Hobbes makes it clear that obligations, at least as they are formally understood, are always self-assumed. This is established in how he defines obligation in chapter 14.

Thus, in *Leviathan*, God's unquestioned "right to command" in no sense obliges human beings, as weak as they are in comparison to God. If, however, we were to engraft into *Leviathan* a definition of obligation found in *De Cive*, Warrender's case for the obligation of human beings to God according to God's "right" could have some ground for justification, for there Hobbes speaks of *two* sorts of natural obligation. The first sort is similar to the use we have treated previously and has to do with how "heaven and earth and all creatures do obey the common laws of their creation" (EW II, 209). In this sense, the conditions of nature itself are said to *naturally* oblige. But the second sort of natural obligation in *De Cive* occurs when hope or fear makes the weaker yield to the stronger. There Hobbes says, "From this last kind of obligation, that is to say, from fear or conscience of *weakness* in respect of the Divine power, it comes to pass that we are obliged to obey God in his natural kingdom" (emphasis mine).

The second form of natural obligation in *De Cive* is quite different from anything we find in *Leviathan* and refers to God's *obliging* men by means of his irresistible power because human beings are so weak and fear the consequences of not yielding. Hobbes's work neither ignores God's power nor human weakness; his text merely excludes these from constituting the formal stuff of obligation. In *Leviathan*, though God may have a right to command because of his power with which he can punish those who do not yield, this does not mean human beings are formally obliged to obey him. Though this second use is dropped by Hobbes in *Leviathan*, Warrender fails to take this into consideration (Warrender 1957, 8).[3] He fastens, instead, on this last sentence of *Leviathan*, chapter 15, and seeks to bolster his position by using a passage from *De Cive*. Warrender cannot find this elsewhere in *Leviathan* and thus makes his fundamental argument concerning obligation in *Leviathan* by relying on a passage from *De Cive*: "Now if God have the right of sovereignty from his power, it is manifest that the obligation of yielding him obedience lies on men by reason of their weakness" (EW II, 209).

Hobbes wrote three versions of his political theory and each version contains revisions of significance, which cannot be ignored when looking from one version to another. If passages are not imported from outside *Leviathan*, we see that God's right to command because of his irresistible power—though we grant God possesses such power—does not mean human beings are *obliged* to obey. Hobbes's definition of obligation in *Leviathan* tells us that if there is no laying aside of right, there is no obligation (EW III, 118–19 [190–91]; Barry 1968, 119–21).

In *Leviathan*, a person's natural obligation to obey natural law is not founded on God's power, but on the self-interested desires prompting reason to seek a way of escape from fear of death, that is, a way of self-preservation. The precepts reason then suggests to all persons shows them a way that their own interest *obliges* them to follow. One might say their fear forces them—but Hobbes avoids saying that. Human beings are left free to choose, even in the presence of fear. Yet the desire for their own good always inclines them in a certain way—so that in this sense, their own nature does seem to force them, but since it is of, or in, themselves, and liberty and obligation in the same thing cannot be, Hobbes is able to resolve the issue: a man's *liberty* to preserve himself cannot be called his *obligation* to preserve himself.

Thus, for Hobbes in *Leviathan*, all obligations are self-assumed, that is, they issue from the liberty of the individual and are not constituted out of the superior power of others. God's right to command, then, even if acknowledged, does not oblige human beings in *Leviathan*.[4]

Why Hobbes Did Not Want to Make Absolute Power Oblige

One may certainly wonder why Hobbes took up the point of the obligation due to absolutely superior power in *De Cive* and then deleted it from *Leviathan*. One must wonder, too, what bearing it has on the notion of God Hobbes presents in the final form of his political philosophy. Three modern commentators have suggested that the change takes place because Hobbes found it necessary to set forth all obligation as self-assumed in order that the absolute liberty of the individual in the state of nature could be established, which would then redound to the freedom of the sovereign; thus, the sovereign Hobbes establishes in *Leviathan*, chapter 17, could not be *obliged* to obey either God or the subjects who covenanted together (Barry 1968, 117–20, 134n12; Orwin 1975, 26–44; Gierke 1934, 60–61).[5]

The liberty, that is, the right of the individual, is absolute in the state of nature.[6] And, as Hobbes suggests, when human beings lay aside right to set up a "sovereign authority by common consent to defend them," they do not invest this authority with a right to all things, a right to reign over the rest (EW III, 346 [397]). Rather, they all originally possessed such a right; the power of the sovereign lies in all others laying down *their* right. Thus, it appears Hobbes's decision not to include this second sort of natural obligation in *Leviathan* was for the purpose of insuring the total freedom of sovereign power, as the separate analyses of Gierke, Barry, and Orwin suggest.

God may still have a right of power to command the sovereign, but the sovereign, not limited by any obligation to that power, retains the right of command over all those who have consented to lay aside their right; this is how the sovereign "benefits" from the obligation of those individuals, now subjects. For they have agreed to lay down their rights in order to set up the sovereign authority, but the sovereign power itself has made no such agreement with anyone.

God's power is unlimited, but then, so too, is the power of Leviathan, for this is not the name of a person, but of an artificial person—Hobbes, indeed, calls it "the mortal god" (EW III, 158 [227]). In a sense, Hobbes has established, at least concerning human beings, two gods. They both have power to overawe all human beings, but since Hobbes's Leviathan-sovereign is independent of the biblical God, not being obliged to him, he is finally superior to him concerning the world of human beings. But, as we have established here, these two gods do not conflict; Hobbes has made one of them final arbiter over all questions concerning authority within a civil association by giving the authority over interpretation of the Bible to Leviathan. Hobbes's removal of the obligation of human beings to obey the law of nature as God's commands by reason of God's infinite power in the state of nature makes room for the establishment of the omnipotent mortal god, Leviathan.

Therefore, Hobbes's saying that the laws of nature are the same as the word of God, who "by right commandeth all things," does not refer to God's right in God's superior power to *oblige* in *Leviathan*. Furthermore, the removal of the understanding that absolute power obliges also frees individual human beings from all authorities they do not themselves set up, and such authority includes, above all, the deity of the Bible. Finally, the argument of the preceding two sections of this chapter only underscores our argument that the freedom or liberty of the state of nature means the complete freedom or liberty of the individual in the state of nature from all restraint of law; nothing originally obliges there but self-interest.

The Last Words in *Leviathan*, Chapter 15

The third and final portion of the concluding sentence of chapter 15, which we have been examining, is that which Warrender takes for his cornerstone: "But yet if we consider the same theorems, as delivered in the word of God, that by right commandeth all things; *then are they properly called laws*" (emphasis mine). We have seen that the major premise of Hobbes's sentence (the "if" phrase that equates dictates of reason that are precepts of self-preservation to the law of the Bible) is ambiguous and misleading, and since this major premise of the sentence is ultimately not true, neither is his conclusion: these nineteen precepts of self-preservation described by Hobbes in chapters 14 and 15 are not properly called laws, and especially not the laws of God. And yet Warrender's argument is built on the premises of this sentence, and finally on one telltale little word, "if."

Warrender is quite right to be interested in this final sentence of *Leviathan*, chapter 15; it is a vital passage since it is the seal on the awkward graft whereby the biblical God is incorporated into the Hobbesian state of nature. But in taking it as the basis for Hobbes's theory of obligation or as the basis for estimating Hobbes's notion of God, Warrender has been mistaken.[7]

The Emphasis of Warrender's Position

Warrender summarizes his position in the fifth chapter of his book under the subtitle "The Ground of Obligation" (Warrender 1957, 97). In this summary he treats the sentence we have just analyzed *and* the sentence that immediately precedes it, that is, the entire last paragraph of chapter 15. These two sentences must be taken together; they cannot be rightly understood separately.[8]

Warrender begins with the first sentence of the paragraph and writes, "Hobbes describes the essential character of law as he sees it, in his assertion that 'law, properly, is the word of him, that by right hath command over others' " (97). Warrender tells us that to make the laws of nature the commands of God, they must be the "word of him who, by right, has command over others." He is preparing to make the case that the laws of nature are the actual commands of God. In its context the phrase has precisely the opposite intent Warrender is trying to give to it, but Hobbes's meaning can only be understood if one looks at this sentence in full:

> These dictates of reason men use to call by the name of laws, but improperly: for they are but conclusions or theorems . . . concerning what conduceth to the conservation and defense of themselves, *whereas law, properly, is the word of him, that by right hath command over others.* (EW III, 147 [216–17], emphasis added)

Warrender chooses to omit the first part of Hobbes's sentence, which tells us that these "dictates of reason" are only conclusions and theorems and *not* proper laws, which statement reflects the argument of the preceding chapters of *Leviathan*. But Warrender proceeds to take the latter part of this sentence without the preceding sentence and without the context of the preceding chapters of Hobbes's book, all of which gives it a very different meaning. He does this in order to set up the final sentence of the paragraph of the chapter as the confirmation of the necessity of God to Hobbes's political philosophy. Thus Warrender has taken a definition of law that Hobbes has specifically stated does *not* apply to the laws of nature and appropriated it as the definitive statement of what Hobbes means by the laws of nature, thoroughly misrepresenting Hobbes's intent.

Warrender does not see that even if these laws of nature *were* the laws of God (as laws are properly, and God is traditionally understood), human beings are not obliged to obey them. He therefore argues,

> It is thus at least a part if not the total requirement for a law to be a law, and hence to oblige, that it be the command of an author whom the subject of the obligation is *previously* obliged to obey. . . . Laws oblige, in that they are the commands of an agent who ought to be obeyed, and the question of why the individual ought to obey the law turns into the question of why he ought to obey the author of the law. (97)

Warrender says laws oblige because their author, the one who commands them, obliges. But how does the author oblige? He first says laws oblige because persons "ought to obey the author of the law." But why ought they? Because Warrender perceives obligation as rooted in a natural law based in duty to a higher power—to God. For Warrender the laws of nature are the commands of him whom one was "formerly obliged" to obey—that is, the command of one whom one is *previously obliged* to obey: "If this general condition that law must be the command of one *entitled* to obedience is applied to the case of laws in the state of nature, the same pattern emerges." Warrender now introduces God as "the agent who ought to be obeyed" and he moves steadily toward the appropriation of the last sentence in *Leviathan*, chapter 15, to confirm his argument: "At the end of his discussion of the laws of nature, Hobbes *asserts* that, considered merely as rational principles, these dictates may not properly be regarded as laws, but only as maxims of prudence unless they are further regarded as the commands of their author, God" (97–98, emphasis added).

Warrender calls the entire discussion one of "laws of nature," though Hobbes originally began the discussion with the term "articles of peace" or "precepts found out by reason"; thus he demonstrates his willingness to view them as *laws* (EW III, 116–17 [189]). He admits Hobbes calls them "dictates of reason" rather than proper laws, but he admits this by using a curious word—the word "asserts"—as if to suggest the laws of nature were imbued with God's authority *before* Hobbes came along to "assert" that they were "merely rational principles." By saying that Hobbes *asserts* that the laws of nature are "only" and "merely" maxims of prudence, Warrender shows his inclination to dismiss Hobbes's genealogy of these "maxims" as "just and merely" rational principles. But the "genealogy," as I am calling it, is worked out with little suggestion of dependence on assertion. Hobbes's arrival at the conclusion that the laws of nature are precepts found out by reason appears to be something he has made an effort to work out, step by step, though there may be grounds to challenge him in his step making.

But Warrender makes no such challenge—he simply dismisses the whole process of the early chapters of *Leviathan* under the label "assertion" with no attempt at analysis to explain this charge. Ironically, this is how he dismisses the whole Hobbesian psychology—indeed, how he claims Hobbes has an "ethical doctrine," that is, a "theory of obligation" independent of his psychology (Hobbes's study of the natural principles or "laws" of human behavior)— Warrender *asserts* it (93). Warrender then terms the "precepts found out by reason" as "merely" rational principles and "only" maxims of prudence, as though that were not sufficient and something more substantial were required of them.

Warrender finally attempts to tie up his case with this final conclusion: "Thus, if the laws of nature in the State of nature are considered as the commands of God, they may properly be regarded as laws, and it is this factor which is responsible for constituting their *obligatory* character" (98, emphasis added). This, at last, constitutes Warrender's thesis—and it confirms his inclination to make God necessary to Hobbes's political philosophy, a God who, by his irresistible power, obliges human beings to obey the laws of nature, which are his commands. Warrender concludes that Hobbes teaches that human beings ought to obey the laws of nature because they are to be considered as God's commands and thus regarded as proper laws that human beings are obliged by God to observe because superior power obliges.

He continues:

> If it is asked with regard to the State of Nature, for example 'why ought I to keep my covenants or to refrain from cruel actions?', the immediate answer is 'because the laws of nature prescribe such behavior.' If it is then further inquired, 'Why ought I to obey the laws of nature?', the reply may be made, 'because these laws are the commands of God, who is entitled to obedience.' (98)

Thus we see how far Warrender understands God to be necessary to Hobbes's theory.

Warrender next makes a case against two possible objections: that Hobbes's treatment of God is confused and that it is pretense:

> If it is denied that God plays an essential role in Hobbes's doctrine, the laws of nature in the state of nature cannot be taken to be more than prudential maxims for those who desire their own preservation. Those commentators, therefore, who have seen the place of God in Hobbes's theory as the product of confusion or pretence on Hobbes's part, have taken this view. They have consequently regarded themselves as *entitled* to take seriously the *first assertion* made by Hobbes in the passages quoted above, to the effect that the laws of nature as they proceed from nature are not commands, but to pass over the second assertion that they are laws as they proceed from God. (99, emphasis added)

Yet an argument is based not on "entitlements" but on reasoning, and Warrender ignores any serious examination of Hobbes's reasoning in arriving at what he (Warrender) calls the "first assertion."

Warrender does not believe that the nature Hobbes describes

when he calls these precepts "immutable and eternal" is a nature independent of God, summoned to fill the space once held by God, and even if nature's laws are made manifest by human beings who find them to be "principles of prudence," or, as Warrender would have it, *merely* and *only* "principles of prudence," for Hobbes they assume a place that transcends the dismissive "only" and "merely" character Warrender wishes to give to them.

Warrender mistakes Hobbes's identification of nature with God for the true purpose of Hobbes's political science. In Warrender's book we find a most explicit claim for the necessity of God to Hobbes's political philosophy (100).[9] He insists that Hobbes's laws of nature are backed up by the power of God (either through punishments and rewards, or by a will that is somehow imperative, even without physical sanctions). This *must* be the case, he claims, for without God's effective pressure, human beings will never be obliged to enter civil association or obey civil power and thus men will never have the guarantee of security in civil society. The notion that human beings might be bound without the effective role of God as guarantor strikes him as unsustainable: "If such a view were sustained, political obligation would turn out like natural law to be no more than another prudential maxim, as there is nothing which the civil sovereign could do that would retrieve this position" (100). But this is precisely what Hobbes says obligation based on natural law is—prudence founded on the desire for self-preservation. Thus we see the extent to which Hobbes departs from the Christian natural law tradition that stretches from Aquinas to his own time.

Why Was Warrender Mistaken?

Warrender develops an extremely problematic passage as pivotal evidence for Hobbes's thoroughgoing participation in the classical-medieval natural law tradition. Several contemporary scholars have remarked on this.[10] The emphasis of Warrender's procedure, including his concept of "validating conditions," is evidence of his strong bias for traditional natural law doctrines, which he seems unwilling to separate from discussion of Hobbesian natural law, though the evidence of the text opposes that tradition. This is why one cannot help sensing that Warrender is forcing things; the interesting question is *why* he does.

I suggest Warrender's inclination to read the older natural law tradition into Hobbes represents both his antipathy toward the notion of a moral order based on the low standard of self-interest, or, to put it another way, his earnest desire to appropriate the "sanctity" or respectability of that older tradition to the new view. If this is so, did Hobbes in some sense not only understand this desire but also try to engineer his use of natural law to satisfy it?

Why is Warrender inclined to see the medieval natural law tradition in Hobbes's *Leviathan*? Does he think that a fundamentally secular view could not underlie Hobbes's work because Hobbes was too much a product of his own time to come to such a modern conclusion, thus forcing Hobbes into a preconceived modern notion about the intellectual mileu of Hobbes's time? Perhaps if Warrender had considered that Hobbes may have had reasons for being less than entirely frank—perhaps if he had been more aware of the prudential style of writing often practiced by philosophers in the early modern era, a style we spoke of in our second chapter, "the tendency to an equivocal defense of Christianity . . . which loves to turn the darker side outwards"—he might have reached a different conclusion (Lange 1881, 225). But the fact remains that Hobbes is ambiguous in those parts of his text to which Warrender was drawn. This very ambiguity may have been purposeful, suggesting Hobbes was inviting such interpretations as Warrender's; Warrender may have been mistaken because Hobbes intended to be misleading. But why would Hobbes be intentionally misleading?

It is clear that if he wished to share his true understanding of truth, or untruth, of Christianity with those readers who were of the philosophical cognoscenti of his time, he would do so in a way that would minimize his exposure to danger. By writing prudently in this respect, he would also be teaching those who understood him best to also be prudent. His ambiguity in this regard could be considered "conspiratorial." But beyond the desire to reveal his discoveries concerning man, science, and traditional religious belief while protecting himself, Hobbes appears to have had a broader intention. Hobbes may have been trying to appropriate the sanctity and authority implicit in the old natural law tradition to make his new use more palatable to the moral and religious attitudes of the largest group of his intended readers, attitudes that I believe are implicit in Warrender. The thought that Hobbes might be inaugurating a new meaning and making a break from the natural law tradition nowhere appears in Warrender's *Political Philosophy of Hobbes* because Hobbes is ambiguous; he wanted to allow the ordered and meaningful world that such ideas traditionally stand for to be found in *Leviathan* by those who needed to find it, who were willing to believe it, partly in order to protect himself, but more importantly, to gain support for his teaching.

Hobbes integrates the old-style natural law into his teaching to satisfy the human need to have obligation legitimated by something higher than human convention. Warrender may have wanted to see Hobbes's egoistic theory of motivation, which we have characterized as his human-rights teaching, "sanctified" for this reason.

One cannot help suspecting that Warrender's 350-page work demonstrates the success of Hobbes's efforts to take advantage of readers' willingness and need to revere something. In Warrender's case, this need for reverence is focused on the idea of obligation, an idea much more difficult to comprehend without a notion of God, however attenuated. For Warrender—and many like him whom Hobbes wanted to persuade—the dignity and respect the principles of obligation and natural law are judged to be worthy of require a notion of God and a related form of religion. By his reading, Warrender can attribute the principle traditionally represented by respect for the divine to the most important matter of the moral authority behind human obligations. Perhaps because Warrender wanted to see Hobbes's egoistic theory of motivation—the teaching we have summarized here as natural or human rights—"sanctified" in this way, he was most reluctant to separate a genuine theism from Hobbes's most fundamental political principles.

It seems probable that Hobbes has presented a trap in this part of his work and Warrender, taking the bait, has been caught in it; it is my view that he was not the first, nor will he be the last, to be so entrapped. Among Hobbes's probable intentions in this particular place would be to convert men and women to a new religious view, a natural religion mingled with the trappings of the old revealed religion.[11] The reinterpretation of the Bible in *Leviathan* has proved an effective part of Hobbes's "trap," as demonstrated by Warrender's ready association of nature's God presented there with notions that are *derived* from the biblical view. It appears that Warrender takes Hobbes's mingling of the old with the new for a serious religious faith.[12]

We note again here that readers like Warrender did not and do not represent the entirety of Hobbes's audience. We have spoken above of other kinds of readers and of their relative importance to Hobbes, but we reiterate that Hobbes thought it most important to persuade that part of his audience that was both religiously inclined and open to the new developments in human knowledge, to approve his teaching.

The intention of this chapter has been to suggest that Warrender was misled into misunderstanding the true basis of Hobbes's political theory because of an ambiguity Hobbes intentionally placed in his work for just such a purpose, an ambiguity necessary to reach his broad and varied audience. How else might we explain why the wording of the final passage in *Leviathan*, chapter 15, is so ambiguous and why it seems contrary to so much that precedes it?

Can Hobbes's Theism Be Separated from the Question of His Christianity?

Our interest in this chapter has been in explaining the ambiguity of Hobbes's treatment of natural law and in how Warrender has not rightly understood Hobbes's true position, a misunderstanding that makes Warrender representative of a certain kind of reader that especially concerned Hobbes. But it is still important to remember that Warrender has also been our subject because he represents the modern scholarship that argues for Hobbes's genuine theism and the sincerity of Hobbes's religious expression. On this ground, we still have somewhat more to do with his argument.

Warrender, opposing the notion that Hobbes was an atheist and contradicting the more popular belief among commentators on Hobbes's work, especially those who wrote before the late nineteenth century, wrote, "The charge that Hobbes's doctrine is essentially atheistical in character has not, however, been well established" (100). He attributes most of the charges of atheism against Hobbes to the indignation of orthodox Christians to the heterodox aspects of Hobbes's philosophy. Such charges, Warrender writes, ought to be distinguished from *atheism*:

> And even when an appeal has been made to Hobbes's text, the question of his atheism has frequently been confused with the more debatable but irrelevant question of whether or not he was in any precise sense a Christian; or a case has been made, as noted above, by relying heavily upon one part of an antithesis and ignoring the other part which completes its meaning. (100)

Warrender concludes that charges of atheism against Hobbes are *ad hominem*. He suggests that textual analysis to demonstrate that Hobbes was indeed an atheist "relies heavily upon one part of an antithesis" while ignoring the other part that completes its meaning. He is probably alluding here to the two sentences of the last paragraph of chapter 15 of *Leviathan*.

Warrender is aware of the tradition that regards Hobbes as an atheist, but he rejects it and so rejects the consideration that Hobbes is being purposefully ambiguous. In fact, it appears that one of Warrender's chief aims was to show that Hobbes has been judged wrongly by those who accuse him of atheism. Thus Warrender uses a quotation from Bishop John Bramhall, Hobbes's greatest seventeenth-century adversary, who accused Hobbes of atheism, as the epigraph at the top of the first page of his preface:

> His principles are pernicious both to piety and policy, and destructive to all relations of mankind, between prince and subject, father and child, master and servant, husband and wife; and . . . they who maintain them obstinately, are fitter to live in hollow trees among wild beasts than in any Christian political society. (Warrender 1957, 1; EW V, 25)[13]

Warrender does not treat this quotation after employing it to preface his 350-page book, but its placement at the beginning of his text is presumably to represent all the erroneous notions of Hobbes that have preceded Warrender's work. The implicit message this conveys is that Warrender will now correct these errors by means of the evidence that is to follow.

Warrender thinks the question of Hobbes's Christianity is irrelevant to the question of his theism and he resorts to a more basic notion that he thinks Hobbes retains, a theism based on "Nature's God" and a "first cause." While Hobbes himself uses language that might associate him with natural religion, he also associates Nature's God with the God of Scripture and once that is done, to what extent can the religion of the Bible be removed from considerations of Hobbes's theism? Warrender would like to divorce Hobbes's treatment of the Bible from claims for his theism, but Hobbes's text will not allow this.[14]

If Warrender's reading of Hobbes on obligation were correct, it would require a theism that included not only a first cause or a God of Nature, but also a revelation that tells human beings something of the character of that God, including a notion of rewards and punishments or including some sense that God has a knowable will for man. How else could human beings know what was expected of them? Reason is not enough. The only revelation in Hobbes's writings to which Warrender can trace such a knowledge of God, is that of the Bible. In other words, Warrender's reading of Hobbes requires some knowledge of God, which can only be gotten through revelation. We must reiterate what has been said about the limits of human knowledge in *Leviathan*—that men and women, by natural reason, can know nothing of God.[15] Once the need for revelation is conceded, it becomes very difficult to discount the Bible and Christianity when one speaks of the theistic aspect of Hobbes's thought. (Furthermore, if Hobbes undermines the Bible with his natural science understandings of the world, as well as with his biblical criticism—both of which we will see evidence of in subsequent chapters—the very book that makes Warrender's reading of Hobbes tenable is being dismissed.)

Yet Warrender says Hobbes's Christianity and his treatment of the Scriptures are irrelevant to the question of his theism. However, if the Bible becomes irrelevant to Hobbes's theism, Warrender undercuts something necessary to his own argument, since that argument requires that human beings have some knowledge of God unobtainable by nature to at least know that the laws of nature are God's will and that God executes punishment on the disobedient. Thus when Hobbes says human beings can only know God by means of revelation, and when the only revelation he speaks of is the Bible, it would seem inappropriate to say that the question of his Christianity is irrelevant. On the contrary, Hobbes's theism, if it is to have any meaning in the sense Warrender wants to give it, that is, if it is to have anything to do with what obliges human beings to seek peace, to leave the state of nature, and to enter civil society, *is* relevant to Hobbes's treatment of revelation, and, indeed, must depend on it. Contrary to Warrender's assertion, there can be no understanding of the role of the divine in Hobbes's thought without turning to Hobbes's treatment of the Scriptures and without concerning ourselves with Hobbes's Christianity.

But what conclusion might one make concerning Warrender's argument? Warrender argued that obligation in Hobbes's *Leviathan* is grounded in obligation to God. He implied by the epigraph taken from Bishop John Bramhall at the beginning of his book (a quotation describing Hobbes as anti-Christian or atheistic), that by his book

concerning obligation in Hobbes's work he would refute this quotation and its unfair verdict against Hobbes. By showing Warrender's
argument is insupportable, we have also shown that Warrender's
claim to have defended Hobbes from the accusation of atheism or
of antipathy to Christianity is also without support. Arguing from
the issue of obligation in *Leviathan* can yield no proof of Hobbes's
Christian orthodoxy nor of a genuine theism.

While Warrender never really claimed Hobbes was a Christian,
arguing instead for a natural theism, which we have seen is untenable, others, not focusing on Hobbes's teaching about obligation,
have argued that Hobbes's political theory is engaged fully in the
defense of Christianity. F. C. Hood, Paul Johnson, and A. P. Martinich have contended that the entire work lies within the realm
of Christian orthodoxy. Herbert Schneider viewed *Leviathan* as a
"passionate sermon to a warring world" by a pious man patiently
waiting for the coming of Christ's kingdom. To address these claims
about Hobbes's religion and to fully understand the relationship of
Hobbes's treatment of Christianity and the Bible to the political
and moral teaching set forth in the first half of *Leviathan*, we now
must turn to the meaning of Hobbes's lengthy treatment of religion
in parts 3 and 4 of *Leviathan*.

I will introduce Hobbes's interpretation of the Bible by considering both the sense of reason he employs in his biblical exegesis and
the premise upon which Hobbes puts reason to work—the state of
nature. Reason is the principal guide Hobbes uses in his biblical
exegesis, but his understanding of reason is distinct from the rationalistic approach to the Bible used by Hobbes's sincerely religious
contemporaries. We shall see that Hobbes's state of nature, from
which all his reasoning about politics and about the Bible ultimately
begins, represents a counterbeginning to the traditional Christian
or biblical account of the human situation.

Chapter Five

Hobbes's Sense of Reason

Antagonism toward the Deity of the Scriptures

The second half of *Leviathan* is a vast and systematic array, spreading over sixteen chapters entirely devoted to Hobbes's interpretation of the Bible. A careful exegesis of Hobbes's treatment of Christianity and the Scriptures shows that for Hobbes, the God of the Bible is the disturber of civil peace and the principal reason that peace and safety are threatened in civil societies throughout Christendom.

The God who in the Old Testament called Abraham from a peaceful and safe life in Haran to dangerous journeyings and mysterious encounters in a land God had promised him, is the God who called Peter in the New Testament from the relative peace and safety of a workaday life of fishing to a life of walking on the waters of troubled seas, exhorting the multitudes to change their ways of living, being threatened by people in power, being imprisoned and finally martyred (Gen. 11:31–12:4, 18:1–33, 22:1–24; Matt. 4:18,19, 14:25–31; Acts 2:14–40, 4:1–30, 12:1–19). This is the God who throughout Scripture called human beings *from* peace and safety to the dangers of faith. Though the Bible calls God the God of peace, the life of faith in him in this world, according to the Scriptures, is full of trouble. Jesus told his disciples, "In the world ye shall have tribulation" (John 16:33; see also Isa. 9:6, Matt. 10:34, 2 Tim. 3:12). This is the God who troubles men and women for *not* heeding his call to risk and who chastises them for loving this world. The notion of "walking with God" throughout the Scriptures often means turning from what seems safe to taking a path of risk and danger

(Genesis 6, esp. v.9; Exodus, esp. chapter 14; I Kings 18, esp. v.30–40; Ps. 1:1; John 14:27; Acts 6:5–7:60; James 4:4).

It is not difficult to understand how the Bible may be appropriated to turn human beings from peace and safety to the dangerous life of faith; England and the world of Christendom of the seventeenth century in general, offered sufficient example of this. Certainly the Bible may be interpreted as teaching men and women to fear God rather than man, and Hobbes understood that the tendency to follow such a teaching was intimately tied to the trouble the life of faith has brought not only to believers, but to civil society in general (Ps. 118:6, Isa. 2:22; also Pss. 23:1,4,5; 27:1–3; 118:8,9; Matt. 10:28; Rom. 8:34–39; Rev. 2:10; EW III, 674–75 [691–92]; EW IV, Dialogue III).

Hobbes's new view of man, government, and God is designed to change all this; he wants to sanctify safety and hallow the love of *this* world, and to do this he does not want people of faith to forsake the world, embrace martyrdom, or have contempt for what others may do to them when they are acting in the name of that faith. He would urge human beings to think of their lives, to save themselves not from the world, as the Bible declares, but from death (Matt. 10:36–40; Acts 2:40; James 4:4; John 2:15–17).

He would have men and women live by a reasoning that above all else makes *this* world safe for human life. This reasoning cannot take precedence in the minds of human beings unless the Bible is either dismissed entirely or is understood in a new way, for the Bible has often been understood to promote a great tension between the world of faith and the natural order of things in the world.

To establish the reasoning that makes peace and safety the chief goal of civil association, Hobbes wants to turn men's eyes from beholding other worlds to the consideration of their situation in this one. At the heart of such a consideration is what he expects and desires them to see in other human beings, and this is developed most powerfully in *Leviathan*, chapter 13, on the state of nature.

To understand Hobbes's sense of reason utilized in *Leviathan* to establish peace and safety through civil association, we must begin by recalling that for Hobbes reason serves the passions—"For the thoughts, are to the desires, as scouts, and spies, to range abroad, and find the way to the things desired" (EW III, 61 [139]). The state of nature, an "Inference made from the Passions" (EW III, 113–14 [186]), is a picture of the world from which reason takes its bearings and, indeed, takes its orders for Hobbes. Such a sense of reason, rather than being synonymous with the revealed word of God, as some theologians in Hobbes's day believed, is instead antagonistic to the teaching of the Bible as the revealed word of God. By exploring Hobbes's sense of reason, one may see more clearly where Hobbes's hostility to Christianity lies and see the tension between Christianity and Hobbes's most important teaching—the far-reaching supremacy of the rights of man over all authorities over human desire.

Hobbes's Sense of Reason: The Importance of Geometry and the Understanding That Preceded Hobbes's Embrace of It

Hobbes presents the human situation as a predicament that arises out of the passions and the liberty human beings have to indulge them. In *Leviathan*, chapters 13 through 15, Hobbes indicates that alongside these passions—especially the fear of violent death—exists the capacity of reason that enables human beings both to gain the things they desire and to escape the predicament such desiring generates (EW III, 116 [188]). This is the reason that serves the desire to make the world anew in a way that will limit the ill effects of too much liberty and too much passion.

In 1640 Hobbes wrote in the Epistle Dedicatory to his *Elements of Law* that he considered the two main parts of human nature to be reason and the passions. He stated that these parts produced two kinds of learning, mathematical and dogmatic. Mathematical learning, Hobbes says, "is free from controversies and dispute, because it consisteth in comparing of figures and motion only" (EW IV; Hobbes 1969a, Epistle Dedicatory). Hobbes added that in such comparisons, "truth and the interests of men oppose not each other." But in dogmatic learning, produced not from reason, but proceeding from the passions, "there is nothing not disputable, because it compareth men, and meddleth with their right and profit."

For Hobbes, religion is a product of passion, above all the passions of anxiety about the unknown of death. Dogmatic learning pertaining to these passions bred the convictions that generated the disastrous religious wars of Hobbes's time. Hobbes says that with such passion-based learning—the dogmatic learning that is against reason—as often "as reason is against a man, so oft will a man be against reason" (ibid.). Therefore, Hobbes explains, all past efforts to establish justice and escape the predicament of the human situation arising out of the passions and the desire to preserve the liberty to indulge them have failed. The various attempts all disagree with each other and "do all invade each other, and themselves with contradictions" because they were all based on the passions (ibid.). As Hobbes says in *Leviathan* of the classical moral philosophers, "Their moral philosophy is but a description of their own passions" (EW III 668–69 [686–87]).

Hobbes thus concluded that the only way to produce a teaching that will truly relieve human beings from the painful situation of their estate in the world is to base such teaching on "the rules and infallibility of reason" (by which he means nondogmatic, mathematical reasoning) and this can only be done by first putting "such principles down for a foundation, as passion not mistrusting, may not seek to displace" (EW IV, 1; Hobbes 1969a, part 1.1.1).

Hobbes explains that the state of affairs in England in 1640 and the controversies encountered in searching for a way out of the predicament that becomes civil war is evidence "that they which have heretofore written thereof, have not well understood their own subject" (ibid.), for had there been a solution produced by any of these thinkers, it might have been applied to their troubles. For Hobbes, an infallible sign of a true teaching is universal agreement. Those who consider "nothing else but the comparison of magnitudes, numbers, times, and motions . . . have thereby been the authors of . . . excellencies," that is, all the products of arts and sciences based on mathematical learning, and in all their work meet no controversy. "To this day," Hobbes adds, "was it never heard of, that there was any controversy concerning any conclusion in this subject" (EW IV, 71–72; Hobbes 1969a, part 1.13.3).

If the learning that produced such success in the natural arts and sciences could be applied to moral and civil life, a way out of the predicament of the human situation—the predicament growing out of freedom and fear, divided loyalties and competing human passions would follow. This enormously successful mathematical learning is free of controversy because it proceeds "from most low and humble principles . . . going on slowly and with most scrupulous ratiocination." This slow process, Hobbes says, begins with "the imposing of names, by which the truth of first propositions is inferred. From two such propositions comes a third, and so on" (ibid.). By such "steps of science" human beings may "build thereon the truth of cases in the law of nature (which hitherto have been built in the air) by degrees till the whole be inexpugnable" (EW IV; Hobbes 1969a, Epistle Dedicatory).

According to Hobbes those men who have written about human nature without laboriously building on such a humble foundation have filled "infinite volumes" but have been so far from removing controversy and doubt about the matters they treat that they seem only to create further and more intense controversy (EV IV, 71–72; Hobbes 1969a, part 1.13.3). If the only learning that removes controversy is one that all can agree upon, then such learning must be built on mathematics, which proceeds from reason alone. Thus, we may better understand the title of the first version of Hobbes's political philosophy, "The Elements of Law, Natural and Political." The term "elements" is reminiscent of another title using this word, a title setting forth the principles of a science, Euclid's *Elements*, which established the principles of the science of geometry. Hobbes's aim is to establish politics as a science after this very pattern first outlined by Euclid.

Hobbes's excitement over the principles of geometry represents his connecting the operations of reason in that science with the problem of moral and political life—the problem of establishing justice by freeing human beings from the ill effects of the passions (EW III, 23–24, 27 [105–8]). By seeing the importance geometry has for Hobbes, we may better understand that for him reason is a tool by means of which human beings can solve the age-old problem of injustice—an astonishingly bold claim for the power of human reason. For Hobbes, we should add, justice means the establishment of a power capable of judging between competing passionate human beings. Hobbes's aim is to establish this power on a sure foundation for the first time.

The story of Hobbes's first encounter with geometry is well known; first recorded by John Aubrey in his *Lives of Eminent Men*, it reads like the story of a revelation:

> He was forty years old before he looked on geometry, which happened accidentally: being in a gentleman's library in _____, Euclid's *Elements* lay open, and it was the 47th Prop., Lib. I. So he reads the proposition. "By G—," says he, "This is impossible!" So he reads the demonstration, which referred him back to another, which he also read, *et sic deinceps*, that at last he was demonstratively convinced of that truth. This made him in love with Geometry. (Robertson 1971, 31)

For Hobbes, reason is a means of escape from the human predicament, but it must be governed in a particular way to perform this role; geometry serves Hobbes as a pattern for the right application of reason to human things.

But what understanding, prior to his encounter with geometry, made Hobbes's response to it so marked? His interest in Euclid appears to have been so pronounced because he was aware of how little human beings can know of the world by any authority other than unassisted reason. Hobbes's excitement about Euclid and geometry suggests his prior awareness that certainty was impossible regarding even what reasoning human beings can know from nature. Underlying this is a great skepticism about the traditional understanding of human purposes and ends, be they derived from classical or religious origins. Hobbes appears to have been searching for a means, a method to attain certainty, and with certainty, a mastery of nature and the world of man.

Hobbes's excitement about geometry is a manifestation of a profound appetite for sure ground to stand on when old truths handed down from both the classical tradition and the Christian one could no longer be viewed as credible. Hobbes's work clearly suggests that he believed the classical and Christian verities could not form the basis for establishing civil peace and order. Furthermore, Hobbes's work clearly indicates he believed that among the still quite vital institutions erected in the name of these old verities, arguments over which interpretation of these truths were true led to violence and war and the destruction of everything that made human life worth living. Geometry was a revelation to Hobbes because it suggested a method by which reason could find certainty, a true basis for justice and a way out of the disorder set in motion by human pride and fear.

We may thus begin to understand why Hobbes's praise for geometry is effusive (EW II, Epistle Dedicatory). He credits contemporary superiority over the ancients to the debt we owe not mathematics in general, but geometry in particular. In the first chapter of *De Corpore*, he explains that the greatest good comes to mankind through the arts of measuring matter and motion, which arts underlie "architecture, navigation, making instruments of all uses . . . etc. By which sciences, how great benefits men receive is more easily understood than expressed." These benefits are not reckoned to all people, Hobbes says, but only to those who have "a clear, exact method."

We come, then, to the importance of philosophy for the establishment of civil peace and safety. Philosophy, which Hobbes first defines as "Natural Reason," is given to all human beings to some degree, but "when there is need of a long series of reason, then most men wander out of the way, and fall into error for want of method" (EW I, 1). Hobbes goes on to say that philosophy is knowledge "of effects or appearances, as we acquire by true ratiocination from the knowledge we have first of their causes" (EW I, 4). And by "ratiocination" he says he means, "computation . . . to collect the sum of many things," including subtraction, multiplication, and division to reach a final sum. Hobbes applies this "computation" to our mental activities, "the ratiocination of our mind," wherein "we add and subtract in our silent thought" ultimately by means of language. The end of philosophy is knowledge, but not, according to Hobbes, for its own sake, but for its usefulness, for "the end of knowledge is power" (EW I, 7). But a problem of power is that there is not enough to go around, and so human beings, for reasons of fear, or desire for glory, compete for it.

The usefulness of philosophy is that it gives power. The usefulness of geometry, by means of which we have a clear and exact method of computing because by it we have "definitions, the explication of our single conceptions, and generation or description," is that it causes all the benefits produced by the science of measuring, building, transporting, and so on (EW I, 71). It is the foundation by which we obtain knowledge, which in turn gives us power.

If the same method that secures for mankind the benefits of natural philosophy—the fundamental ingredient of which is manifested in the science of geometry—could be applied to moral and civil philosophy, those studies could be rendered useful, as well. "But the utility of moral and civil philosophy is to be estimated, not so much by the commodities we have by knowing these sciences, as by the calamities we receive from not knowing them" (EW I, 8). And the worst calamities—war, and especially civil war—"bring slaughter, solitude and the want of all things."

The knowledge of the rules of civil life, "the duties which unite and keep men in peace," could prevent these calamites, but a clear method to gain the knowledge of these rules has been lacking:

For what shall we say? Could the ancient masters of Greece, Egypt, Rome and others persuade the unskilful multitude to their innumera-

ble opinions concerning the nature of their gods, which they themselves knew not whether they were true or false, and what were indeed
manifestly false and absurd; and could they not persuade the same
multitude to civil duty, if they themselves had understood it? (EW
I, 8–9)

According to Hobbes, the ancients were excellent persuaders, as we
see in their effective argument where ultimate ignorance was no
handicap; they understood the power of the appeal of certain ideas
and used that appeal, but they failed to persuade men and women
about the principles that preserve civil association because no
skillful rhetoric could accomplish that task; real knowledge was
required, which knowledge they did not have.

Though mankind had not heretofore discovered a science that led
to peace, Hobbes is astonishingly optimistic that he has discovered
a sound moral and political science, the rudiments of which the
multitude of human beings would be capable of learning. All that
had been lacking was a proper method. According to Hobbes, the
ancients "increased only words, and not knowledge." Hobbes says
that what their writings chiefly lacked was "a true and certain rule
of our actions, by which we might know whether that we undertake
be just or unjust" (EW I, 9). There is no point, Hobbes concludes, in
being bidden "to do the right, before there be a certain rule and
measured right established, which no man hither hath established"
(ibid.).

But could it not be said against Hobbes here that such a rule was
considered to be in the Bible? But that was precisely the point—the
Bible represented the "dogmatic learning" human beings could not
rely on. It was a product of human passions, and of human pride
and fear. Thus, because passion-based learning is subjective, no
universal agreement about it can be achieved. But of course once a
mathematical basis of knowledge is established, a basis all can
agree on, that basis can provide a means of understanding the
Scriptures, too.

Therefore, to escape the civil wars and great calamities of mankind that come from not knowing civil duties, human beings ought
to turn to the pattern to be learned from "those few writings of
geometricians which are extant," since they ought to "be thought
sufficient for the taking away of all controversy in the matters they
treat of" and of more value than "those innumerable and huge
volumes of ethics" produced by ancient masters (ibid.). Geometry,

when applied to human things, can show the way to certainty, not opinion, and with certainty, agreement, upon which peace may be built and power established.

Reasoning As Addition and Subtraction

Hobbes's *Leviathan*, beginning with the phrase, "Concerning the thoughts of man," proceeds according to a mathematical pattern of learning to reason out slowly definitions of what thoughts are—both their causes and effects. What human beings sense and remember sensing, he argues, is the source of all thought. From these causes and effects of thought, he proceeds to explain trains of thought, and so continues until he writes, "Speech consists in names and their connections, whereby men register their thoughts . . . without which there had been amongst men neither commonwealth, nor society, nor contract, nor peace, no more than amongst lions, bears and wolves" (EW III, 18 [100]).

Hobbes says that without "names and their connections" there is no reckoning "of number, of magnitude, of swiftness, of force, and other things, the reckonings whereof are necessary to the being, or well being of mankind" (EW III, 23 [104]). It is above all by means of speech, Hobbes indicates, that human beings may proceed to an exact science whereby they may master nature, including their own nature.

Thus, in part 1 of *Leviathan*, beginning with the procedure of giving apt and clear definitions, Hobbes builds an understanding of human beings upon which a basis for certainty may be constructed. For Hobbes, truth "consisteth in the right ordering of names," and thus to find precise truth, we "need to remember what every name stands for, and to place it accordingly."

Thus we come to the essential importance of geometry: "in geometry, which is the only science that it hath pleased God hitherto to bestow on mankind, men begin at settling the significations they call definitions, and place them in the beginning of their reckoning" (EW III, 23–24 [105]). With this form of marking meanings, human beings may determine the consequences of words. As geometricians add and subtract lines, figures, angles, proportions, and so on, "logicians teach the same in consequences of words" and "writers of politics add together pactions to find men's duties" and "lawyers, laws and facts, to find what is right and wrong in the actions of private men. In sum, in what matter soever there is place for additions and subtractions, there is also place for reason; and where these have no place, there reason has nothing to do at all" (EW III, 30 [110–11]).

A Special Help for Reason Hobbes Calls "Method"

For Hobbes, reason is "nothing but reckoning." It is not an inner light from God, as Richard Hooker might have said, nor a corrupt and fallen instrument, as Martin Luther or a strict Calvinist might have put it. Hobbes argued in the second chapter of *Leviathan* that human beings excel all other animals in this, "that when he conceiveth anything whatsoever, he was apt to inquire the consequences of it." In chapter 5, he adds another aspect of this same supremacy: that a man "can by words reduce the consequences he finds to geometrical rules, called *theorems* . . . that is, he can reason, or reckon, not only in number, but in all other things" (EW III, 33 [113]). Thus reason is not seen as flawed, nor as a light from God, but as an excellent tool and nothing more.

However, reason can reach absurd conclusions due to "want of method" and to various errors of assertion, ascription of names, and use of metaphors. Reason, then, Hobbes argues, is not born with men, but gotten through hard work in "apt imposing of names" and in "getting a good and orderly method in proceeding from the elements, which are names, to assertions, to syllogisms . . . till we come to knowledge of consequences . . . and this is it that men call Science" (EW III, 35 [115]).[1]

By means of this science, patterned after that first science, geometry, begining with the causes of thought in human sense, Hobbes does nothing less than Euclid does at the beginning of his *Thirteen Books of Elements*—he gives definitions. He then proceeds to develop the consequences of these definitions in order "to begin a method of seeking": "The discourse of the mind when it is governed by design, is nothing but *seeking* . . . a hunting out of the causes of some effect, present or past; or of the effects, of some present or past cause" (EW III, 14 [96]).

This seeking must proceed according to a strict method utilizing careful definitions of terms in order to reduce the consequences of effects or causes to rules or theorems. This procedure or method is vital to the establishment of what Hobbes calls mathematical learning, and for Hobbes it is the only way human beings can produce sure knowledge. Without this method, prudence—learning based only on experience and not on extrapolation from experience to general or theoretical knowledge of man and the world—is the best human beings can do with their reason. Hobbes writes of prudence:

> As he that forsees what will become of a criminal, reckons what he has seen follow on the like crime before; having this order of thoughts, the crime, the officer, the prison, the judge, and the gallows. Which kind of thoughts is called prudence . . . though such conjecture, through the difficulty of observing all circumstances, be very fallacious. (EW III, 14–18 [97])[2]

However, Hobbes says it is not prudence that distinguishes man from beasts, for animals learn from experience to make conjectures concerning future actions, too. Yet these conjectures always have elements of uncertainty in them. But with method, a "special help" as Hobbes calls it, human beings may enhance their rational capacities to great power. Hobbes writes,

> Those other faculties . . . which seem proper to man only, are acquired and increased by study and industry; and of most men learned by instruction and discipline; and proceed all from the invention of words and speech. For beside sense and thoughts, and the train of thoughts, the mind has no other motion . . . [but] by the help of speech, and method, the same faculties may be improved to such a height as to distinguish men from all other living creatures. (EW III, 16 [98–99])

By means of this orderly and careful method, proceeding from the simplest elements of names "aptly chosen" to assertions, to syllogisms, Hobbes develops a knowledge of consequences and effects concerning man that he shows represents far more certainty than that knowledge upon which prudence is built. In part 1 of *Leviathan*, he continues with this procedure to definitions of the passions and considerations of their effects, arriving at last at the proposition that is his clearest picture of the human predicament: the state of nature.

The development of Hobbes's "geometry," or science of moral life, generated on the foundation of the state of nature and the "articles of peace" reason discovers there, continues in part 2 of *Leviathan*, where Hobbes explains how civil association is built

upon the basis of the elements identified in part 1. In the final
paragraph of the first half of *Leviathan*, Hobbes indicates that
knowledge attained by this careful method constitutes the first true
political science. He calls it "the science of natural justice." At the
beginning of the second half of his work, Hobbes gives his project
another name, summarizing the first half of *Leviathan* as "political
reasoning" (EW III, 358–59 [407–9]).[3]

The state of nature introduced in chapter 13 ought to be considered the first axiom of Hobbes's science of natural justice or "political reasoning." The state of nature, based on the careful ordering of
elements developed in the preceding twelve chapters, becomes the
foundation from which all further propositions of Hobbes's moral
and political science will take their beginnings. It is the unchanging
basis from which reason figures a way out of the human
predicament.

"Figuring Out" a Political-Moral Science

Hobbes shows man as a kind of designer, an engineer who seeks to
figure things out, which term seems particularly fitting for Hobbes
and his political-moral science based in geometry. One may compare the work of man—and that of Hobbes in particular—to that of
God in creation (see Hobbes's introduction to *Leviathan*). The
picture I have in mind is William Blake's painting of the hoary-
headed, bearded "Ancient of Days," whose image in Blake's art
holds a geometer's compass in hand, busily figuring out the dimensions of the world he is making with a draftman's precision.[4] One
might think this is an image of God making the world, since the
term "Ancient of Days" is a biblical one referring to God, and the
description in the book of Daniel matches the image in Blake's
painting (Dan. 7:9, 13, 22). In *Leviathan*, Hobbes transforms the
designer of the world from deity into man; as the Ancient of Days
holds a compass and makes the world by means of a kind of
figuring out in Blake's image, so Hobbes teaches that man holds the
compass, man creates his own world. But to do this, the draftsman-
designer must himself be positioned on something solid. We are not
told what ground the Ancient of Days crouches upon in Blake's
images—and the biblical notion of creation *ex nihilo* excludes this
problem entirely in reference to the God of the Bible. But for *his*
solid ground, Hobbes chooses a man's own passions and his natural

liberty to do what he pleases, and he states such "givens" in what he calls the state of nature. Just as Blake's picture of God must presuppose some "place" for the divine draftsman to be as he designs a world, so Hobbes must have a place for human beings to stand as they do the same thing, and the place Hobbes finds is seen in its fullness in his famous—or infamous—state of nature. With this "state," Hobbes gives human beings a natural beginning—as opposed to a supernatural one, but with such a beginning, unless men and women use their reason to find a way out, they are certain to meet a nasty and brutish end after a short life. Figuring from this beginning, too, Hobbes redesigns Christianity to make it fit the project he inaugurates on the basis of the state of nature and the natural rights he finds there.

There is a distinction, then, between the direction nature seems to take man—toward an early death—and the order created by human beings on the basis of the state of nature using the motivation of the passions and the tool of reason. If human beings can create an order in the world according to their determination not to die violently and too soon, they would appear to be defying nature, and they defy this end by means of reason. This is the understanding that we might say "puts reason to work" for Hobbes; this is why, to borrow Blake's image, Hobbes and all human beings crouch, making plans. They are prompted by the fear of violent death, the hope for self-preservation, the appetite for pleasure, the desire to defy the nature that delares their mortality. Hobbes's passion for geometry and the extremely hopeful teaching concerning method that develops from it, are signs of his belief that he has discovered something dependable in a world he understands is fundamentally unknowable. For Hobbes, reason is no guide to finding absolute truth, but reason, with the help of a method and proper use of speech, can build a science that will provide great safety and security for mankind, greater than has ever before been thought possible.

Hobbes teaches that his "science of natural justice" or "political reasoning," that is, his "geometry" of political and moral life, frees human beings from arguable opinion and gives them the great liberty of certainty. But what does Hobbes teach that human beings can be certain about? For Hobbes, certainty emerges only concerning those things that human beings can understand (and thus potentially even control). Thus human beings can be certain about only what they make themselves. Man may control what he can "figure out."

The "Last Sum" of the Reasoning Called Science
"Is Not Absolute but Conditional"

Hobbes's reason, then, does not discover "truth"; it creates it. It works from within "givens" that human beings postulate themselves to produce useful ends; it does not discover the ends of things, that is, the meaning or truth given by something higher than or precedent to man. The description of human beings made up of definitions of how they behave, of their thoughts, and of their passions, is not comprehensive, but it is clear and accurate enough to be extremely useful for the project at hand. The description is true enough to *work*.

One might argue with Euclid's first axiom, that "things which are equal to the same thing are also equal to one another." It assumes that things that occupy the same space are equal to one another (Heath 1926, Introduction). Nonetheless, for the purpose of geometry, it is infinitely useful. So we may argue about people in the state of nature: such a notion assumes most human beings fear violent death above all things. These are all axiomatic; we cannot prove them with certainty, but, asserted and assumed, we can build a useful, workable structure. Hobbes admits,

> No discourse whatsoever, can end in absolute knowledge of fact, past or to come. For, as for the knowledge of fact, it is originally, sense; and ever after, memory. And for the knowledge of consequence, which I have said before is called science, it is not absolute, but conditional. No man can know by discourse, that this, or that, is, has been, or will be; which is to know absolutely: but only, that if this be, that shall be: which is to know conditionally. (EW III, 52–53 [131])

Though the "last sum" or conclusion of the reasoning called science is "conditional knowledge, or knowledge of the consequence of words," such reason is infinitely useful because it produces conclusions human beings can agree upon, based as they are on strictly defined—mathematically defined—calculations. Reason cannot show man absolute truth, nor is reason God's truth, immanent in man, but it is a human faculty by which human beings can build conditional knowledge for their own ends.

The Challenge of "Dogmatic Learning" to Science

These definitions and axioms of Hobbes's science of natural justice are not comprehensive because they do not fully describe what a human being is. They are comprehensive *enough* and as thorough as reason can be, but reason cannot know all things, as Hobbes often admits. Theology and matters of the origins of life are things beyond certainty and comprise the realm of dogmatic learning, of quarrels, of war, and ultimately, for Hobbes, of fear. Hobbes's concern is with what reason *can* know, for with such knowledge, the mathematically patterned knowledge we have spoken of above, comes agreement and subsequently peace.

Hobbes's axioms of political life represent the place in his political thought where he is most vulnerable to criticism. If they are challenged by "non-mathematical" learning, that is, by what he terms "dogmatic learning," their usefulness is undermined. When he considers dogmatic learning, Hobbes means religious learning above all, but Hobbes would say Aristotle's *Ethics*, which emphasizes nobility of character, is also a form of dogmatic learning, and thus it, too, poses a threat to the political findings of mathematical learning (EW III, 668–69 [686–87]). If matters of religion or matters to do with pride in nobility of character, which Hobbes understands to be matters of passion, undermine the first principles of a solution based in reason, there can be no lasting solution to the problem of establishing peace, safety, and, consequently, justice.

For Hobbes, reason is to be an instrument of human passion, and the primary passion it should serve is the desire to avoid violent death. The greatest challenge to Hobbes's view of man, a view which makes this world's good the final end of man, is the prideful view that thinks it knows there is a God who is there, concerned with what human beings do, and capable of inspiring human beings to defy civil authority when they believe such authority violates the will of God. The arrogance or pride of man as it grasps views that see beyond this world, leads human beings to act in ways that are *against* their best interests in this world.

So, too, the pride of man fires such views as those celebrated in Aristotle's *Ethics*—that nobility of character is the aim of human life over even self-preservation—leading human beings to give up their lives for even a disrespectful word spoken against themselves or their God. Such pride, married to a life of religious conviction based on the Bible, or based on ethical conviction to do with ideas of nobility of character, constitutes the general culprit in the most troublesome kind of mischief against the peace and safety of human beings and commonwealth. For Hobbes, reason cannot be safely

employed by such prideful views and thus must operate independently of all such "dogmatic learning."

This, then, is Hobbes's sense of reason; it is a reason not at all
equivalent to the natural word of God as Thomas Aquinas or
Richard Hooker would understand reason-as-the-natural-word-of-
God to be, for it is utterly divorced from the divine authority of the
God of the Bible. Hobbes makes this difficult to see because he has
cleverly veiled his picture of the natural word of God with the
vestments of biblical connotation.

All Reasoning Ultimately Serves Passions

We must now indicate a kind of irony in Hobbes's use of mathematical learning to develop a political science capable of the kind of
success for which it is celebrated in the physical sciences. Despite
the distinction Hobbes makes between mathematical and dogmatic
learning, between learning based on reason and learning based in
the passions, Hobbes's project reveals that reason must always
ultimately serve some passion. Hobbes's "political reasoning" is
based in the passion of the fear of violent death at the hands of
human beings because that passion represents the inclination in the
lives of men and women *freest* of controversy. Though the very fact
of our mortality engenders religion, Hobbes's teaching is that the
fear of violent death at the hands of men is a fear far more immediate than our apprehension concerning the fact of our ultimate
mortality. Thus, though men and women may theoretically say
they will fear and obey God, and even accept martyrdom tomorrow
in the name of their religion, for most men and women most of the
time, fear of the violence of man today is the guiding passion,
not fear of what God may do tomorrow. As we have seen, the
predominance of the passion of fear in the present is viewed by
Hobbes as so dependable that the entire project of his political
science founded on mathematical learning is built upon it; this is a
principal lesson of chapter 13 of *Leviathan*. On this passion of self-
preservation presented as the state of nature (the human fear of
what other people may do today, not of what God may do tomorrow), Hobbes ultimately builds the structure of civil association,
applying his "geometry" of human things to politics and religion.
The notion of the fear of the unknown that Hobbes says engenders
deity, which Hobbes describes in chapters 11 and 12 of *Leviathan*, a

notion that could conceivably compete with fear of violence at the hands of men, finds no place in *Leviathan*, chapter 13, where the latter fear reigns unchallenged in Hobbes's description of the state of nature.

Political Reasoning As "The Natural Word of God"

Hobbes commences the second half of *Leviathan* with one long sentence summarizing the entire first half of the work. This sentence is placed precisely between the two halves of the book and juxtaposes them. It begins, "I have derived the rights of sovereign power, and the duties of subjects, hitherto from the principles of nature only." His sentence continues with his definition of the principles of nature: they are what "experience has found true, or consent concerning the use of words has made so." Hobbes adds that by "principles of nature" he means that which we may *learn* "from the nature of men, known to us by experience," *and* that which we may *make* by consenting among ourselves "from definitions of such words as are essential to all *political reasoning,* universally agreed upon" (emphasis mine).

The second sentence of the opening paragraph of chapter 32 introduces the second half of *Leviathan*: "But in that I am next to handle, which is the nature and rights of Christian Commonwealth, whereof there dependeth much upon supernatural revelation of the will of God; the ground of my discourse must be, *not only the natural word of God,* but also the prophetical" (emphasis mine). In the first sentence Hobbes says he has derived the rights of sovereignty (and duties of subjects) from nature *only,* but he adds, quite strikingly, in the second sentence, that this knowledge constitutes "the natural word of God." Hobbes indicates in the second sentence that his aim now, in turning to matters of "supernatural revelations of the will of God" (which he also calls "the prophetical" word of God), is to *confirm* that which in the first half of *Leviathan* he derived from the principles of nature only. Hobbes is informing his readers that the prophetic will confirm the natural, for *both* are the word of God.

Let us note that Hobbes has indicated in these first sentences of chapter 32 that the principles of nature can mean what consent about the use of words *makes* true. Human beings, in Hobbes's terms, can make truth. Human beings can create natural principles through a process beginning with words we all agree upon, that "are essential to all political reasoning."

"Political reasoning" is that method Hobbes patterns after the science of geometry, which is exercised ultimately to get human beings out of the state of nature and into civil association; it is a term that represents the entire argument built upon the foundation of natural rights and the state of nature. If we understand this, let us also remember that in the second sentence of the second half of *Leviathan*, Hobbes indicates that the precepts of nature derived through his "political reasoning" are "the natural word of God" (EW III, 359 [409]).

Thus, for Hobbes, principles derived from the consent of human beings about the use of words, and according to a method based in human reason, have now become "the natural word of God." But from whence this divinity? Is the voice of human beings the voice of God? Or is reason somehow divine for Hobbes? We have shown that Hobbesian natural law is not the Thomistic kind, where reason is the voice of God manifested in human hearts as conscience. Hobbes, whose intention here is to associate the divine with his sense of reason, calls his "political reasoning" the "natural word of God" and then equates it with what he terms the "supernatural" or "prophetic" word of God; but are they equivalent? While Hobbes's sense of reason does make human beings *like* gods, since by it they can order the world and make nature serve their interests as human beings, his equation of it to "the natural word of God" is deceptive; indeed, it is another example of Hobbes's purposeful use of ambiguity, of which we have spoken before.

But let us turn from Hobbes's effort to appropriate the authority of divinity to his sense of reason and consider further the nature of this sense of reason. To do this we must consider the foundational premise from which reason operates for Hobbes. If Hobbes's view of man is characterized by the human potential to extend man's independence over his own natural end, Hobbes's aim may be said to be mastery of nature, particularly his own nature. But the problematic aspect of the mastery of nature cannot be appreciated unless one sees the view of man it emerges *from*. The medieval view was that man was between nature and something higher than man. But Hobbes's man begins on the foundation of the state of nature and emerges as the being who orders nature alone, depending on nothing but himself. With this autonomy, man's place as a being "at home" in the universe with a great figure above him giving him meaning and comfort tends to dissolve.

The Context of Hobbes's Sense of Reason: The State of Nature versus the Fall of Man

If we compare the situation human beings seek to escape in the first half of *Leviathan* to the human situation described in Scripture and the role reason plays in providing an escape from that biblically described predicament, an important distinction becomes apparent. The human being we see in part 1 of *Leviathan* is not estranged from what he or she ought to be. He sees no golden age behind him and ahead of him he seeks peace, safety, and prosperity, but no change in himself. His being is determined by his passions and his freedom to pursue them, and there is no sense of sin attached to these. He seeks to maximize the freedom to indulge his passions. He is compelled by his desire to live—and by fear of dying—to change his way of living, to make reasonable arrangements, we could say, but he is not asked to change his very way of being, nor is there a sense in which he understands himself to be estranged from what he ought to be. There is no imperative to become a new sort of person. He is prodded by his own interests not to change himself, but to change the world to make it safe for what he is. The Hobbesian man described in *Leviathan* is not dissatisfied with himself, but with the state of nature, which is to say, he is dissatisfied with the world that inhibits his freedom. Reason's role is to show such a person how to escape the extremely inconvenient situation in which he finds himself placed by nature, and still be himself. Thus, we may say Hobbes accepts human beings as they are.

The human situation described in Scripture is altogether different. It involves a history, a genealogy that has no place for a timeless and autonomous state of nature, even though the biblical view confirms the *description* of the human passions found in Hobbes's state of nature. The biblical vision, however, has no place for an *acceptance* of the selfish interests based on naturally free human passions, while Hobbes's teaching implies they are acceptable, but that self-interest must rein them in for the sake of peace and safety. There can be no statement of a "state of nature" in a biblical sense without revealing that this situation is a *consequence* of something:

human beings made choices that led them away from God; this is what the teaching of the Fall in Genesis chapter 3 means. Human beings, in the biblical view, would not merely be unhappy in the situation of the state of nature because of the danger to themselves and their liberty; they would be unhappy because of an awareness of estrangement from what they ought to be. They would be understood as unhappy not only because of their *situation*, then, but because of *themselves*.

The New Testament states that without the law there is no imputation of sin, and in this Hobbes's state of nature and the Bible agree. Hobbes says this is the case because until there is a person or a group of persons whom all agree should make laws, there is no law; once there is law, then the capacity to break it becomes evident, and so there is, technically, sin, or missing the mark— transgression of the law. This is true in the Bible, too, for as St. Paul writes, "I had not known sin, but by the law; for I had not known lust, except the law had said, Thou shalt not covet" (Rom. 7:7). Thus, for Hobbes, there is no sin in the state of nature, for there is no law.

Yet the Bible also speaks of a "law of the mind" (Rom. 7:23). It is by this term, which refers to the conscience, that St. Paul argues the heathen know right and wrong by nature. The traditional law of nature as received through the medieval Christian teaching is identified by Aquinas with St. Paul's "law of our minds," or the conscience; Aquinas also calls this "the law of righteousness" (Rom. 7:23; Thomas Aquinas n.d., 55–57, 71 [*Summa Theologica* 94:1,6]). As we have seen, there are principles of self-interest Hobbes calls "articles of peace" or "laws of nature" in the state of nature. Do these constitute conscience as St. Paul or Thomas Aquinas understand conscience? I do not believe so. As one commentator has written: "Conscience is that faculty in me which attaches itself to the highest that I know, and tells me what the highest I know demands that I do. [It may look toward God, or toward] whatever it regards as the highest, and therefore conscience records differently in different people" (Chambers 1963, 134).

In Hobbes's state of nature the rules that govern human behavior—the "articles of peace" otherwise known as the laws of nature (EW III, 115–16 [188])—are the highest "rules" human beings know. These rules are found out because the passion for self-preservation drives human beings to them; they do not become rules in the state of nature because of any connection to a lawgiver who acts on

human conscience and who commands humanity to love one another and worship God—but we have discussed this already in
chapters 3 and 4, above.

Nonetheless, at the end of *Leviathan*, chapter 30, we see that
Hobbes speaks of conscience as a place where the law of God reigns.
Here Hobbes identifies the law of God with the laws of nature, yet
in this identification the biblical law of God is not actually involved
at all, but rather Hobbes's laws of nature, which have supplanted it.
The passage reads:

> the law of nations, and the law of nature, is the same thing. And every
> sovereign hath the same right, in procuring the safety of his people,
> that any particular man can have, in procuring the safety of his own
> body. And *the same law*, that dictateth to men that have no civil
> government, what they ought to do, and what to avoid in regard of
> one another, dictateth the same to commonwealths, that is, to the
> consciences of sovereign princes and sovereign assemblies; there being
> no court of natural justice, but in the conscience only; where not man,
> but God reigneth; whose laws, such of them as oblige all mankind, in
> respect of God, as he is the author of nature, are *natural*; and in respect
> of the same God, as he is King of kings, are *laws*. (EW III, 342–43 [394])

Hobbes says here that "the same law" that dictates to human
beings in the state of nature what to do and what not to do, dictates
the same "to the consciences of sovereign princes." He says there is
no court of natural justice except in the conscience, where not
human beings, but God reigns.

Hobbes's language here, appearing as it does to speak in tones of
the Thomistic tradition, suggests that these articles of peace or laws
of nature found out by reason function as a "law of the mind" and
constitute principles of conscience that Hobbes would have us
understand are equivalent to the word of the God of the Bible.

Hobbes would persuade us that the human being he places in the
new creation of his state of nature is the natural man St. Paul
speaks of, and that both have a conscience that may be troubled by
a departure from the ways of the God of the Bible, a departure we
might term "unrighteousness." But the difference between them
may be seen when the character of Hobbes's person in the state of
nature is compared to that of St. Paul's person who is said to be
without law.

If we compare the teaching of *Leviathan*, chapter 13, with that of
St. Paul's Epistles (for example, Rom. 3:9–19 and 7:15–25), we see

that the human being found in Scripture is unlike human beings in Hobbes's state of nature because the conscience of the person St. Paul sees in the former state troubles that person. He is not free of a sense of unhappiness about who he is, a sense no amount of safety can remedy. For such a human being, reason ultimately points not to physical peace and safety—Hobbes's great goal—but to a resolution of travail within. The biblical view is that man is "fallen"; something occurred in the past and human beings find themselves estranged from a peace that is more, shall we say, "existential" than physical. Thus, St. Paul wrote that the convert to Christianity finds the world a new place, not because the world has changed, but because *the convert* has (2 Cor. 5:17). Hobbes's man in the state of nature, however, is freed from whatever might inhibit a human being in this way; his feelings toward his own behavior are not traceable to the imputation of Adam's sin, but rather toward his sense of physical security. Hobbes's use of reason does not take this "existential unquiet" that is traceable to the story of the Fall into account.

Hobbes is able to see man in this way through what we may call his special "spectacles"—a reasoning that is always ready to behold "the state of nature" in human hearts and that pays attention to no accepted authorities that general human experience cannot corroborate; thus the Bible is left aside, as is the God of the Bible. These "spectacles"—this vision—allow him to penetrate the clothing of mores, of cultural conditioning, to see human beings stripped of everything except naked passions, the most powerful of which are pride that makes a person think himself superior to others and a dominating fear of violence from other human beings. These passions, and ones associated with them to do with anxiety concerning human vulnerability, give rise to religion, according to Hobbes. Thus, because he understands religion is only a product of the passions (*Leviathan*, chapter 12), Hobbes's vision enables him to see the world free of the strictures associated with the God of the Bible.

Hobbes, comprehending human pride and self-interested action by means of unassisted human reason alone, differs essentially from the Bible because the Bible condemns these things as diverging from the righteousness of God, constituting sins against him, while the implicit teaching of the state of nature in *Leviathan* is that pride and untutored self-interest are merely violations of man's best interests in this world. Thus, human beings in the state of nature stand uncondemned—there has been no Fall; they are in a terrible situation and need to find their way out, and the way out is by means of reason that discovers articles of peace or laws of nature, that is, a standard by which to judge how to behave so as to best secure peace and safety. The way of Hobbes's articles of peace or laws of nature, then, is not the way of the redemption of the God of the Bible; it is not the way of Christ's sacrifice for humanity's sins, which event is at the heart of authentic Christianity (which is why the symbol of the cross is at the center of orthodox Christian faith). In Hobbes's state of nature, the prudential maxims of the law of nature work in human beings to tell them they are unsafe; they do not burn in people's souls to tell them they are unrighteous.

The human being Hobbes shows us in the state of nature in *Leviathan* may be understood through two different principles concerning the human psyche, both of which we may illustrate by a passage of Scripture. In the Bible's book of Job, Satan argues with God saying, "Skin for skin, yea, all that a man hath will he give for his life," and though this saying is placed in the mouth of the Satan, it indicates a true biblical view of the power of human self-interest (Job 2:4). It is also part of the vision instituted in Hobbes's teaching, as Hobbes indicated this attitude characterized most human beings most of the time.

However, the second principle of Hobbes's vision of the human psyche (which may be illustrated through this same passage from Job) is antithetical to the spirit of the biblical teaching implicit in Job, for Hobbes's teaching is that *there is no higher law human beings can trust* that will contradict or limit the view expressed by the question—"What will a man not give for his life?" The Bible, on the other hand, teaches limits to the law of self-preservation, for it indicates there are things more precious than one's own life. Though one may say the Scriptures even teach one to love one's own life "for no man hateth his own flesh" (Eph. 5:29), it always does so in the context of the greatest commandments that state that human beings should love God above all else (Deut. 6:4–5, Lev. 19:18, Matt. 10:36–38, 22:37–40). Thus we see that the man called Job is not an example of Hobbesian man, but is rather an example of the teaching of Scripture, for his story shows he loves God more than his life.

Since no law except the law of self-interest limits human self-interest for Hobbes, this characteristic of his view of man ultimately supports a theoretically extraordinary human freedom. I use the qualifying term "theoretically" here because ultimately, in Hobbes's view, God is no longer present to limit freedom. Yet human freedom is only theoretically very great, for, while God is no longer understood as present to check human liberty, human self-interest is seen to go very far all by itself toward checking extremes of self-interested behavior, for men and women willingly limit their own liberty as they discover the natural rules of safe action. This is the source of Hobbes's "articles of peace": human beings find it in their interest to check their natural liberty for the sake of peace and safety. Hobbes's work shows that these two "tenets"—the passion for self-preservation and an assumption of great liberty from law in pursuing one's interests—are the defining concerns of most men's character and that this is not so difficult to apprehend if human beings will but consider themselves and others with sufficient thoughtfulness.

This, in short, is the message of *Leviathan*, chapter 13, the "news" Hobbes brought back from his journeys to the state of nature (see Bloom 1987, 162). Hobbes teaches that this vision of the human situation should be considered fundamental to the way we see all human beings, for all are equally free and generally prone to do what is necessary to preserve themselves—and furthermore, to please themselves. All human beings, Hobbes teaches, are prone to act as though there were no law against any pleasures they might pursue if given the right opportunity. As Hobbes says, there is nothing to accuse mankind for in whatever they may do in the state of nature (EW III, 114 [187]). This is the natural freedom that underlies the natural-rights teaching of the first half of *Leviathan;* it is the original basis for what today is called human rights.

The distinction between the view of man instituted in Hobbes's state of nature and that founded on Genesis, chapters 1 to 3, is hidden beneath Hobbes's claim to have harmonized biblical revelation and natural reason (EW III, 359 [409]). Yet the tension between the vision Hobbes would give to human beings via the state of nature, and the vision of the Scripture is very great. Scripture answers Cain's rhetorical question to God—"Am I my brother's keeper?" with St. John's declaration, "He that loveth not his brother abideth in death" (Gen. 4:9 and I John 3:14). Chapter 13 of *Leviathan* gives no such answer. In fact, the duties of human beings toward God implied by the condemnation of Cain and the rule of love enshrined in the First Epistle of St. John are antipathetic to the freedom implied in the natural rights of man that leads to the war of all against all that is the state of nature.

Have we not seen that in the state of nature the reigning power is self-interest in the satisfaction of human desires? For some human beings this is experienced chiefly in self-defense, but for others, natural liberty is the opportunity to enjoy power over others. In either case, Hobbes says, "the desires and passions of man are no sin. No more the actions that proceed from those passions, till they know a law that forbids them: which till laws be made they cannot know: nor can any law be made, till they have agreed upon the Person that shall make it" (EW III, 114 [187]).

As for Hobbes's laws of nature or "articles of peace," we have seen that these articles are principles of self-interest that teach human beings the safest and most profitable way to satisfy their desires. We may reprove ourselves for failing to prudently follow these, that is, for failing to pursue our own interest in the most satisfying manner, but is such reproof the same as the reproof of St. Paul's "law of our minds" or Aquinas's "law of righteousness"? It is not.

Thus, when Hobbes speaks of conscience as a place where the law of God reigns, as he does at the end of *Leviathan*, chapter 30, identifying the law of the God of the Bible with the laws of nature, he is mingling elements of a traditional teaching concerning natural law and conscience with his own new view, so that he *appears* to be writing in the vein of Christian natural law tradition. Yet "laws" operating in the state of nature are founded only on self-interest, as we have demonstrated. Hobbes says that these natural laws are God's laws because God is the author of nature, and that God is also King over kings, and these natural laws have the authority of the king who made them, but he is being as purposefully ambiguous and as duplicitous, as we have shown him to be in the last words of chapter 15 described in our chapter 4, above.

Hobbes's Reasoning Serves Rights, Not Duty to God or Man

Hobbes's state of nature and the sense of reason instituted there are indicative of the state of human beings without divine revelation, and thus the state of human beings without knowledge of God's command to love and without knowledge of the injunction to be one's brother's keeper. But Hobbes nevertheless explicitly connects the law of nature, these "precepts found out by reason," with the revealed word of God in the Bible (EW III, 359 [409]; see also note 4 in chapter 4, above), but with his connection, the individual's freedom or right to be left alone takes precedence over any notion of the individual's duty to be concerned for the welfare of others. Thus, we may say that Hobbes's sense of reason serves the right to be left in peace above the duty commanded by God to love one's neighbor or watch out for one's brother (see Minogue 1963, 26).

In *how* Hobbes arrives at this position and *what* he suggests by it, he does something new: he publicly sets forth a plan (in a skillfully disguised teaching antipathetic to authentic Christianity) by which his "political reasoning" will provide the rules for civil association. He bases his entire project on his greatest "discovery," the state of nature and the natural or human rights he found there. Thus, he legitimates self-interest in a new way by demonstrating that human beings have rights: that they are free to be self-interested since there is no condemnation in it. He boldly appropriates God and the Bible for the support of his plan.

However, when Hobbes looks at man in *Leviathan*, chapter 13, his vision of the role of reason arises from the fear of death, not the fear of God. Love appears unreasonable; it is better for human beings to settle for a safety that is attainable—this world's peace and the rights and reason that show the way to it.

Chapter Six

Hobbes's Departure from Orthodoxy

Can Revelation Be Harmonized
with Hobbes's Sense of Reason?

This chapter marks the beginning of a survey of the first three chapters of the second half of *Leviathan*, where Hobbes begins his detailed exegesis of the Bible. In this chapter, which addresses the very beginning of *Leviathan*, chapter 32, I will show that Hobbes's departure from the theological bearings held by his religious contemporaries actually represents a departure from Christian orthodoxy. But is there such a thing as orthodox Christianity? Before we can say Hobbes departs from orthodoxy, it must be established there is such a thing, and this, too, will be included in our objectives. Our study here is made necessary in order to refute fully that group of modern scholars who finds Hobbes's treatment of the Bible in part three of *Leviathan* to be within the tradition of Christian rational theology extant in Hobbes's own day.[1] In the discussion of Hobbes's departure from orthodoxy, the principal means by which Hobbes does so, which we described in chapter 5, will remain before us: his application to Scripture of an autonomous reason based in his new view of man.

In his conclusion to part 2 of *Leviathan*, Hobbes summarizes the concern of the entire first half of the work as "the constitution, nature, and right of sovereigns, and . . . the duty of subjects, *derived from the principles of natural reason*" (EW III, 357 [407], emphasis mine). The principles of natural reason begin with the axiomatic state of nature, where the passions of men and women know no true law. This natural freedom is the bedrock upon which civil association is first generated: political life emerges out of the desire of human beings to maximize their freedom by minimizing the deleterious effect of its common possession by all. The principles of natural reason are broken down by Hobbes into "the constitution, nature, and right of sovereigns, and . . . the duties of subjects," but the fundamental basis of all these principles is man's initial natural rights.

When Hobbes turns to the second half of *Leviathan* and to his extensive treatment of the Bible beginning in chapter 32, he wishes his readers to see that the principles of natural reason based on natural rights and those of divine revelation are actually but two sides of the same coin. He joins natural rights and the Bible, seeming to make the Scriptures confirm his teaching of great human freedom to preserve oneself, and, indeed, to please oneself.

In the beginning of the chapter, Hobbes alerts us that in turning to supernatural revelation "we are not to renounce our senses, and experience; nor, that which is the undoubted word of God, our natural reason." But since it has already been shown that Hobbes's sense of reason serves a view of human nature unimpeded by any higher authority than the passions that rule the individual human heart, when Hobbes says we are not to renounce such reason we must not hastily embrace his statement that it is "the undoubted word of God." In fact, we shall come to understand that when this reason is applied to Scripture, traditional orthodox views of the word of God and the tenets of Christianity are significantly altered.

In the second and third paragraphs of chapter 32 Hobbes sets the tone for the rest of the chapter, and, indeed, for the rest of the work by attempting to ally natural reason and Scripture. These paragraphs, upon close examination, are quite revealing concerning Hobbes's problematic equation of the word of God and human reason; they also reveal a good deal concerning the exegesis of the written word of God he is about to undertake. Hobbes writes:

> For they [our senses, our experience, our natural reason] are the talents which he hath put into our hands to negotiate, till the coming again of our blessed Saviour; and therefore not to be folded up in the napkin of an implicit faith, but employed in the purchase of justice, peace and true religion. For though there be many things in God's word above reason; that it is to say, which cannot by natural reason be either demonstrated, or confuted; yet there is nothing contrary to it; but when it seemeth so, the fault is either in our unskilful interpretation, or erroneous ratiocination. (EW III, 359–60 [409–10])

Hobbes makes use of the Scriptures in the quotation above with a blending of the two accounts of Jesus' parable of the talents, passages of Scripture worth examining in view of Hobbes's use of them to establish the role of reason that will be exercised throughout the rest of the work (Matt. 25:14–30; Luke 19:12–27).

In the parable a nobleman representing Christ goes away "to a far country to receive a kingdom." His servants understand that he will return after a long time. As he is about to depart he calls his servants to him and gives them money—the talents—with which they are to trade for the benefit of the master until his return. Each, then, trades, except for one, who, fearing he will lose his talent and incur his master's anger, puts his money in a napkin and hides it away. In Hobbes's references to the parable, this "hiding away" refers to a failure to use natural reason suggesting that relying instead on "an implicit faith" is a fault. In the parable as Christ tells it, when the master finally returns he finds his servants have used their talents profitably and he rewards them. But when he comes to the servant who has hidden his talent he is extremely angry. In the account in Matthew, the servant is "cast out into outer darkness" by the master, while in Luke he loses everything and there the text suggests that he is sentenced to death (Luke 19:20–27).

Hobbes insists that the talents each man is given are natural reason, which he warns should not be "folded up in the napkin of an implicit faith." If they are, it is to each man's own peril. Thus Hobbes is saying that failing to use reason and relying instead on an implicit faith—and the context here is the use of it to understand the meaning of the Bible—is displeasing to God.

Hobbes's use of this parable is to establish that natural reason is the God-given means by which human beings are to understand the Scriptures, secure justice, peace, true religion, and their entry into the kingdom of God. If human beings fail to use it, the parable seems to suggest, the most severe penalties will follow.

Thus, as Hobbes appropriates the parable, human reliance on reason is far more to God's liking than the Christian virtue of simple trust in God—a very curious conclusion, since the parable was not told originally to praise the use of natural reason at the expense of faith and the "napkin of an implicit faith" Hobbes criticizes is nowhere condemned in the Scriptures. On the contrary, faith of the unquestioning sort that Hobbes associates with the fearful servant receives no disapprobation at all—ever, but is instead

always praised. Christ even upbraids his disciples for their lack of it
(Matt. 18:1–6, Luke 18:15–17, John 20:24–29; see also Matt.
6:30–34, 8:23–27, 9:22, 15:21–28, 17:14–20, 18:1–4; Luke 5:18–26).
The meaning Hobbes gives to the parable is a bold misuse of the
text, but it clearly intimates the role reason is now to play, not as a
complement to faith, but as its master.

Hobbes's Controversial Prescription for Things "Above Reason"

In Hobbes's time when people said that revelation was above reason
and not contrary to it, they usually understood that this meant
reason operated within presuppositions of faith—and that made all
the difference. Hobbes appears to share this general understanding
when he writes in the first paragraph of chapter 32: "For though
there be many things in God's word above reason; that is to say,
which cannot by natural reason be either demonstrated or confuted;
yet there is nothing contrary to it" (EW III, 360 [409]). Hobbes goes
on to declare, following his statement that natural reason and God's
revealed word are not at odds, that there is a proper manner of
response when the revealed word speaks of things that he calls
"above reason; that is to say, which cannot by natural reason be
either demonstrated or confuted"; Hobbes indicates he has a pro-
gram that defines this proper response. In it he prescribes how
human beings should proceed when the precepts or the narrative of
the Scriptures are "above" reason:

> Therefore when anything therein written is too hard for our examina-
> tion, we are bidden to captivate our understanding to the words; and
> not to labour in sifting out a philosophical truth by logic of such
> mysteries as are not comprehensible, nor fall under any rule of natural
> science. For it is with the mysteries of our religion, as with wholesome
> pills for the sick; which swallowed whole, have the virtue to cure; but
> chewed, are for the most part cast up again without effect. (EW III,
> 360 [410])

This passage brings to our attention three things of importance
that help us see that Hobbes's sense of reason does not operate
within presuppositions of faith: first, the meaning of "we are bidden
to captivate our understanding"—with some emphasis on the words
"we are bidden"; second, the implication of the analogy that com-

pares Christianity to "wholesome pills for the sick"; and, finally, the fact that Hobbes totally ignores the advice and rule he gives himself in this passage concerning things "above reason."

Taking his last point first, one cannot help wonder what the purpose of this passage is when, in the following chapters Hobbes ignores its advice and, indeed, fully demonstrates a contempt for it. The rest of the book, fully half of the work, some 354 more pages in the Molesworth edition, consists, in one sense, of *nothing but* a "labour of sifting out philosophical truth by logic of such mysteries as are not comprehensible nor fall under any rule of natural science." The lesson Hobbes wishes to bring out in the parable of the talents in the preceding paragraph alone contradicts this advice.[2]

The next thing to note from Hobbes's prescription for response to things "above reason," which helps us see that his sense of reason does not operate on the presuppositions of faith, is that he says men should "swallow and not chew," for chewing these hard-to-understand precepts will not cure the sick, as it were. The important implication here is that "the mysteries of our religion," as Hobbes has termed them, are the remedy for a "sickness," which is the human problem of anxiety about the future—especially about death. The aspects of religion that are not above reason, that are not mysterious, and that are accessible to natural reason have no medicinal value and are not at issue since they do not address fully the vital question and will not be that which divides human beings from their civil duties. But ascending into the mysteries "above reason" destroys religion's power to "cure," not because the mysteries will cease to provide answers to vital questions but because involvement in the heart of the matter of religion introduces multiple interpretations of things pertaining to the deepest human loyalties.

When human beings enter into the mysteries of religion concerning the vital matters of life and death, the inclination, motivated by fear, to follow their private opinions is at its height. When such high matters are at stake and a variety of directions are presented to them, human beings who are not taught where their loyalties should properly reside will invariably divide according to their opinions, leading potentially to anarchy and the state of nature where fears reach their height. Where opinions about vital matters are multiplied, then fears are ultimately multiplied, too.

Hobbes's metaphor of the pills suggests the problem before him: wanting to know the mysteries of religion, which, in fact, are the mysteries of life—what is man? why do we exist? what happens in death?—leads men and women to grapple with their greatest fears. Human passions are inflamed over these issues as by nothing else, for men see not only their immediate preservation but also their eternal destiny come into question. A single interpretation of the great questions addressed by religion may render death less fearful by decreasing the likelihood of men and women being tossed about, wondering if they are secure in their beliefs. A unitary attitude toward the great questions assists human beings to live in relative peace concerning matters of the greatest passionate interest, but multiple interpretations promote divided opinions and loyalties and bring the fearful state of nature closer.

Through arguments over resolutions to the "sickness" of the fear of death, human beings bring on conditions in which the sickness develops into an epidemic as they go to war over the meaning of life and death. Hobbes would solve the problem, ending the debate by placing the sovereign, Leviathan—and above all, the natural rights he represents—above the dispute and allowing him to resolve it. Hobbes justifies this through his argument that the sovereign is the product of natural reason, which is the word of God. Thus the product of the natural word of God, that is, the product of human reason, which is the person of the sovereign, determines the meaning of the Bible. But in doing this Hobbes would disregard legitimate disagreements about the meaning of the mysteries of Scripture, as though the Bible had no truly authentic interpretation—a "literal meaning," as the English Reformers termed it—that stood independently of the interpretations of men.

Thus Hobbes suggests that natural rights and the political reasoning based upon them, whose supremacy requires human beings be certain about the priority of peace and safety above all else, may eclipse the faith defined in the Bible. The welfare and safety of natural or human rights, is to be prior to the question of the individual's judgment of his status before deity. But it is important to see that Hobbes "softens" this implication through his repeated argument that the sovereign power called "Leviathan" is itself a manifestation of the word of God and is thus the only legitimate judge of matters to do with faith and Scripture.

As prescribed by Hobbes's natural-rights teaching, manifest in the person of the sovereign, the sickness of society caused through contentions about matters of the very highest concern, though they are "above reason," is cured by swallowing the pills of revealed religion without "chewing," as Hobbes puts it; "chewing" is reasoning, and that is what causes the trouble.[3] In matters of the highest importance to religion, natural reason—"the natural word of God," which gives rise to Leviathan in Hobbes's teaching—instructs human beings to accept the sovereign's interpretation of the Bible. No "chewing," no private reasoning (at least not concerning public matters of religion) is to be encouraged, since it potentially undermines the only authority that can guarantee peace and safety. Thus we see that Hobbes's reference to religion as "pills for the sick" that need to be "swallowed whole" points to a treatment of Scripture by human reason that goes beyond the bounds of what is traditionally considered authentic Christian faith.

The final point I wish to explain from the passage quoted at the beginning of this section will also reveal that Hobbes's teachings operate outside the presuppositions of biblical faith. In the opening phrases of the paragraph, Hobbes writes, "Therefore, when anything therein is too hard for our examination, we are *bidden* to captivate our understanding to the words." Hobbes explains the meaning of this in the succeeding paragraph, "by the captivity of our understanding is not meant a submission of the intellectual faculty to the opinion of *any other man*; but of the will to *obedience where obedience is due*" (EW III, 360 [410], my emphasis). But while Hobbes rejects submission to the opinion of "any other man," this is exactly where he ends up. For Hobbes the problem of those things that are "above reason" is not simply captivating or submitting our intellectual faculty to them, but rather finally submitting to an interpretation—and an interpretation must finally be made *by some man*—of what they mean: "obedience *where* obedience is due."

As readers of *Leviathan* understand, the power to whom "obedience is due" and the final judge of revelation is to be the civil sovereign, but, as we have established, the sovereign represents the culmination of a process directed by natural reason ultimately in the service of natural rights. For Hobbes, human beings are not to be concerned with submitting natural reason and the evidence of the senses directly to things in Scripture that are "above reason"; they are instead instructed to submit natural reason and conclusions from the evidence of the senses to the authority to whom interpretation by nature and, as Hobbes would have it, by Scripture, is given.[4] This represents a subtle but profound alteration of the issue with which we began: if anything is too hard for us to comprehend, we are bidden to captivate our understanding to the words, not of Scripture, but of the final interpreter of Scripture. Human beings are not to use their independent reason, susceptible to passion as it is, but are instead to rely on the product of the method Hobbes has applied to moral and political life, the carefully crafted creation of natural reason realized in the sovereign "Leviathan." Leviathan and the rights of man this sovereign represents are thus found to be the only legitimate authority concerning the meaning of the product of divine revelation—the Bible.

Hobbes's contemporary critic George Lawson wrote of Hobbes's new doctrine of placing Scripture interpretation in the hands of his Leviathan: "His design is to take all power from the Church, Dethrone Christ, and confer all Spiritual power in matters of religion upon the civil Sovereign, and this directly contrary to express Scripture" (Lawson 1657, 156–57). Lawson argued that the sovereign, being the product of consent and placed higher than all authorites, even above Scripture (since Leviathan also decides what is canonical and what is not), actually represents human beings supplanting God's will with the will of man, since human beings consent to give the sovereign such power.[5] Lawson's criticism also thus confirms the argument given here that natural rights, being an understanding of humankind that regards man as naturally free from all authority, is the first principle of Hobbes's teaching.

This section of the chapter shows, then, that Hobbes's prescription (for the proper manner of response when Scripture speaks of things which he calls "above reason") does not preserve the supremacy of faith over reason, but, on the contrary, actually replaces that faith with Hobbes's "political reason," which is inimical to the tenets of orthodox faith.

Hobbes and the Theology of His Contemporaries

In writing that natural reason is "the undoubted word of God," Hobbes was endeavoring to elevate the status of natural reason, as many of his contemporaries wished to do. These contemporaries may be said to wish to lift it up for the purposes of advancing faith, from the rather low place it held for the Reformers. Hobbes, in writing that reason was "the undoubted word of God," also aligned reason with the Scriptures, but not for the same purposes as did the so-called rational theologians. The "ascent of reason" meant something quite different for Hobbes than it did for a whole range of seventeenth-century theologians. Neither the Cambridge Platonist Benjamin Whichcote, nor the Arminian Hugo Grotius, much less such conservative scholars as Hobbes's first published critic, Alexander Rosse, subscribed to the notion of reason's equivalence to the word of God we see in Hobbes. By surveying the views of these men, it will be possible to define to some extent what "orthodoxy" means and also show that Hobbes was not of their number. If the rise of natural rights and "political reasoning" in Hobbes is accomplished in an eclipse of Christianity, we must see in what manner and to what extent Christianity truly is eclipsed in his teaching.

Alexander Rosse, author of the first published criticism of *Leviathan*, wrote, "He [Hobbes] saith that our natural reason 'is the undoubted word of God.' But I doubt Leviathan himself, for all his great strength and power, cannot make this good; for God's word is infallible, so is not our natural reason, which faileth in many things" (Rosse 1653, 32–34).[6] Rosse, at least in this passage, is representative of the English Reformers, such as Cranmer and Tyndale, and indeed, the first great Reformers, Luther and Calvin, who based their views on Scripture and looked with great disfavor on notions of independent natural reason. Luther's position was to "inveigh against Aristotle and against the 'whore,' human reason" (Holborn 1959, 128).

The Reformers' approach to the authority of Scripture was conservative; that is, they wished above all to conserve the text as utterly authoritative. James Pilkington, who prior to the accession of Mary, was Regius Professor of Divinity at the University of Cambridge, argued that "Scripture cometh not first from man, but from God; and therefore God is to be taken for the author of it and not man . . . Matthew 10:20 . . . 2 Peter 1:21" (Hughes 1965, 21–22).[7] The Reformers such as Pilkington argued that the Scriptures are the word of God, addressed to man, and man—including his reason—is fallen, lost in sin. For such men, a person understands the Scriptures not by natural reason, which is not reliable, but by the gift of God through the Holy Spirit. The Spirit, then, both gives the word and, through the grace of the Spirit, also interprets it. Pilkington wrote that no matter how much men tried, they would understand nothing of the Scriptures unless God gave them his Holy Spirit to give them understanding. Autonomous reason, therefore, does not help. William Tyndale, distinguished for producing the first printed Scriptures in English, wrote:

> The Scripture speaketh many things as the world speaketh, but they may not be worldly understood, but ghostly and spiritually: yea, the Spirit of God only understandeth them; and where He is not, there is not the understanding of the Scripture, but unfruitful brawling about words . . . "the natural man understandeth not the things of God . . . I Corinthians 2:11." (Hughes 1965, 24–25)

Reformers like Pilkington and Tyndale believed that through the Holy Spirit believers would understand the Bible in the only proper sense, its true, natural, "literal" sense, as they called it. The medieval Schoolmen divided the ways of understanding the Bible into various "senses" of Scripture, but the Reformers argued that the "literal" comprised them all—allegorical, proverbial, and analogical—and that the appropriate facet of the literal would be made plain to the inspired reader. Thus, according to William Whitaker, Regius Professor of Divinity at the University of Cambridge under Elizabeth, there could not be a variety of interpretations of a passage, but only one true, genuine sense: "We must not bring any private meanings, or private opinions, but only such as agree with the mind, intention and dictate of the Holy Spirit" (Hughes 1965, 29).

This attitude of the English Reformers, an attitude held by the English Church under Henry VIII and Elizabeth and endorsed by Calvinists of the Anglican Church under James I, was still held by many believers in the 1630s. The notion of reason implicit in this view was embraced by the conservative Calvinists in the Anglican Church, against both Catholics and the religious partisans of Archbishop William Laud. But the Laudians turned aside from such Lutheran-Calvinist tenets and held another sense of reason that took the name of one of its inaugurators, Arminius. To the Calvinists of the Anglican Church such as Daniel Featley, author of *Pelagius Redivivus, or Pelagius Raked Out of the Ashes by Arminius and his Schollers* (1626), the Arminianism of Laud was an embracing of grave error: "Arminianism is 'plausible to corrupt reason', but the holy Scripture, 'to which natural reason must bow and strike sail', gives no support to 'this new model of God's counsels fram'd in man's brain' "(Trevor-Roper 1988, 145).[8]

It is this new sense of reason linked to Arminius that the modern Hobbes scholars such as Paul J. Johnson and Herbert Schneider seem to see in Hobbes and bring to his defense when they argue for his orthodoxy, piety, and Anglicanism (Ross, Schneider, and

Waldman 1974; Reedy 1985, 16–21). The sense of reason held by those who could be called Arminian has its pedigree in theology going back to Richard Hooker and Erasmus. We shall see that the notion of reason used by these rational theologians and that used by Hobbes travel along similar lines for a time, but then diverge to such a degree that the former condemn Hobbes for his usage and some finally accuse him of atheism.

The seventeenth-century, English rational theologians' notion of the independence of reason may be traced to the figure of Erasmus. The message of Erasmus was "tolerant, unsuperstitious, rational. . . . It was an appeal to primitive Christianity, as interpreted by the exact scholarship of the Renaissance and human reason" (Trevor-Roper 1988, 42). Erasmus's edition of the text of the Bible, published in 1519, with its exegetical annotations, contained unorthodox opinions, making Erasmus the inaugurator of a new biblical exegesis characterized by a rationalistic approach. Erasmus was highly esteemed among many of the rational theologians in England, first and most notably, by Richard Hooker.

Hooker speaks of the "Law of Reason," saying "[it] is the law whereby man in all his actions is directed to the imitation of God" (Allen 1941, 186). Hooker, echoing Aristotle, reasons that since human beings' actions always imply an end or goal, that goal must be understood as a "good" they seek to obtain. "To will is to bend our souls to the having or doing of that which [we] see to be good" (Allen 1941, 187; Hooker 1970, 1:220–21 [Bk. I, vii.2]). Hooker writes, "The object of will is that good which Reason doth lead us to seek" (ibid.). Thus "reason is the director of man's will, by discerning that which is good . . . for the laws of right doing are the dictates of right Reason" (Hooker 1:222 [Bk. I, vii.4]). Hooker sometimes calls the law of reason the "Law of Human Nature." He says, "The Law of Reason or Human Nature is that which men by discourse of natural reason have rightly found out themselves to be all forever bound unto in all their actions" (Allen 1941, 188; Hooker 1970, 1:233 [Bk. I, viii.8]).

Men and women find this law in the Bible, but it can also be found "imprinted in the minds of all the children of men" (Allen 1941, 188; Hooker 1970, 1:334 [Bk. II, viii.6]). As commentator J. W. Allen explains Hooker's view, "Implanted in every man are intuitions as to what is in harmony with the purpose of God in creation. . . . By reasoning upon intuitions as to right and wrong, men can deduce general principles which constitute the law of reason" (ibid). For Hooker, reason was "an emanation of the divine *lex aeterna*, the substance of a pre-established moral order" (Orr 1967, 157; Hooker 1970, 1:204 [Bk. I, ii.6]).[9] Hooker sees reason as a natural light understood to be connected to the God of the Bible, of whom for Hooker we know much through the authority of the Bible. But for Hobbes reason is not attached to the divine in this way. It is, rather, separated from such a relation through Hobbes's skepticism about human knowledge. As Hobbes says, we can by reason know nothing of God except that there is some First Mover.

Still, Hooker held to a view of reason that allowed him to stand critically before Scripture. By reason, Hooker understood that God's moral nature clearly "demands that salvation be available to all" (Orr 1967, 147; Hooker 1970, 1:269–70 [Bk. I, xiv.3]). Since the moral law "was apprehended by reason," the findings of such reason took preeminence in the interpretation of Scripture (Orr 1967, 147; Hooker 1970, 1:232–33 [Bk. I, viii.8]). Thus for Hooker, the justice required by a moral law to which, by reason, he determined the Bible pointed, made it necessary for him to refuse certain Calvinist interpretations of Scripture (such as the understanding that many were excluded from salvation by means of the doctrine of predestination), even though the biblical text seemed to uphold it. The greater message of the Bible as a whole demanded a different view as far as Hooker was concerned, and human reason mediated it. Thus Hooker did not subscribe to the strict predestinarianism that seemed to be supported by Scripture because such a notion of God was contrary to reason.

For Hooker human beings *begin* with reason and conscience and because of the testimony of these things they finally trust Scripture. "Man would not serve and honor God 'but for the light of natural reason that shineth in him, and maketh him apt to apprehend the things of God' " (McLachlan 1951, 53; Hooker 1970, 374 [Bk. III, viii.11]).[10] Hobbes's guides are, on the other hand, first of all, the more fundamental human passions that are served by reason, such as fear of violent death at the hands of men.

Hooker differs greatly from Hobbes, but we also see the groundwork in Hooker for a set of notions very different from those held by Pilkington, Whitaker, and Tyndale. For Hooker, reason is not damnable. Human beings have a natural light, which is reason, and with it they find the way to the supernatural light of Scripture. The Puritans opposed to Hooker denied reason such power. Yet Hooker still had this much in common with them: he "denied that God had given to man such natural reason as could lead to a knowledge of salvation" (Hunt 1973, 61). Nature teaches nothing of the resurrection, for example, nor of the doctrine of redemption, including the Trinity; for such knowledge the revealed word is needed: "for Nature is no sufficient teacher what we should do that we may attain unto life everlasting" (Hooker 1970, 1:331–32 [Bk. II, viii.3]). Thus Hooker denies that the heathen who have heard nothing of God can be saved. But we see in him both a new freedom given to reason and the early foundations of the greater movement of rational theology.

With Hooker and others such as Lancelot Andrewes and John Overall, theologians and Masters of Cambridge colleges, anti-Puritan "Erasmianism"—later to be known as Arminianism—was inaugurated in England, where it received strength from the Continent not only from the writings of Arminius, but from the greatest name of the time associated with the role of reason in approaching revelation, Hugo Grotius. Grotius was in a large sense the intellectual heir to his countryman, Erasmus, whom Grotius called "the master and teacher of the whole human race" (Trevor-Roper 1988, 52).

The rationalism of Erasmus and Grotius was associated with another name of the time—Socinius. Socinianism was "technically a denial of the doctrine of the Trinity and thus a forerunner of Unitarianism" and thus the Arminianism of Archbishop Laud and the Anglican Church under Charles I was not Socinian in this sense. But Socinianism had a more common meaning; it "was little else than the application of reason to Scripture" (Trevor-Roper 1988, 95).

This was something Hooker did, and the followers of Archbishop Laud, but always within certain bounds, so that doctrines such as the Trinity or the necessity of the gospel to salvation remained undisturbed. Reason was instead the instrument to bring men and women to Scripture, to defend Scripture from the interpretations of extremists, particularly those of the Calvinist position with their stark predestinarian views, as well as those interpretations that give the authority of interpretation into the hands of the Roman Church. But a less reserved application of reason tended to undermine "not only the doctrine of the Trinity but also some other important truths." Thus Socinianism "was feared and condemned by Roman Catholics and Calvinists alike. The Roman Church had condemned such rationalism in Erasmus. Calvin himself had condemned it in the 'libertine' discipline of Erasmus. . . . Socinus merely gave a belated name to a particular form of Erasmusism, as Arminius, too, would do" (Trevor-Roper 1988, 95).

Hugh Trevor-Roper writes that in the early seventeenth century a uniting of the Arminian and Socinian senses of Erasmianism occurred in Holland and that Grotius was a central figure in this event. Grotius "began by attacking Socinianism . . . but study of his enemy led him to discover a large area of agreement" (ibid.). In time the two terms were linked more and more so that "in the 1620s, when 'Arminianism' was made a charge against the new Laudian clergy, the added accusation of 'Socinianism' was not far behind" (ibid.).

What was the influence of the rationalism of Erasmus through thinkers like Hooker and Grotius, on the rational theologians some have linked to Hobbes? The Oxford Rationalists, such as Chillingworth, John Hales of Eton, and Henry Hammond associated with the home of Lord Falkland in Great Tew near Oxford, all embraced the writings of Erasmus, Hooker, Grotius, and the Socinians, yet the theology of none of these men can be identified with that of Hobbes. Hobbes was welcome at Great Tew and was acquainted with many of Falkland's guests; some scholars have also suggested he was greatly influenced by them. Yet other scholars have argued that Hobbes's intellectual pedigree runs not through the theological thinkers of Great Tew, but rather through natural philosophy associated with Bacon and Galileo, and with the Epicurean materialism of Gassendi.

The scholar Perez Zagorin has questioned the alleged close relationship between Hobbes and the men of the Great Tew group, citing "the profound difference in intellectual interests existing between them in the 1630s. . . . During that period . . . Hobbes was entirely preoccupied with natural philosophy . . . geometry and mathematics. The interests of the Tew circle, on the other hand . . . centered on . . . theological and religious debates" (Zagorin 1985, 593–616).

Zagorin describes how Clarendon, an intimate of the Tew circle and Chillingworth, found *Leviathan* "full of impieties" and unorthodox opinions. He adds, "As Clarendon says, Hobbes's materialism and scepticism were responsible for his reaching conclusions that contradicted widely believed . . . interpretations of the Christian faith."

But another modern scholar has argued that Hobbes was a mainstream Anglican whose views were "substantially indistinguishable from those of his friends at Lord Falkland's home near Oxford, Great Tew," including especially John Hales and William Chillingworth (Johnson 1974). He also associates them with Chillingworth's godfather, William Laud, and with the Cambridge Platonist, William Cudworth, seeming to be unaware that the Cambridge Platonists were among Hobbes's most virulent opponents.

This Hobbes scholar, Paul Johnson, who represents one group of the modern commentators who argue in defense of Hobbes's piety, argues repeatedly that Hobbes *follows* Chillingworth and concludes that Hobbes's view of Christianity "was substantially identical with that held by leading Anglican thinkers in the first decades of the century" (Johnson 1974, 122). Johnson writes that, "given the close relationship between Hobbes and the Falkland circle, it is not unlikely that Hobbes's views were directly influenced by Chillingworth." He bases his argument on the apparent congruence of Hobbes and Chillingworth on a "simplified Christianity, which made salvation depend on accepting but a small number of propositions clearly laid down in Scripure."

Trevor-Roper's investigations of the Great Tew circle describe these men and the genealogy of influences that affected them (Trevor-Roper 1988, 186–206). According to Trevor-Roper, the men who gathered at Falkland's estate at Great Tew, including Falkland, Hales, Chillingworth, Hammond, and Edward Hyde, Earl of Clarendon, were all charged in their day with "Socinianism." The biographer John Aubrey, who was Hobbes's friend, called Falkland, "the first Socinian in England" and John Hales, "one of the first" (Trevor-Roper 1988, 186–87). Though we must note here that in the two senses of the term "socinian"—strict (or anti-Trinitarian) and broad (that is, subscribing to "the use of reason generally in matters of faith"), members of the Great Tew circle were of the latter form.

Trevor-Roper describes the background out of which the Tew group understood the capacities of reason and suggests the context of its understanding was the crisis of skepticism of the day:

> by 1620, the operations of natural reason threatened to undermine Christian doctrine. . . . In the previous century, this danger had been less apparent. Protestants had then used natural reason to undermine Catholic doctrine and Catholics—in particular the Jesuits—had sought to retaliate in kind. By now each had succeeded to such an extent that even the agreed-upon central truths of Christianity were at risk. The central truths were symbolized by the incomprehensible doctrine of the Trinity: hence the united front against Socinianism. (200)

This crisis also explains something of the extreme paths some took—from those of Descartes and Hobbes to put human knowledge on a new, surer foundation, to those who fled into conversions to Catholicism, or to radical sects, seeking certainty, to those who sought escape from the burden of doubt in suicide (Trevor-Roper 1988, 202).

Both Falkland and Chillingworth struggled with doubts about faith, Chillingworth converting to Catholicism and then back again to the Protestant faith, seeking certainty. When he returned to England from the Continent upon his reconversion to Protestantism, he "sought a canon of certainty from which natural reason could operate . . . as an alternative to the acceptance of infallible authority" (Trevor-Roper 1988, 205). In other words, his adherence to reason was in response to disillusionment in received authority. As he sought certainty in matters of faith, he, along with Falkland, read the writings of the church fathers. They decided finally that their works did not provide a foundation for certainty (ibid.). Chillingworth found that these sources all argued among themselves, thus increasing his skepticism rather than lessening it. His efforts pushed him "further back in search of a secure basis for reason" (Trevor-Roper 1988, 206). This led him to Grotius and Hooker, and through their writings he came to accept that "absolute certainty was unattainable." Seeking some foundation "on which to build, he settled for a lesser degree of certainty, 'moral certainty,' which is attainable by natural reason" (ibid.).

This, then, is the context of Chillingworth's use of reason—and we see it as one primarily centered around faith; Chillingworth was a sincerely religious man, to whom questions of theology were paramount. His famous work, *The Religion of Protestants*, is completely concerned with theology and questions of belief. Chillingworth believed, in Trevor-Roper's words, that

> religion must have a moral foundation, and natural reason is itself an emanation of the moral order written by God in the hearts of men. Such natural reason, recognizing its own limits, is essential to faith. . . . It is the only means to interpret Scripture as well as to eliminate error. . . . It is not infallible . . . but it is the only criterion we have: probability is the most to which we can aspire. (Ibid.)

This was Chillingworth's response to the "crisis of skepticism." It was a notion of reason that looked for certitude in the realm of faith. It was not understood to be merely a computational tool, but, as with Hooker, it was seen to hold a spark of the divine. Chillingworth was an Anglican and an Arminian, as were all the men of Great Tew. But now our question must be, was Hobbes one of their kind?

Chillingworth's defense of human reason—like that of Falkland and John Hales—"operated within a wholehearted acceptance of Christianity" (Orr 1967, 72). Hobbes's rationalism, on the other hand, according to Robert Orr,

> was rooted in a total scepticism as to human capacity to know divine truth. . . . As a substitute for a single, unknowable, true religion, Hobbes postulated a single, knowable and *authorized* religion; i.e. just as the king's authority comes, not from above but from below, so the authority of religion comes, in the end, not from its revealed character but from the individual's need for peace. (73)

Chillingworth opposed this reduction of Christian faith to the worldly needs of peace and safety. Sounding like the Puritan George Lawson, who wrote against Hobbes, Chillingworth—who never read *Leviathan* (he died in 1644)—anticipated Lawson's reaction to that work in his remarks concerning other Erastian works: "What can follow from [such Erastianism] but perhaps, in the judgement of carnal policy, the temporal benefit and tranquility of temporal states and kingdoms, but the infinite prejudice, if not the desolation of the kingdom of Christ?" (Orr 1967, 73). As with Lawson, Chillingworth "contrasted the Erastian viewpoint, which he thought every Christian was bound to oppose, with his own conviction that 'There is a King of kings and a Lord of lords by whose will and pleasure kings and kingdoms stand and fall' " (ibid.).

Chillingworth, like Hobbes, was apt to see reason as a legitimate manifestation and instrument of human freedom and thus entitled to doubt and criticize all received opinion. He "evok[ed] a notion of reason as primarily a critical faculty, which scrutinizes and appraises evidence for propositions" (Orr 1967, 157). But he was unlike Hobbes—and like Hooker—in subscribing to "a medieval-scholastic conception of the law of reason which sees the mind as the receptacle of divinely implanted truths plainly written for all to perceive" (156–57).

Hooker and Chillingworth resemble Hobbes in that they both give reason a certain autonomy—Chillingworth more than Hooker—but neither of them give it the kind of autonomy Hobbes does, since both genuinely—and unambiguously—connect it to the God of the Bible. Chillingworth believed that human beings could not finally know whether the tenets of Christianity were true or false—and so there was bound to be controversy concerning such tenets:

> If some doctrines are agreed on by Christians as being of fundamental importance, the tenability of their interpretation rests, not on authoritative decrees, but on the fact that these beliefs are the outcome of rational discussion and mutual criticism. These two techniques are not in themselves infallible, but they are the best we possess. To attempt to secure unity of opinion . . . by raising rational apprehension to the level of authoritative finality is to fall into an error whose effects are at once corrupting and subversive of religion itself. (153)

Chillingworth is skeptical of what human beings can know, as is Hobbes, but his first priority is faith, the securing of as sure a standing as is possible before God, a God who has given man reason in order to help him approach divine truth. Chillingworth's reason, marked with a skepticism about the capacities of human beings to know truth, including what the Scripture tells them about God, nevertheless always bows in genuine belief before the God of the Bible and it never serves a view of man independent of the claims of the Bible. While Hobbes's harmonization of reason and Scripture is a subjugation of Scripture to reason, Chillingworth ultimately makes reason serve Scripture (Orr 1967, 155ff).

We see that Chillingworth and Hobbes were not of the same stamp and that Hobbes was not an orthodox Anglican if similarity to Chillingworth is understood to qualify him for that description. Perhaps before the writing of *Leviathan*, on the evidence of *De Cive* alone, Hobbes might have seemed less heterodox. Clarendon, also associated with the Tew circle, apparently read *De Cive* and did not condemn Hobbes for any of its contents, while *Leviathan*, particularly the second half, elicited a great critical response from him in which Hobbes's impiety was the principal charge. It seems clear, then, that it is as wrong to connect Hobbes's position on matters of religion to the influences of the Great Tew circle—and particularly to Chillingworth—as it is to consider him an orthodox Anglican.

Another group of religious thinkers that might be called "rationalist theologians" at the time in England were the Cambridge Platonists, or "Latitudinarians." These men were less tied to the Anglican Church than the Tew circle and they brought still another sense of reason to theology and the interpretation of Scripture: "They sought, in a word, to marry philosophy and religion, and to confirm the union on the indestructible basis of reason. It was the first elaborate attempt to wed Christianity and philosophy made by any Protestant school" (Tulloch 1874, 2:14).

They were interested in the mechanical philosophy of Descartes, whose work they thought could be brought to the support of Christianity and in their own writings they drew chiefly on Plato, and "follow[ed] out in a theological direction the Platonic course of thought" (Tulloch 1874, 2:24). "This Platonic revival" was vital, they thought, "to meet the development of naturalism in a direction which threatened the distinctive principles of religion and the Church" (2:25). In their view Hobbes was the principal thinker leading this threatening development. Thus, "While Platonism . . . may be said to have originated the movement, Hobbism was the means of concentrating its thought and giving dogmatic direction to it" (2:26).

The inaugurator of the movement was Benjamin Whichcote, who in 1644 became provost of King's College, Cambridge. Whichcote wrote, "to go against *reason* is to go against God. . . . Reason is the Divine Governor of man's life; it is the very voice of God. . . . Reason discovers what is natural, and reason receives what is supernatural" (Tulloch 1874, 2:100–1). For Whichcote, morality "rests on the Divine." Man is "endowed with divine reason . . . the idea of good and evil are as absolute as the axioms of geometry" (Tulloch 1874, 2:300). For such a man, Hobbes, who thought the terms "good" and "evil" are meaningful only in terms of the subject, "there being nothing simply and absolutely so" (EW III, 41 [120]), was the bearer of the gravest error. Whichcote saw reason not as a tool of man, but as a link between man and the divine mind, of which Scripture was a manifestation. Some of the strongest attacks on Hobbes come from among these Cambridge men such as William Cudworth and Henry More.[11]

Hobbes's Departure from Orthodoxy

In Christian thought in Hobbes's time, reason was not considered the enemy of revelation by many theologians so long as it operated within the boundaries of the principal tenets of Scripture, boundaries that varied from one Confession to another. But with Hobbes the divine sources and special coherence of the Bible itself are challenged to such a degree that in Hobbes's own time, his biblical criticism was viewed as destructive of the very heart of the Christian religion (Popkin 1982, 138).

Hobbes obscures the liberty he gives to reason by emphasizing that revelation is "above" and not "contrary" to reason, thus making himself appear an orthodox Christian user of reason. But Hobbes's statement that he places revelation above reason does not actually make revelation less susceptible to the solvent power of autonomous reason—it only sets it apart from direct and counter-productive entanglement with the assertiveness of human freedom given new power in Hobbes's natural-rights teaching. Christian understandings of reason implied a boundary line for Hobbes's religious contemporaries, across which the submissive heart of the believing Christian did not tread, where reason throws up its arms and falls on its knees, submitting to the words found in Scripture. This Hobbes's reason does not do; it walks on, independent of all authorities except the passions it serves.

The term "Christian orthodoxy" is hard to define and it is therefore difficult to say someone is outside of it. However, although the task of defining it in a precise way may be difficult, indicating what it is *not* is less so. Anglican divines, the Oxford rationalist theologians, Puritan clergymen, and the Cambridge Platonists, among others, were each offended by Hobbes's application of reason to revelation. Reason, as concerns divine revelation, was to operate within certain broad bounds beyond which Christian faith was violated; across the spectrum of faith from Catholicism to Anglicanism to Puritanism, if nothing else at the time could be so named, this may be termed as a kind of limit of orthodoxy and in this important sense Hobbes departed from orthodoxy and, indeed, was well outside of it. The effects of the application of Hobbes's sense of reason to the Bible—the subject of the chapters to follow—will reveal further the extent to which Hobbes's use of reason departed from Christian orthodoxy and from authentic Christian faith. Thus we conclude that modern interpreters of Hobbes's religious expression, failing to properly understand that Hobbes's putative harmonization of Scripture and reason is not to be relied upon, mistakenly identify Hobbes with authentic Christian theologies, thus distorting Hobbes's thought. Their erroneous interpretations of Hobbes's relationship to Christianity prevent an accurate perception of the stark and radical teaching that underlies Hobbes's political theory.

Chapter Seven

Leviathan Chapter 32: The Biblical Prophets Are Not Trustworthy

We now come to Hobbes's extended exegesis of the Bible. In this chapter and the two succeeding chapters, through close reading of *Leviathan*, chapters 32, 33, and 34, Hobbes's antipathy toward what most believers would regard as the central tenets of Christianity will be displayed. In this portion, the aim will not be only to show Hobbes's antipathy toward these traditionally Christian ideas, but also to reveal more fully why Hobbes goes to such lengths to reinterpret and incorporate the Bible in his work. We shall consider at length why the view of human freedom we have characterized as human rights, set forth in the first half of *Leviathan*, is presented by Hobbes in conjunction with a reinterpretation of the Bible.

Who Is a True Prophet?

Early in chapter 32, Hobbes asks a question: How can human beings who believe in God and who believe that God cares for them know that care through the mediation of another human being, the so-called prophet? Hobbes's discussion of prophets and the signs or marks by which a prophet is known is his answer to this question. It is an answer that poses a troubling problem for orthodox faith.

He reasons that without some distinct proof any person may claim to have had an extraordinary experience of divine revelation. The great danger in this claim is that anyone making it can justify words and actions of disobedience to civil authority, ultimately threatening the peace of civil association. Hobbes intends to show that all contemporary claims to divine revelation are completely illegitimate, but in doing so he implicates not only claims in the seventeenth century, but all such claims in all times.

Hobbes writes that while some may understand God to be speaking plainly to them, such confidence is hard to transfer to others: "For if a man pretend to me, that God hath spoken to him supernaturally and immediately, and I make doubt of it, I cannot easily perceive what argument he can produce, to oblige me to believe it" (EW III, 361 [410–11]). There was no shortage in England during the first half of the seventeenth century of those who claimed God's authority for their actions—chapter 32 may be viewed in part as Hobbes's response to such claims. But he also makes an exception to the rule he lays down for preventing claims of divine authority— the sovereign.

The sovereign can declare God's will and can claim the authority to interpret prophecy. This authority ultimately comes out of Hobbes's argument concerning the state of nature, natural law, and the authorization of civil association, or, as Hobbes terms the knowledge that encompasses these things, "the natural word of God." For the further justification of this *natural* word, Hobbes appropriates the *revealed* word of God—the Bible—but this appropriation is very unusual, meriting careful examination. The effect of a double justification of sovereign power is the exclusion of all other human beings from access to divine authority pertaining to matters of public dispute; such power is to be the province of Leviathan alone.

In other words, in a commonwealth there is *one* person or sovereign power that may legitimately speak to other human beings about nonprivate matters claiming God as his or its authority. Hobbes says this *before* any mention of the signs or marks of a true prophet, thus allowing one person or authority to speak as interpreter of God's will without any of the signs of true prophecy, which he is about to explain are necessary in all other cases.

However, Hobbes's sovereign cannot therefore practically take great liberties with Scripture. The sovereign has to deal with the Bible as a "given"—its power being the weight of human fears associated with fear of God, fear of death, desire for approbation of other men, tradition, and so on. The sovereign *governs*, but this does not give him the power to recreate the nature of man or to rewrite human history; prudence, not arrogance, must be the sovereign's watchword.

The sovereign, then, according to the "laws" of self-preservation which all human beings find applicable to themselves, will not simply push his own agenda against all the passions that define human nature—against all that multitude we see pictured in the famous frontispiece of *Leviathan*, for to do so would be pure folly. The sovereign governs human beings as they are, not as they ought to be, or as the sovereign wishes they would be. Thus the sovereign's great freedom is qualified by how human beings actually are and by the potential for resistance the sovereign understands is implicit in that understanding.

In other words, theoretically the sovereign has the authority to declare the Bible is not God's word and suspend its authority as divine law, but the rational principles found out by reason—that is, Hobbes's understanding of natural law—oblige the sovereign to tread softly here. The traditions of the people the sovereign governs "oblige" him to do so because to violate popular opinion— particularly popular faith in the Bible—would not be conducive to peace, which principle is a sort of summary or first principle of all the natural laws Hobbes enumerates. The same natural law might, in another circumstance, lead the sovereign to declare, for example, that the host and the wine offered in Christian communion are nothing more than bread and fermented grape juice (see Allen 1941, 230).

Hobbes argues that those of his day who say God has spoken to them "in the Holy Scriptures" are not to be understood to say that God has spoken "immediately" to them, but has rather done so by various means: a prophet, an apostle, the church. Furthermore, if a man says God has spoken to him in a dream, Hobbes says this means nothing more "than to say he dreamed that God spake to him" (EW III, 361 [411]). Hobbes explains that for a man to claim to have received God's direct revelation in a dream is not sufficient to persuade anyone to truly believe God actually spoke to the person, since "dreams are for the most part natural, and may proceed from former thoughts" (ibid.). Hobbes adds that many dreams come from "self-conceit, and foolish arrogance, and false opinion of a man's own godliness," which makes men think they "merit the favor of extraordinary revelation." Hobbes offers similarly naturalistic explanations for the seeing of visions, hearing voices, and receiving inspirations.[1] These explanations are not necessarily unorthodox; they might be interpreted as counters to a religious enthusiasm that was considered error in legitimate Christian circles.

After his naturalistic explanation of dreams, visions, and inspirations, Hobbes seems to concede that these means of knowing the divine will may still actually exist, but their possible existence should compel no one to obey those who claim to have experienced them: "So that though God Almighty can speak to a man, by dreams, visions, voice, and inspiration; yet he obliges no man to believe he hath so done to him that pretends it; who, being a man, may err, and, which is more, may lie" (EW III, 362 [411]). This acts as an antidote to those who in Hobbes's time caused civil strife by claiming God's will as their justification for rebellion. But there is nothing in Hobbes's catalogue of skepticism regarding supposed prophets of his own time that prevents it from being applied even to those who generally were held to be true prophets and dreamers—including, though not explicitly, the apostles of the New Testament and the prophets of the Old, such as Moses and all the rest of those considered to have authored the books of Scripture. Though Hobbes never calls these prophets liars, he suggests that human beings *claiming to be* prophets, and, as we shall see, *prophets themselves*, can lie, and thus tacitly casts doubt on the reputation of the most esteemed prophets, the authors of the Scriptures.

Two Biblical Stories

There is, then, a doubt about prophecy, but at the same time Hobbes appears to assume human beings *can* know there *are* true prophets of God. His arguments have the appearance of presuming that true prophecy does exist; the difficulty is merely that certainty about prophecy is hard to attain. Yet beneath this appearance there is an implicit question of the veracity even of Scripture. This doubt is manifest in a questioning of how human beings can be sure that any man—even a so-called prophet—is a person to whom God truly speaks. Hobbes's pointed retelling of two biblical stories emphasizes his doubts about prophecy and the Bible and will serve to illustrate both his skepticism concerning revealed religion and his purposes in reinterpreting the Scriptures in *Leviathan*.

The first story is of the prophet Micaiah and four hundred lying prophets, and the second is a story of a man of God—a true prophet according to Scripture—who was deceived by another man—an older man of God who, according to the Bible was also an authentic prophet. Hobbes describes the two cases:

Of four hundred prophets, of whom the king of Israel asked counsel, concerning the war he made against Ramoth Gilead, (I Kings, xxii.) only Micaiah was a true one. The prophet that was sent to prophesy against the altar set up by Jereboam, (I Kings, xiii.) though a true prophet, and that by two miracles done in his presence, appears to be sent from God, was yet deceived by another old prophet, that persuaded him as from the mouth of God, to eat and drink with him. (EW III, 362 [412])

Hobbes's reason for citing these particular biblical narratives is to emphasize that the Holy Scriptures themselves indicate that natural reason is the best way to know the divine will. These two examples thus set the stage and provide the context for the proofs of true prophecy Hobbes will subsequently describe. In these examples Hobbes argues that there are indeed true prophets, but, while doing so, he undermines faith in the ability to know who they are. This in turn leads to the conclusion that natural reason alone is the best way to determine such things. Thus, Hobbes's exegesis of Scripture in the second half of *Leviathan* begins to teach what the first half of *Leviathan* teaches, that the greatest conclusion of natural reason places the power to make determinations about divine will solely in the hands of the sovereign authority, Leviathan, who sets up all law.

The first example, from 1 Kings 22, has to do with the kings of Israel and Judah meeting to decide whether to go to war with Syria, whose army was gathered together. Ahab, king of Israel, wants to go, but Jehoshaphat, king of Judah, hesitates, desiring to ask "at the word of the Lord" about the matter. Ahab obliges, calling together the prophets—about four hundred men—who all advise the kings, "Go, and the Lord will deliver them into your hands." Jehoshaphat is nonetheless still uneasy and asks Ahab, "Is there not here a prophet of the Lord *besides*?" (which is some indication that these four hundred *were themselves* considered to be the Lord's prophets). Ahab admits there is yet one prophet, Micaiah, of whom he adds, "But I hate him, for he doth not prophesy good concerning me, but evil." Jehoshaphat pleads with Ahab to call him, too, and Ahab relents. When Micaiah comes he first agrees with the other four hundred, saying "Go, and prosper." But Ahab answers, "I adjure thee, tell me nothing but that which is true" (v.16), at which Micaiah then prophesies Ahab's defeat and death.

At issue here is the honesty of prophets, for only Micaiah told the truth, and even then not right away. The example shows that prophets can lie—both the four hundred prophets and one more besides. How, then, can these prophets be trusted? But the story of Micaiah only prepares the ground for the example Hobbes makes more of, the story of the two prophets of 1 Kings 13.

There the Scripture recounts that a man of God came out of the land of Judah to prophesy against the idolatry of Jereboam of Israel. The prophet or man of God arrives at the altar of idolatry, and prophesies against it. When he does this two miracles occur—the stones of the altar are ripped apart, as by an invisible hand, and Jereboam's hand, which was stretched out to arrest the prophet, withers. Jereboam begs the prophet to pray that his hand be healed. The prophet prays and Jereboam's hand is then restored. Jereboam, very grateful, invites the prophet to dine with him. The man of God answers, "I will not go in with thee, neither will I eat bread . . . in this place: for so was it charged me by the word of the Lord, saying, Eat no bread, nor drink water, nor turn again by the same way that thou camest." So the prophet leaves by another route.

Meanwhile, an old prophet living nearby hears of the word and works of the man of God from the land of Judah. He finds him and invites him home to dine. The younger prophet tells him the same thing he told the evil king Jereboam, that the Lord forbids it. But the old prophet says, "I am a prophet also as thou art; and an angel spake unto me by the word of the Lord, saying, Bring him back with thee into thine house, that he may eat bread and drink water. But he lied unto him" (v.18). By means of a lie, then, the young prophet is thus persuaded, but as soon as he eats and drinks in the house of the old prophet, the word of the Lord *truly* comes to the old prophet and he cries out, "[Thou] hast eaten bread and drunk water in the place, of the which the Lord did say to thee, Eat no bread." He then predicts the death of the young prophet for his disobedience, which occurs shortly afterwards.

Here again a prophet is held up as a deceiver. Of all the examples of prophets in Scripture that might have presented a different face on this issue, why does Hobbes choose to speak of these stories from 1 Kings? His aim is to emphasize the need to rely, finally, on natural reason concerning matters to do with the divine will. But the overall effect of achieving his grand end, the means to which included this insertion of these examples in the argument, is the undermining of the status of the rank of "true prophet of God." Hobbes has already made it clear that there are good grounds for doubting persons who claim to have spoken to God—grounds in natural explanations that reveal how human beings err and deceive themselves and willfully lie. By the examples of Micaiah and the man of God from Judah, the problem of this latter ground for doubting—the willful lie—is applied not only to those who are not true prophets, *but also to those who are.* The lesson Hobbes draws from these passages is not so much that true prophets can be the objects of deceit (as was the younger prophet in 1 Kings 13), as that *a true prophet may himself be a deceiver.*

If true prophets can lie, the position of human beings seeking to know the will of God by some means other than reason—by some direct revelation from the Almighty—is very precarious. The problem with prophets is that no person can be sure of them: "How then can he, to whom God hath never revealed his will immediately, saving by the way of natural reason, know when he is to obey, or not to obey his word, delivered by him that says he is a prophet?" (EW III, 362 [411–12]). Thus, beginning with an inclination to trust reason above the claims of revelation, and after examining these cases from Scripture itself, Hobbes concludes that if one prophet can deceive another, "what certainty is there of knowing the will of God, by other way than that of reason" (EW III, 362 [412])?

We see, then, that natural reason seems a safer way to know God's will. What does this mean for the authority of the very books of Scripture? Does it finally indicate rejection of the idea of divine revelation and a belief that the Scriptures are the work of men? Hobbes does not go that far explicitly; but his first critics clearly saw what his interpretation of these passages suggested and said so, as Edward Hyde, the earl of Clarendon's comments on this passage reveal:

> Mr. Hobbes is much concerned to weaken the credit of Prophets, and of all who succeed in their places; and he makes great use of that Prophet being deceiv'd by the old Prophet in the first of Kings, (ch.13) when he was seduced to eat and drink with him. Whereas he might have known, that that Prophet was not so much deceiv'd by an other, as by his own willfulness, in closing with the temptation of refreshing himself by eating and drinking; chusing rather to believe any man of what quality soever, against the express command that he had received from God himself. (Clarendon 1676, 197)

Clarendon notes that Hobbes takes no interest in the traditional reading of this passage, with its lesson to the believer to learn from the experience of the young prophet that it is better to obey the original instructions of God than to try to figure things out according to natural reason. But Hobbes wishes to *encourage* the use of reason—and, ultimately, to encourage trust in the sovereign that reason sets up; his aim is not to warn of any tension between reason and divine revelation.

Hobbes has now implicitly brought us to the point, as Clarendon confirms, where all the prophets may be suspect and where the only person left standing is the sovereign, who, established on the principles of natural right in *Leviathan* parts 1 and 2, remains the one authority who must be trusted. Although Hobbes's momentary argument against prophecy does not explicitly lead to the abandonment of revelation, his use of this story shows the extent to which Hobbes favors reason over revelation as he seems to leave us looking askance at the biblical prophets, wondering.

Yet after his minor note of doubt, Hobbes goes on to sound major notes that seem to express faith in the existence of true prophets. The explicit notion Hobbes wishes to leave us with is that such prophets do exist, but his argument in the rest of chapter 32 is that in all cases human beings should trust the authority of the sovereign first; trust in the Scriptures comes on the sovereign's word (EW III, 362 [412]).

He says, after all, in the beginning of chapter 32, that the duties and rights of sovereigns expressed in the first half of *Leviathan* constitute the "natural word of God." We are thus taught that in the reinterpretation of the Bible being inaugurated in chapter 32, the lesson of the first half of *Leviathan*, featuring Hobbes's "science of natural justice" (or his "political reasoning" or the "natural word of God"), "trumps" the traditional understanding of Scripture. The Bible is retained, but the project based on the state of nature and mathematical learning sets all standards for biblical interpretation and ultimately determines all exegetical questions.[2]

Hobbes's Test of True Prophecy

At the conclusion of his treatment of the two examples from 1 Kings, Hobbes returns, as though nothing in his treatment of those passages were unorthodox, to the preference for reason as the best indicator of the will of God. Hobbes has elevated reason by casting doubt on prophecy. But at the same time he reassures the reader who may be troubled by what he has said by putting this argument away and returning to the very Scripture he had doubted only a moment before. Thus he responds to his own question of doubt (How then can a man know if he should obey the word of him that says he is a prophet?) saying, "To which I answer *out of the Holy Scripture* . . ." [my emphasis].

His arguments have amounted to a campaign of doubt about the Scriptures but now, from that very Scripture that is so questionable, he will reassure us that there are, indeed, two ways to know which prophets are not deceivers. Hobbes explains that along with the way of the natural word of God—or natural reason—which human beings themselves exercise to establish a sovereign civil authority in the first place, human beings have been given two marks or proofs from the revealed word of God—Holy Scripture—by means of which they can establish the veracity of a prophet and help themselves confirm whom they ought to obey. After the two biblical stories Hobbes retells, the rest of chapter 32 is dedicated to explaining these marks of true prophecy. How he establishes these two marks will help reveal the extent to which he is willing to reinterpret the Bible to confirm his own premise that the revealed word of God will not contradict the natural word of God.

Hobbes's first mark of true prophecy is the doing of miracles, but it is qualified: "God will not have miracles alone serve for arguments, to approve the Prophets' calling." Hobbes says the performance of miracles is a proof required for obtaining the status of true prophet, but miracles unaccompanied by the second mark are explained as a test of man by God, or, as Hobbes puts it, they are God's "experiment of the constancy of our adherence to himself." Hobbes gives his own example of this from Scripture from Exodus 7: "For the works of the Egyptian sorcerers, though not so great as those of Moses, yet were great miracles."

His second mark for the verification of true prophets pertains to such a person not teaching any other religion "than that which is established." Hobbes changes this second mark further along in the same paragraph saying, "how great soever the miracle be, yet *if it tend to stir up revolt against the king, or him that governeth by the king's authority*, he that doth such a miracle, is not to be considered otherwise than as sent to make trial of their allegiance" (EW III, 363 [412], emphasis added).

Hobbes writes, referring to the biblical passage from which he derives his two marks of prophecy, "For these words, 'revolt from the Lord your God,' are in this place equivalent to 'revolt from your king.' " But let us consider this passage of Scripture:

> If a prophet rise amongst you, or a dreamer of dreams, and shall pretend the doing of a miracle, and the miracle come to pass; if he says, Let us follow strange Gods, which thou hast not known, thou shalt not hearken to him, etc. But that prophet and dreamer of dreams shall be put to death, because he hath spoken to you *to revolt from the Lord your God.* (Deut. xiii. 1–5.) (EW III, 363 [412], emphasis mine)

Hobbes's analysis of this passage enables him to make a connection between God and king that the Scripture in Deuteronomy 13:1–5 does not make, but making such a connection clearly has the effect of making illegitimate any prophet's words spoken against a king and the established religion that supports him, which is precisely Hobbes's intent. Scripture plainly shows that Moses ruled Israel by God's authority, and thus any person who might have performed a miracle that tended to undermine Moses' authority was stirring up revolt against God. Since the Children of Israel did make God their king, as Hobbes reminds us—"For they had made God their king by pact at the foot of Sinai, who ruled them by Moses only; for he only spoke with God, and from time to time declared God's commandments to the people" (ibid.)—revolt from the Lord *is* in this case, as Hobbes says, revolt from their king (Exodus, chapters 19 and 32). But Hobbes's innovation here is to suggest that no prophet of God will ever speak against an established religion or a king's authority; that is, his innovation is to generalize from Scripture to disallow any voice that might speak against any established political authority. But note that by means of his interpretation of Deuteronomy 13 he would confirm the equivalence of the natural word of God with what he calls "the prophetic word."

Is Hobbes's second mark of true prophecy a reliable test for the verification of prophets if we apply this mark to the test of careful scriptural exegesis? In Scripture, can no one claiming to be a prophet of God speak against an established religion or speak words that tend to undermine a king's authority and *truly be such a prophet*? What then can we say about the life of Moses himself?

In Exodus, Moses, by means of miracles, shows the Children of Israel that he is their deliverer, sent from God to lead them away from the authority of the sovereign of Egypt. If Hobbes's stipulations concerning true prophets were to apply to Moses in Egypt, then

Moses himself fails the test, since his miracles tended, to use Hobbes's words, "to stir up revolt against the king."

Edward Hyde, earl of Clarendon, also argued that by this standard Moses himself was not a true prophet:

> For if those marks, and conditions which he makes necessary to a true prophet, and without which he ought not to be believed, were necessary, Moses was no true prophet, nor had the Children of Israel any reason to believe, and follow him, when he would carry them out of Egypt. . . . [since] Moses had no other credit with the people, but by the miracles which he had wrought in their presence, and in their sight; and that which he did perswade them to, was to revolt and withdraw themselves from the obedience of Pharaoh, who was, during their abode in Egypt, the only King they knew and acknowledged. So that in Mr. Hobbes's judgment the people might very well have refused to believe him; and all those Prophets afterwards who prophesied against several Kings ought to have been put to death; and the Argumentation against the Prophet Jeremy was very well founded, when the Princes said unto the King, Jer 38.4 "We beseech thee let this man be put to death," for thus he weakeneth the hands of the men of war, when he declar'd that the City should surely be given into the hands of the King of Babylon. (Clarendon 1676, 196–97)

It is not true, then, that genuine prophets according to the Bible never spoke or never could speak prophecy tending to undermine the authority of a king and that no prophet ever did miracles and at the same time spoke words undermining a king's authority; Hobbes's interpretation of Deuteronomy 13, whereby he gives us two marks of true prophecy, is bold—and inaccurate.

Hobbes's bending of this passage and his usage of Moses ("him that governeth by the king's [God's] authority") is to justify, by means of the prophetic word of God, his foundation of sovereign authority in natural reason, that is, in the natural word of God. Thus Hobbes makes the Leviathan-sovereign not only ordained by the God of the Bible for the sake of human order, but also ordained by God to be "prophet-proof," since by this passage of Scripture (Deuteronomy 13), no one claiming God's authority can legitimately publicly judge the sovereign. Hobbes thus appropriates this passage to maintain the sovereign above all authority and to prevent others from usurping the authority of God in opposition to the interests of Leviathan. Hobbes strains to make this passage fit his own purposes and this is an indication of the forceful bending of

Scripture required to make the principles of biblical faith synonymous with Hobbes's natural reason.

Contrary to Hobbes's argument, the Hebrew prophets spoke
words and performed acts that threatened the authority of kings of
ancient Israel and Judah on numerous occasions. Samuel's anointing
David king over Israel while Saul still reigned is one example; even
the young prophet of 1 Kings 13 is an example of a prophet speaking
and doing things that worked to overthrow the "established religion" of Jereboam, and the young prophet's actions could not have
helped tending toward the undermining of the authority of that
king of Israel.

Hobbes uses the passage from Deuteronomy 13 to illustrate the
authority of sovereign civil power over the realm of prophecy and
to demonstrate that the supreme civil magistrate is to be the
sole authority over the meaning of the revealed word of God. He
established such a claim for civil power previously under the aus-
pices of natural reason alone in the first half of *Leviathan*; now,
beginning in chapter 32, he is seeking to establish his position by
means of Scripture.

By indicating that the authorization of Scripture as the word of
God, as well as the final meaning of Scripture, both rest with
Leviathan's power alone, Hobbes aims to eliminate the problem of
divided loyalties. If the sovereign is the only one authorized to
interpret Scripture, all other interpretations become invalid. Hobbes
thus excludes the possibility that obedience to God may mean
disobedience to Leviathan.

The passage from Deuteronomy that Hobbes takes for his proof
was originally concerned only with those who would turn the
people from the God of the Bible or God's representative, Moses,
not with all those who would turn human beings from their worldly
governors or whatever religions their civil associations accept, but
Hobbes wishes to universalize Deuteronomy 13:1–5 to demonstrate
that no voice speaking as the voice of God will ever speak against
any established religion or established political authority.

Generalizing from Moses seems to suggest that in all subsequent
regimes in the nations of Christendom, the people have made a pact
with God, as in Exodus 19, making God their king and their earthly
sovereign his latest Moses, who, as such, is the only one in the
realm who has authoritative communication with God, that he
may, "from time to time [declare] God's commandments to the
people" (EW III, 363 [413]). The effect of Hobbes's use of Deuteron-

omy is not only to admonish human beings not to revolt against civil authority, a long-established tenet of the Christian church, but to indirectly suggest that the sovereign created by Hobbes's convenant of *Leviathan*, chapter 17, is protected by the sanctity associated with a pact with God.

Hobbes's interpretation makes the gospel into a guarantor of the principle of no rising up against rulers, which is orthodox enough to have precedents in Augustine, Luther, and Calvin. However, Hobbes's effort here also implicitly suggests that he is indirectly making Christ into a converter of human beings into obedient hearers of the authoritative word of kings, "who from time to time [will] declare God's commandments to the people" (EW III 363 [413]). This is not orthodox in the least. The king is the minister of God, sent by him "for the punishment of evildoers, and for the praise of them that do well" (1 Pet. 2:15). He is to be honored as one ordained by God for the task of maintaining order, but not to be seen as Moses, the voice of God to man (1 Pet. 2:17; Rom. 13:1–6).

The gospel urges obedience to the powers of this world concerning matters of civil life and these passages from 1 Peter and Romans provide the basis for the biblical view that the king—or whatever kind of sovereign power exists—has a God-given role in bearing the sword to punish evildoers. However, the sovereign power is to be obeyed according to the New Testament not because he is a prophet, but rather for the same reason believers are admonished to have an "honest conversation among the Gentiles," that is, that they may advance the cause of the gospel, either through converting others, or giving others no cause to persecute them (1 Pet. 2:12–17). Human beings are not to take up arms under those interpretations of Scripture that lead to the biblical principle of nonresistance to civil authority, but they are not to obey commands that go against the word of Scripture, either (Augustine 1985, 293–304). This means they are to choose martyrdom rather than obey.

There was no room given in Scripture, however, to disobey Moses, for according to the Bible he truly spoke with God and was told by God that he should be *as God* to Israel (Exod. 4:16, 7:1, 18:19, 20:19). In the Christian tradition, the example of obedience to Moses on the basis of Deuteronomy 13:1–5 is not usually held to be the biblical standard for obedience to all civil authority (Romans 13 and 1 Peter 2 traditionally have performed this function). Yet this is what Hobbes would seem to suggest by means of his interpretation of this passage. Hobbes's choice of Moses as a model for his principle of obedience to Leviathan suggests the nature of the obedience he wishes to ensure. Hobbes's Leviathan is to be a sovereign against whom there is no rising up (Prov. 30:31), and Hobbes appropriates Moses to help guarantee this.

The example of the Christian martyrs is indication enough that the message of Christ was not that believers were above all to be model citizens of the city of this world, though they were called to be exemplary up to a point. The martyrs' deaths suggest instead that they were suspected of crossing some line beyond which civil authority could no longer tolerate them, a line having to do with loyalty to another kingdom. The lives of the Christian martyrs also do not lead us to conclude that believers understood the Bible to teach that the kings of this world are ultimately sitting in the seat of God's prophets, though this is where Hobbes's appropriation of Deuteronomy 13 ultimately places them.

However, Hobbes does make provision for passive resistance; he says a believer may refuse to obey the sovereign power and take the penalty of his actions. A person can choose martyrdom in Hobbes's teaching, though this seems to be the course he urges only upon leaders of Christian communities, while intimating that the flock may, for example, bow to idols so long as they keep a different attitude in their hearts (EW III, 492–95 [526–30]). But this contradicts the teaching of the martyrs of the faith described in both Testaments (Daniel 1, 3, and 6; Hebrews 11 and 12). Hobbes's argument here seems to work to diminish the potential threat of passive resistance by suggesting that believers may outwardly appear as friends of the world and receive no condemnation for it from the God of the Bible. But the place given to this loophole whereby Christians may escape the stern strictures of the gospel to testify of their faith and confess their belief before others has an insignificant position in an obscure corner of Hobbes's interpretation of the Bible (ibid.). The importance of Hobbes's allowance of passive resistance to sovereign authority in these matters ought to be judged accordingly. But why does he bother to allow it? He "allows" passive resistance under the rubric of each person's liberty or natural right, and it presents no great problem so long as only a few choose it. Hobbes counts on self-preservation to predominate in the minds of believers once they have been freed from biblical interpretations that would lead them against their interests in this world. Hobbes knows that his reinterpretation—lowering the requirements of faithfulness to Christ—means he is not really giving up very much by allowing such passive resistance in his teaching of the meaning of Christianity.

While Hobbes does not explicitly declare that God speaks to kings—not even to Christian kings—"face to face" as the Scripture says God spoke to Moses, he does say that authorization of Scripture as the word of God and final interpretation of Scripture rests with the sovereign power alone. Thus, Hobbes implicitly suggests the potential in every king or supreme civil magistrate for this very thing—Leviathan does "hear from God." Hobbes's use of Deuteronomy 13 and of Moses as the pattern for the authority of sovereigns over subjects only confirms this.

It is very important to understand that Hobbes comes to his conclusion concerning the supremacy of sovereign power first of all by means of reason unassisted by Scripture. While arguments based in natural reason were used by theologians such as Augustine or Tyndale, they used them only to support what was already outlined in the sacred writings. These theologians approach Scripture from below, as it were, and employ reason in looking up to the Bible. But with Hobbes it is the reverse. His use of Deuteronomy 13 to teach nonresistance to kings and that the kings of this world are alone in the position of determining God's will and God's word, differs from traditional Christian teachings that subscribe to the principle of nonresistance to sovereigns. Hobbes boldly chooses a novel passage and interprets it in a peculiar way because he is motivated more by the wish to use the Bible to support his political teaching founded on natural reason, than by the desire to confirm the authentic standing of the Scriptures.

Hobbes argues that rule by the principles of "the science of natural justice," that is, by the principles based upon natural rights portrayed in the first thirty-one chapters of *Leviathan*, is also established—and therefore hallowed—by the revealed word of God in the Bible. In order to accomplish this, as we see early-on in chapter 32, he must make the Scriptures, like Deuteronomy 13:1–5, say things they do not actually say.

For Hobbes, a sovereign's authority is founded ultimately on natural rights.[3] Finally, therefore, by means of natural rights alone, the sovereign has the authority to be the sole and final interpreter of the Bible, and thus to sit in Moses' seat and, if need be, as Moses did, "from time to time deliver the word of God to the people." The sovereign rules by the consent of human beings, whose consent allows him to exercise the complete freedom from authority all persons formerly possessed in the state of nature—this is what natural rights means. His natural right or freedom from all authority extends to declaring what the Bible means or even declaring *which* books of the Bible are authentically inspired by God. If this suggests the sovereign's ear alone may extend within range of the voice of the God of the Bible, then, as Hobbes understands it, the Bible ought to support this. As Hobbes argues, the revealed word of God is in harmony with the natural word, that is, with human reason based on the principles of natural right and self-preservation. It is this rule of reason that governs Hobbes's interpretation of Scripture in *Leviathan*, chapter 32, as he introduces "marks" of true prophecy. His aim is to prevent any teaching that might lead human beings to disobey civil authority in the name of the God of the Bible.

Hobbes *uses* the Scriptures, then, but the true basis of his argument, while appearing to come down on the side of genuine Christian faith in the vein of a Tyndale or an Augustine, is finally the natural rights that employ unassisted reason to obtain those things desired by human passions. The first two parts of *Leviathan* establish natural human rights as the rule that governs Hobbes's theology. For Hobbes the natural word of God—natural reason—shows human beings who the authority over them *should* be, and since, as Hobbes seeks to demonstrate, the prophetic word will never contradict the natural word, the civil sovereign established by reason is the final authority in all things.

The hard fact of the power of the sovereign over the revealed word of God (that he sits in Moses' seat and "from time to time delivers the word of God to the people") is to be softened by hiding that authority within a church that mediates the sovereign's will to the people. The sovereign allows the church its freedom—up to a point—but the sovereign is the final authority. The sovereign is "bound" in all of this by the principles of nature that lead to peace—a kind of prudence. His own good obliges him from taking his freedom too far.[4] He will not, or should not, speak outlandishly—nor act in too public a manner—against the Christian tradition. But the rule that governs Hobbes's teaching emerges clearly when we are able to see how he uses the Bible to argue that to speak or act in any way contrary to Leviathan is to revolt against God.

Christ and St. Paul Brought to the Support of Hobbes's Test

Hobbes turns to the New Testament to defend further the two marks of prophecy he contends are essential to the establishment of true prophetic authority. He first treats the very highest Christian biblical authority, the words of Christ, to show that without these two marks no prophet should be believed. He writes:

> *In like manner*, after our Saviour Christ had made his disciples acknowledge him for the Messiah, (that is to say, for God's anointed, whom the nation of the Jews daily expected for their king, but refused when he came,) he omitted not to advertise them of the danger of miracles. "There shall arise," saith he, "false Christs . . . and shall do . . . miracles, even to the seducing, if it were possible, of the very elect." (Matt. xxiv.24.). (EW III, 363–64 [413])

This is a curious passage containing telltale hints of Hobbes's novel intention. Hobbes begins with the phrase "in like manner" as preface to this passage from the Gospel of Matthew since Christ's words are employed here to warn, as Hobbes does in the preceding passages concerned with the Old Testament, "that false prophets may have the power of miracles; yet are we not to take their doctrine for God's word." But did not Christ himself perform miracles—and did he not speak words that tended to undermine the religion of the Jews that was already established, which teaching Hobbes calls the proof of false prophecy?

But we note that Hobbes takes the trouble to include the context of Christ's remarks: "*after* [emphasis mine] our Savior Christ had made his disciples acknowledge him for the Messiah, (that is to say, for God's anointed, whom the nation of the Jews daily expected for their king, but refused when he came)." He writes in this way here, beginning with the word "after," in order to emphasize that Christ himself was legitimately king *before* he instituted any *new* religion, so that the Jewish religion was not then to be considered the established one, and thus he—Christ—was no false prophet.

It should be recalled that according to Hobbes's biblical interpretation, any person who teaches against the established religion is not a true prophet. Note, therefore, that Hobbes takes additional pains to add in parentheses that he understands "Messiah" to mean king. Hobbes seems to want to emphasize that Christ did nothing "against" established religion until "*after*" Christ had made his disciples acknowledge him for Messiah *and king*. But even *before* the time Jesus' disciples do acknowledge him as Messiah (Matt. 16:13–20), Scripture shows Christ was going about doing miracles and saying things that could be termed "undermining the established religion," thus fulfilling one of the marks of false prophecy.

Since his kingship at this time was hardly known even by his disciples, to all others, especially to established authority, Christ would appear as a miracle-working subverter of the established religion and thus as no true prophet. Thus Hobbes wants Christ's "kingship" to be no secret—for Christ's rule as king must be as legitimate as possible in terms of the understandings of *this* world so that Hobbes may use this biblical story to legitimate his teaching about the sovereign of *Leviathan*.

In other words, if Christ, at the place in the gospel account where he *appears* to undermine the established religion of the Jews, is shown actually to be the *legitimate* king, then the religion of ancient Judaism is no longer that which legitimately presided over Israel. Instead, the presiding religion has become that of Jesus, the newly come king. This is the logic of Hobbes's argument as it allows Hobbes to take from Christ the onus of being a subverter of "established religion" and all that implies against Hobbes's painstaking interpretation of Scripture.

Thus the Pharoah-undermining God and his viceroy, Moses, and the Herod- and Caesar-undermining Christ pass unnoticed in Hobbes's exegesis, since this aspect of the lives of Moses and Christ undermines Hobbes's project of legitimating the authority of the sovereign of *Leviathan* by means of Scripture. Since Hobbes wanted to institute a biblical doctrine that disqualified as true prophets those who taught a religion other than the established one, he could not allow his readers to look too closely at the biblical accounts of the lives of Moses and Christ, for they both do precisely this.

Hobbes employs a final passage from the New Testament to support his "two marks of true prophecy," this last from St. Paul's Epistle to the Galatians:

> St. Paul says farther to the Galatians. *(Gal.i.8.) that if himself, or an angel from heaven preach another gospel to them, than he had preached, let him be accursed.* That gospel was, that Christ was King; so that all preaching against the power of the king received, in consequence to these words, is by St. Paul accursed. For his speech is addressed to those, who by his preaching had already received Jesus for the Christ, that is to say, for King of the Jews. (EW III, 364 [413])

Hobbes reminds us that Paul writes in Galatians that if any prophet, or if he himself, or if even an angel, preaches any other gospel than that which he, Paul, has preached, he should be considered accursed (Gal. 1:8). It is important to observe that Hobbes is careful to say that the gospel Paul refers to here is *that Christ was king*. Paul's words to the Galatians prove, Hobbes says, that Paul considered all preaching against "the power of the king received" as "accursed" (EW III, 364 [413]). What is Hobbes's intention here?

Hobbes says that the gospel is a declaration of kingship, and this is not untrue, but the emphasis Hobbes gives to this passage makes Paul's "gospel" a declaration of a principle of worldly political authority. Hobbes emphasizes that Paul's words are applied to the Galatian church, a group of men and women who have already accepted Christ's kingship—"For his speech is addressed to those, who by his preaching had already received Jesus for the Christ, that is to say, for the King of the Jews" (ibid.). Thus Hobbes stresses the Galatian Christians' role as *subjects* of a king.

The manner of emphasis is what is suspect here, since the bare contents are no departure from a traditionally accepted understanding of the passage. But Hobbes's next phrase shows that the *intent* of his emphasis is a departure from traditional Christian views regarding obedience and resistance to kings. He extrapolates from the uncontroversial and long-accepted notion of Christ's kingship to say that Paul was actually arguing here that the Gospel of Christ says *anyone* preaching against *any* civil sovereign is accursed, that is, condemned by God. With this, Hobbes's exegesis now becomes controversial. Hobbes writes, "That gospel was, that Christ was King; *so that all preaching against the power of the king received,* in consequence to these words, is by St. Paul accursed" (EW III, 364 [413], emphasis mine). This leap turns the meaning of the Scripture in Galatians 1 from a condemnation of those who would subvert the Kingdom of God into a condemnation by God of anyone who would undermine the authority of *any* king.

Of course, Hobbes does not note that Paul preached Christ—a new king and a new religion—to the Galatians, and in doing this unavoidably undermined the established authority of *some other king* in authority in Galatia at that time, and, no doubt, of some *other established* religion, as well.

Hobbes's prescription for the identification of true prophets includes one last element: he speaks of those who preach "true doctrine" *without* accompanying, corroborating miracles. He writes that their words alone are "an insufficient argument of immediate revelation":

So that it is manifest, that the teaching of the religion which God hath established, and the showing of a present miracle, joined together, were the only marks whereby the Scripture would have a true prophet, that is to say, immediate revelation, to be acknowledged; neither of them being singly sufficient to oblige any other man to regard what he saith. (EW III, 365 [414])

Hobbes says, "if a man that teacheth not false doctrine, should pretend to be a prophet without showing any miracles, he is never the more to be regarded for his pretense, as is evident by Deuteronomy XVIII. v. 21,22" (EW III, 364 [413]). But this passage from Deuteronomy says only that if a prophet prophesies and "the thing follow not," people need have no fear of him. It does *not* say that prophets cannot be authentic unless they perform miracles—though that is what Hobbes wishes to make it say. Furthermore, a brief survey of the Old Testament prophets reveals that there were many authentic prophets who did no miracles, but Hobbes wishes to close the position of God's spokesman to those who have not performed such acts. Samuel, David, Jeremiah, and Ezekiel were prophets who performed no miracles and none of the "Minor Prophets" performed miracles, either. This serves as the last lock and chain on the box that safely seals up the notion that God is presently speaking to man through new prophets, but where does this place the prophets who performed no miracles, such as Jeremiah or Ezekiel, for Hobbes?

We conclude, then, that the test of true prophecy described by Hobbes was instituted by him to discredit any who claim to hear the voice of God and use such claims as authorization to rebel against the supreme civil power established by natural reason. But more importantly, it was instituted by him to appropriate the Bible for the legitimation of Leviathan; Hobbes's interpretation of the Bible concerning the marks of true prophecy represents his effort to establish that Scripture supports the findings of his political science.

Are Prophets Trustworthy?

At one moment Hobbes's treatment of prophets in chapter 32 leaves us doubting if such persons can be trusted, but at the next, Hobbes seems to banish the doubts he has brought with the breezy reassurance that the Scriptures are authoritative after all and will "supply the place" and "recompense the want of all other prophecy" through "wise and learned interpretation, and careful ratiocination" (EW III, 365 [414]). Yet Hobbes's concluding words in chapter 32, that the Scriptures, rationally interpreted, can be our guide, seems out of place after the doubts he has raised at the beginning of the chapter concerning the veracity of prophets. Can careful study relieve the unease he has created?

We can ask this question only because our efforts have brought us a little closer to the reactions Hobbes's work provoked in his own time. We have been able to reach *below* the apparent good sense Hobbes's explicit argument might make to an unprepared modern reader, to identify the doubt that is implicit beneath. Without some excavation that includes digging into Scripture, Christian theology, and Hobbes's own contemporary critics, Hobbes's admonition at the beginning of chapter 32 "not to bury the talent of natural reason," which will reveal "all the rules and precepts necessary to the knowledge of our duty both to God and man" (EW III, 365 [414]), might seem perfectly acceptable. Without a careful analysis of Hobbes's text, a casual modern reader might see only a persuasive religious exposition whose author seems to possess a great knowledge of Scripture and Scripture-based faith.

But this is not the conclusion of this analysis. Instead, with these first excavations, it is possible to see that it is not the Bible's divine authorization that is the most fundamental presupposition of Hobbes's work. We may see that Hobbes is teaching us there are difficulties with prophets having to do with the limits of human knowledge and the capacity in human beings for deceit. We may see that Hobbes is actually pointing us not to prophecy, but to the Bible's reasonableness according to a human reason that is employed by the human passions it serves. The purpose of the part of chapter 32 regarding the marks of true prophecy, which was discussed above, is to show that the Bible supports the findings of Hobbes's "science of natural justice" if it is interpreted to *emphasize* its congruence with those findings of human reason. However, the price for doing this appears to be the neglect or disavowal of traditionally orthodox understandings of Scripture.

By suggesting in chapter 32 that the biblical prophets are not to be trusted, Hobbes shows himself to be antagonistic to one of the chief principles of Christianity. But his antagonism is couched in an interpretative style the analysis of which reveals both his reluctance to be explicitly skeptical and his interest in appearing to be a believer. The new world of Hobbes's political science based on human rights that Hobbes aimed to establish required the support of a religion that had been subordinated to the worldly interests of human beings. Hobbes thus reinterpreted the Bible to help establish his new view of man and civil association.

The Bible poses no problem for Hobbes so long as it is made into the school where human beings will learn the lessons of this natural word of God—the lessons of his "science of natural justice" or "political reasoning"—and allow those lessons to rule biblical interpretation. It is this notion of reason that Hobbes will continue to employ in his treatment of the Scriptures in chapter 33, where he examines not only the trustworthiness of the prophets, but also of something that believers understand the prophets gave the world—the written word of God itself.

Chapter Eight

Leviathan Chapter 33:
The Bible and Political Reasoning

The Authority of the Scriptures Depends on the Sovereign

In *Leviathan*, chapter 32, Hobbes intimates that prophets may be deceivers. In chapter 33, he casts doubt on the authorship of the Pentateuch and then suggests that the New Testament may have been tampered with by an early council of the church. Yet in each case he seems to banish doubts by proceeding as though these discoveries have no effect on the authority of the Bible. It seems that for Hobbes, the great questions of the Scriptures are not to do precisely with who wrote them or with tampering that might have occurred in the assembling of the canon or with the fact that sometimes human beings are deceivers. These, Hobbes seems to say—after he has brought them up (and *why* has he brought them up?)—are uncertainties we may ponder, but they are not to be taken as unsurmountable. The big question, Hobbes indicates, is who finally stands behind them, that is, who determines their authority. The determiner, Hobbes has demonstrated in chapters 1 through 31, is the sovereign.

We turn in chapter 33 to the relationship between Hobbes's answer to this great question about the Bible and the uncertainties Hobbes brings concerning the independent authority of the Scriptures. In examining this relationship we will seek to determine why Hobbes launches a campaign of doubtful suggestions about prophets in chapter 32 and, in chapter 33, about the written record, the written word of God.

Hobbes begins chapter 33 by describing the books of Scripture as

155

"the rules of Christian life," adding that they are not only rules, but laws. He writes, "because all rules of life, which men are in conscience bound to observe, are laws; the question of the Scripture, is the question of what is law throughout all Christendom, both natural and civil" (EW III, 366 [414]). But how are laws known to human beings and how are they legitimately *law*? Hobbes has worked this out with care in parts 1 and 2, as he reminds us here: "Seeing therefore I have already proved, that sovereigns in their own dominions are the sole legislators, those books are only canonical, that is, law, in every nation, which are established for such by the sovereign authority" (EW III, 366 [415]). We are here to understand that Hobbes has established that the sovereign of each Christian commonwealth is above all other authorities in that commonwealth.

But we should not forget the context of these first lines of chapter 33. Hobbes appears to concede that the Bible has some authority over the sovereign because it determines what laws he cannot constitute ("For though it be not determined in Scripture what laws every Christian king shall constitute in his own dominions, yet it is determined what laws he shall *not* constitute"), but he immediately reasserts the full extent of sovereign rights by telling us that only the sovereign can legitimately make the Scriptures into law (EW III, 366 [415]). So Hobbes's seeming admission that there are some laws the sovereign "shall not constitute" appears to be a remark that, whatever its purpose, means something other than what it actually states.

If the sovereign has the authority to say what is canonical, the sovereign is entitled to say what is and what is not Holy Scripture. The right of the supreme governor of a Christian commonwealth thus includes the authority to regulate the content of the Bible—and it is the duty of subjects to accept such regulation. If the purpose of chapter 33 is to explain the rights of the supreme governors of Christian commonwealths and to explain the duties their subjects owe them, we now begin to see to what extent these rights and duties are to be governed first by the sovereign who is established by political reasoning and to what extent they are to be governed first by Scripture (EW III, 365 [414]).

The Authority of Scripture Depends on Political Reasoning

In Hobbes's opening remarks to the chapter, he states the question before us as "the question of Scripture." Why is this question of

Scripture, which Hobbes also calls the question of what is law throughout Christendom, the issue? Hobbes has alerted us that his purpose overall in *Leviathan* is to establish the rights of sovereigns and the duties of subjects, and he poses the question of what constitutes law throughout Christendom in chapter 33 to show how these rights and duties may be derived from the Bible, as well as through natural reason. Since Hobbes's arguments place the sovereign above Scripture, the most serious question of Scripture appears to be how Scripture itself may be made to prove that the supreme governor of each Christian commonwealth has final authority over what it says.[1] Thus, the question is how the Bible can be made to authorize one who, in the last analysis, has authority over it. For if the case is otherwise, and the Bible is the final authority, the question of Scripture, as Hobbes sees it, will not be resolved by any supreme civil magistrate, and, in Hobbes's view (and, indeed, as the events in England from 1640 to 1660 bore out), there will be, instead, a number of authorities declaring the meaning of the Bible. These will be rivals for the sovereignty in every commonwealth in Christendom.

For Hobbes, the question of Scripture, then, is not first of all a question of what God has said to man, but rather one of *who* will rule in Christian commonwealths. For if the authority of Scripture does not rest with the sovereign, there will be a tendency for loyalties to be divided and peace to be threatened. The peace of this world is Hobbes's goal; the question of Scripture in some sense, then, is finally how it may be shown to support such peace.

It is noteworthy that Hobbes calls the question of Scripture the question of "what is law throughout all Christendom, *both natural and civil.*" With these two branches of law, Hobbes leaves out those rules of life that pertain to the supernatural or prophetic word of God. He omits, therefore, what Christ called the first and great commandment: "Thou shalt love the Lord thy God with all thy heart, and with all thy soul, and with all thy mind" (Matt. 22:37–38; Deut. 6:5). Natural law—the discovery of human reason—cannot show human beings they ought to love God, though human reason may instruct men and women to acknowledge an unknown and mighty power—a natural religion—as Hobbes had suggested in the twelfth chapter of *Leviathan*. Here in chapter 33 Hobbes implicitly relegates the Bible—the spiritual or divine law—to what human reason can figure out, that is, to civil law that itself emerges out of natural law. We recall again that the sovereign emerges out of the precepts discovered by natural reason; the sovereign then becomes the maker of civil law (*Leviathan*, chapters 13 through 18, and 26). The category of divine law is swallowed up, then, by natural law—by the findings of natural reason.

Hobbes now proceeds to the canon of Scripture according to the Church of England—that is, according to the authority of the civil sovereign who is understood to be head of that church. The rest of the chapter is a discussion of that canon. The contents of the canon Hobbes lists contain nothing that would seem unusual to a seventeenth-century Englishman. Yet whatever Hobbes's ensuing examination is to reveal, the essence of his argument rests on what he has posited at the outset of the chapter, namely that the canon is composed as it is because the sovereign has judged it ought to be composed in this way. It is not the content of Scripture, but who determines the content that is decisive. This is Hobbes's controversial conclusion, since he is saying that the authority of the Bible depends on the findings of the *political reasoning* that set up the sovereign in the first place. Remember that Hobbes described parts 1 and 2 of *Leviathan* as "political reason" at the outset of chapter 32. It is that process by which Hobbes determines "the right of sovereign power and the duty of subjects . . . from the principles of nature only" (EW III, 359 [409]). Hobbes's declaration that the authority of the Bible depends on political reasoning attracted criticism from former friends, like Clarendon, and from his avowed adversaries from both Anglican and Puritan parties.[2]

Once the power of authorization is confirmed in the first sentences of chapter 33, Hobbes turns to survey the canon of Scripture. In the course of Hobbes's survey, including analyses of who wrote the various books, and when, the doubt about the veracity of Scripture first suggested in chapter 32 again becomes apparent as Hobbes suggests problems concerning Moses' authorship of the Pentateuch, problems of authorship with other books of Scripture, and tampering with the content of the Bible by the Council of Laodicea in the year 364 A.D. It is interesting that this tends further to justify the reasonableness of leaving the choice of the contents of the canon to the sovereign: it is reasonable according to the laws of nature and because of the very uncertainty of the authority of Scripture.

The first paragraph of chapter 33, then, indicates that the authority of the Scriptures depends on the sovereign. Hobbes here advances the notion that reason, not revelation, ought to rule political life. Yet we shall find out as we follow Hobbes as he turns to the canon that he wishes to establish a clear role for revelation, too. But what sort of role?

Doubts about Moses and Questions about the Canon

My aim in finding out the role of revelation in Hobbes's teaching in this chapter is, first, to show that he undermines the authority of Moses and of Scripture generally and that in the place of divine authority represented by Moses, the prophets, and the apostles, he elevates the authority of the civil sovereign. After doing this, I shall then ask what his purpose in doing this is, which will then permit me to address the problem of why he seeks to retain the notion of revelation while also seeking, on another level, to undermine it.

In the seventeenth century, Moses was traditionally regarded to be the author of the first five books of the Old Testament, the Pentateuch, but Hobbes wrote, "the five books of Moses were written after his time, though how long after is not manifest" (EW III, 369 [418]). This was a controversial idea and disturbing to generally agreed-upon Christian belief.

Hobbes begins with the assertion that the primary authority for Moses' authorship of the Pentateuch is simply that it is *called* the five books of *Moses*. This is no argument, he says, and he proceeds to cite evidence for another conclusion:

We read in the last chapter of Deuteronomy, verse 6th, concerning the sepulchre of Moses, "that no man knoweth of his sepulchre to this day," that is, to the day wherein those words were written. It is therefore manifest that those words were written after his interment. For it were a strange interpretation, to say Moses spake of his own sepulchre, though by prophecy, that it was not found to that day, wherein he was yet living. But it may perhaps be alleged, that the last chapter only, not the whole Pentateuch, was written by some other man, but the rest not. (EW III, 368 [417])

This, indeed, *was* the Jewish tradition, as Alexander Rosse, another of Hobbes's contemporary critics, protested: Joshua wrote the last chapter of Deuteronomy long after Moses' death (Rosse 1653, 34–35).

Hobbes thus turns to other texts in the Pentateuch to prove that Moses was not the author of the five books: "consider that which we find in the book of Genesis (xii.6) 'And Abraham passed through the land to the place of Sichem, unto the plain of Moreh, and the *Canaanite* was then in the land;' which must need be the words of one that wrote when the Canaanite was not in the land; and consequently, not of Moses, who died before he came into it" (EW III, 368–69 [417]). Though he does concede that Moses still wrote a large portion of Deuteronomy, he proceeds from that admission to declare that the rest of the books of the Old Testament were written long after the events described in them. He argues that the entire Old Testament was assembled in its present form "after the return of the Jews from their captivity in Babylon." He says that according to the Apocrypha, the Scriptures were set forth in their present form by Esdras (that is, Ezra), whom he then cites, quoting from the second book of Esdras (2 Esd. 16:21–22).

In this passage Esdras speaks to God, declaring God's law has been burned so that none can know it. He prays God will send his holy spirit into him and inspire him to write "all that hath been done in the world, since the beginning, which were written in thy law, that men may find thy path, and that they which will live in the latter day, may live." The passage concludes with an admonition from God to Esdras: "And it came to pass when the forty days were fulfilled, that the highest spake, saying, The first that thou hast written, publish openly, that the worthy and unworthy may read it" (EW III, 373–74 [422]).

This is Hobbes's account of how the Old Testament came into being. On the following page of the Molesworth edition of *Leviathan*, Hobbes seems even more certain of this, for where he suggested Esdras as a *possibility* on the former page, on the latter he writes, "The books of the Old Testament are derived to us, from no other time than that of Esdras, who by the direction of God's spirit, retrieved them, when they were lost" (EW III, 375 [423]). Thus this apocryphal story becomes one of Hobbes's arguments employed to shake the traditional authority of Scripture.

Hobbes insists repeatedly that the biblical phrase "unto this day," and such phrases as "the Canaanite was *then* in the land" in Scripture refer to events that took place long before these written accounts were completed, thereby implying that the authors of the various texts in which such phrases occur could not themselves have been witnesses of the events these books relate to us. Thus Moses, who died before the conquest of Canaan, could not have referred to a time when the Canaanite was *not* in the land.

Hobbes goes on to cite the story in the Book of Joshua concerning

Joshua's setting up twelve stones in the middle of the Jordan River to mark the passage of Israel across that natural divide, "of which the writer saith thus, 'They are there unto this day' (*Josh.* iv.9)." This statement could not have been written by Joshua, "for," as Hobbes puts it, " 'unto this day,' is a phrase that signifieth a time past, beyond the memory of man" (EW III, 370 [418]). This exegesis becomes the second argument Hobbes uses to shake the traditional authority of Scripture. But both this argument and that taken from Esdras were problematic for Hobbes's contemporaries.

Concerning the first argument, that Moses did not write the first five books of Scripture and that Esdras did, it ought to be mentioned that the New Testament writers believed that it was Moses who wrote them; Christ and the gospel writers declared Moses' authorship and the Jews of the time of Christ certainly believed the Pentateuch was Moses' work (Mark 7:10; Luke 16:31; John 1:17; Acts 6:11–15). Beyond this, the book of 2 Esdras is the least esteemed of all the fifteen books of the Apocrypha: Esdras was the only one excluded from the Septuagint and the Vulgate.[3]

Hobbes was very much ahead of his time in his argument against Moses' authorship, which much current biblical scholarship tends to support in part, although modern biblical studies would not support Hobbes's alternative theory—that Esdras received the Scripture himself by revelation. We shall see how dangerous Hobbes's view was taken to be.

Hobbes's skepticism about the authorship of the Pentateuch was controversial because the reliability of the Bible for almost every educated person in his time rested on the testimony of trustworthy witnesses, foremost of which was Moses; if the first five books of Scripture were not his writings, the conviction that the Bible was the truth of God would be shaken. Hobbes was thus viewed as a threat to religious belief, along with others of the very first bold expositors of the same teaching about the authorship of Scripture, Benedict Spinoza, author of *A Theologico-Political Treatise*, Isaac La Peyrere, author of the infamous *Men before Adam*, and Father Richard Simon, author of *The Critical History of the Old Testament*. These men all doubted Moses' authorship. Richard Popkin recites an account of a meeting between Simon and La Peyrere in which the former told the latter, " 'It seems to me that your reflections are going to ruin the Christian religion entirely' " (Popkin 1982, 138). All these men together were regarded by many to be intent on that effect. Popkin writes of another testimony of this attitude: "An unsympathetic reader [of Simon's], the English Jurist, Sir Matthew Hale . . . said that belief that La Peyrere's interpretation of the Bible was true "would necessarily not only weaken but overthrow the Authority and Infallibility of the Sacred Scripture" (ibid.).

Moses' authorship of the Pentateuch served as the foundation for its authenticity, and to doubt this brought into question not only his work, but the entire balance of Scripture. To again cite Richard Popkin's research, as Tom Paine, certainly an enemy of traditional Christian belief, later wrote: "Take away from Genesis the belief that Moses was the author, on which only the strange belief that it is the word of God has stood, and there remains nothing of Genesis, but an anonymous book of stories, fables . . . or downright lies" (ibid.). And, as Popkin brings out, once one part of the Bible comes to be doubted, there is very little to stop book after book and epistle after epistle from also being doubted until there is no word of God left.

Though Hobbes was more conservative in his exposition concerning both Moses' authorship and questions about the authenticity of the accounts given in the Bible than Spinoza and these others, his was the very first of these to be published. His conservatism may be considered an act of caution, though his critics clearly perceived the seriousness of the doubts he inaugurated in *Leviathan*.

In Hobbes's other argument to discredit the authority of Moses, he uses a phrase in the twelfth chapter of Genesis, "the Canaanite was then in the land," to claim the post-Mosaic authorship of the book. He also claims the phrase repeatedly used in the book of Joshua, "unto this day," is evidence that a post-Joshuan author wrote that book of Scripture. Hobbes concludes, "the facts registered are always more ancient than the register" (EW III, 371 [419]).

Concerning this objection, even for many nineteenth- and some twentieth-century interpreters of the Bible, Hobbes's doubts could not be accepted. Admittedly, such interpreters are of the more traditional stamp, but for them the phrase, "the Canaanite was then in the land" need not refer to Moses' experience at all. Moses, according to such traditional readings—which have in common the seventeenth-century view of the authority of the Pentateuch—is simply recording the situation in the land at the time of Abraham's migration there.[4] Hobbes also argued that the phrase "unto this day" established Joshua as being written "long after" the time of Joshua, and this interpretation, too, was questioned up to the nineteenth and twentieth centuries—while it was considered extremely unorthodox in the seventeenth.[5]

But the more important question is not now defending the authorship of Moses or Joshua, but determining what Hobbes is doing here. Why has he decided to make this criticism of Scripture? Let us recall that Hobbes was not the first to note these passages, yet other interpreters of Scripture found ways to continue to believe that, for example, Moses himself wrote the Pentateuch.[6] Hobbes does not consider those earlier defenses of orthodoxy and instead uses these passages as the determining proof to force a reappraisal of the tradition of authorship. He then places the responsibility for the authorship of the Old Testament on Ezra (that is, Esdras), although the passage he has cited in 2 Esdras appears to refer only to the Law, that is, to the Pentateuch. Whereas Hobbes had previously conceded that a large portion of Deuteronomy *was* written by Moses, he now attributes not only the five books of Moses but the Old Testament as a whole to Esdras.[7]

Unlike Moses and Joshua, the other books of the prophets are not individually opened to Hobbes's doubts; and the histories—Judges through Chronicles—contain no internal record of their authorship for Hobbes to contradict. It is agreed that the poetry of Psalms and Proverbs may well have been assembled from preexisting records at some time after the days of David and Solomon. If all Hobbes were arguing was that the pieces were *assembled* in their Septuagintal form by Esdras that would be one thing; Jewish tradition accepts this so that Esdras, for his editorial work, is even considered a "second Moses." But Hobbes does not simply say that; he goes further.

Even though Hobbes's quotation from Esdras only refers to the Pentateuch and even though his survey of the other books of the Old Testament makes no attempt to criticize the authorship of any of the books of the prophets (except Jonah), he says "the books of the Old Testament are derived to us, from no other time than that of Esdras, *who by the direction of God's spirit retrieved them when they were lost*" (EW III, 375 [423], my emphasis).

Hobbes elevates Esdras to a supremely important position, denying that what was considered the canon of the Old Testament survived prior to the time of Esdras (or Ezra) and the Jewish return from Babylon. It is plain from Hobbes's argument that if Esdras had not recovered these books, he considers that they would have been lost in perpetuity. In citing Esdras, Hobbes does affirm the possibility of divine revelation—this is a common thread between Esdras and the traditional story of Moses. But why is Hobbes so keen to discredit Moses? What is his purpose in explaining the existence of the entire Old Testament according to the words of the obscure and generally questioned account of Esdras? Before answering this, let us follow Hobbes through the remainder of the chapter.

He moves on to the New Testament, by his treatment allowing the greatest possible grounds for suspicion of its authority. According to Hobbes, the canon of the New Testament as we now know it was not assembled until the year 364 A.D. by the Council of Laodicea, and his opinion of the character of that conclave suggests the greatest skepticism.

He writes that at the time of the council the great doctors of the church would not deign to think of kings and emperors as shepherds of the people but as sheep, and of non-Christian kings as wolves. He describes the leaders of the church as men dominated by ambition who sought to have their word treated not as counsel, but as law, and who thought of themselves not as preachers but as absolute governors. Hobbes speaks of the great doctors who had gathered at Laodicea as men who "thought such frauds as tended to make the people the more obedient to Christian doctrine, to be pious." But after such criticism Hobbes writes, "Yet I am persuaded they did not therefore falsify the Scriptures, though the copies of the books of the New Testament, were in the hands only of the ecclesiastics; because if they had had an intention so to do, they would surely have made them more favourable to their power over Christian princes, and civil sovereignty, than they are" (EW III, 375 [423]). He makes the likelihood of tampering large, but seems to dismiss its occurrence. Why does he do this?

Hobbes acknowledges that the traditionally received writers of the New Testament all saw the Savior and that "consequently whatsoever is written by them, is as ancient as the time of the apostles" (EW III, 374 [422]). He hypothetically legitimates the written work of the apostles, then, but he distinguishes between their erstwhile accounts and the books of the New Testament in their present form. Thus we have in these New Testament works a parallel with the works of the Old Testament: Hobbes acknowledges the *existence* of both Old Testament Moses and New Testament Matthew, of both Old Testament Joshua and New Testament Mark, but in all cases he sets up a distinction between the *existence* of the authors and their testamental *work*, that is, between the *persons* whose names are associated with the writings and the *writings* themselves as found in the canonical Scriptures. He finds passages in the Old Testament by which to claim Moses and Joshua were not the authors of the books that are credited to them, and he finds grounds to suspect tampering with the works of the apostles in the New Testament. Without explicitly denying the identification of the lawgiver Moses with his five books and of the apostle with his written gospel, he nevertheless finds it worthwhile to suggest the possibility of such a thing.

Hobbes is willing to doubt the authenticity of Moses' authority and suggest the possibility of falsification of the apostles' words. But he ultimately appears to retrieve all the writings from troublesome doubt: first, in the case of the Old Testament, by means of the suddenly important Esdras, and then, in the New Testament, by bringing to our attention its favorable disposition toward the supremacy of Christian princes over the church, an attitude running counter to the interests of the ambitious council members at Laodicea.

Hobbes then concludes: "I see not therefore any reason to doubt but that the Old and New Testaments, as we have them now, are the true registers of those things which were done and said by the prophets and apostles" (EW III, 376 [424]). This is a curious remark. Hobbes has compressed our ability to believe the Old Testament into our ability to trust in the faithfulness of Esdras, and our ability to believe the New Testament into our capacity to trust men he describes as ambitious perpetrators of frauds, who, for unknown reasons, resisted what Hobbes views as an excellent opportunity to manipulate the Scriptures—to falsify them—to forward their immediate interests. These backhanded reasons for faith in scriptural authority appear ironic, even sarcastic, especially when Hobbes then declares he has no reason to doubt the Scriptures. Returning anew to the confidence he expressed in the Scriptures earlier in the chapter (EW III, 366 [415]), a confidence founded now on a somewhat different ground, he states: "But it is not the writer, but the authority of the Church, that maketh the book canonical" (EW III, 376 [424]).

His reference to the church here is made in the same sense as when, earlier in the chapter, he wrote, "I can acknowledge no other books of the Old Testament to be Holy Scripture but those which have been commanded to be acknowledged for such, *by the author-*

ity of the Church of England" (EW III, 366 [415], emphasis mine).
The Church of England is mentioned there in the context of
Hobbes's argument "that sovereigns in their own dominions are the
sole legislators; those books only are canonical, that is, law, in
every nation, which are established by the sovereign authority." He
speaks further of the "obligation . . . to obey the authority . . . of
their lawful sovereign." Thus Hobbes's reference to the Church of
England ultimately refers to the authority Hobbes would set above
that church, that is, the civil sovereign. Hobbes's reference to the
church at the end of the lengthy section on the books of the Bible
(EW III, 376 [415]), declaring that it is the church that decides the
content of the canon, is actually a reference to the authority under
which the church, in Hobbes's view, resides.

The implication of reiterating that sovereign power determines
the canon after concluding a long discussion of the authorship of
Scripture, is that the entire discussion is in the service of establishing the supremacy of the natural word of God, which in turn is the
means by which the primacy of natural rights is established. On the
basis of this natural word of God, we see that the sovereign is
supreme and thus determines the meaning and even the content of
the prophetic word. The natural word of God is thus established as
superior to the prophetic word. Since the civil law is what the
sovereign, established by natural law, wills, that, too, emerges as
superior to the prophetic word and may thus legitimately declare
what is and is not the prophetic word (EW III, 252–56 [313–16],
262–65 [322–23]). No matter how questionable the background of
the books of Scripture—and Hobbes seems to go out of his way to
make this background doubtful, indeed—it is the sovereign who
makes them authoritative.

This is our first conclusion as to why Hobbes has told us stories
about Esdras and Laodicea. Certainly these are things to make us
wonder about the authoritativeness of the canon, even as in chapter
32 we are shown reason to wonder about the trustworthiness of
prophets. In both chapters, Hobbes reassures us by arguing that the
sovereign instituted by natural law, by the natural word of God, by
political reason in the service of natural rights, will provide the
authoritative word that can resolve all wonderment.

Let us now consider more exactly the connection between
Hobbes's sowing of doubt on the one hand and his desire to confirm
the sovereign's authority to make these now-questioned writings

into Holy Scripture, on the other. Is Hobbes perhaps underscoring the great dangers inherent in examinining the Bible by historical analysis? Is he showing how susceptible to undermining the foundations of Christianity are without the authorizing power of the supreme magistrate? Is Hobbes's pioneering sally into higher criticism done in order to drive home the point that unless the civil authority guarantees the unity of religion by determining what writings are true and presiding over what those writings mean, dissensions among religious parties will go even further to destroy the most basic notion of the Scriptures and Christianity?

In this sense, has Hobbes, usually considered antagonistic to orthodox faith, performed a sort of apologetic service in defense of the faith? He points out the way reason may go on devouring the world of the divine, but he also shows that unless the civil sovereign is allowed the authority to put a stop to the kind of doubting exegesis Hobbes himself is practicing in chapter 33, there will be no peace whatever through which faith may survive. Hobbes seems to consider that critical abuse of the Bible will make civil peace impossible, but he also seems to reveal that this same critical treatment of the Bible can become so dangerous *for religion* that only the authority of the civil sovereign can protect it. Thus Hobbes's work suggests a world in which the sovereign as supreme authority over the Scriptures will seem less of an evil than the unrestrained application of reason to the Bible.

Hobbes's treatment of the Bible is itself representative of what partisan quarreling over the meaning of the Scriptures can lead to. It is almost a self-accusation of skepticism, done in the name of his great project, the securing of civil peace. I think Hobbes's questioning of who wrote the Scripture, his bringing of a radical rationality freed from the most traditional presuppositions of Christian faith to the exegesis of the Scriptures, represents the potential effects of religious denominational quarreling over a whole range of questions. If one side uses the Bible to prove there is no legitimate resistance against civil authority while another argues for the legitimacy of tyrannicide, the final victim will be the Scripture itself, tortured this way and that and thus not only losing its ability to support faith, but also losing its capacity to support any civil peace whatever.

Hobbes's argument shows the potential result of quarreling: it reduces the awe, it lowers the degree of authority the Bible will have over human beings. His exegesis is then only a formal reproduction of the effects of tendencies going on all around him; his formal resolution suggests what he considers the only way to prevent the worst realization of these tendencies: biblical religion must depend on the civil sovereign. Hobbes shows that the growth of doubt makes people of faith wish for a king who will put a stop to it. Nor is Hobbes unaware that his own work represents a spread of doubt—and only the word of the sovereign of *Leviathan* can put a stop to such things. It is, then, a sort of self-accusation, but with a purpose; it is an advertisement for his own resolution, that the first priority among human desires should be peace and safety, and perhaps it is also even a warning to the clergy about their contentions. Thus only Leviathan, the truest product of reason, can legitimately put a stop to the unrestrained and undermining foraging of reason into the mysteries of faith: the reason of the law of nature can tell faith-devouring reason when to stop—this latter aspect of reason is not justified in going on, devouring faith indefinitely.

Reason curbs reason and therefore seems to defend a kind of faith. Hobbes shows reason clearly controls faith and that it must be used to provide a faith for religious human beings who deeply need and want it. Nevertheless, the true status of faith for Hobbes, as revealed by his letting unrestrained reason have its way as we have glimpsed in this and the preceding chapter, can be found in the text of these chapters of *Leviathan* by those true Hobbists who want to see it.

The Purpose and Scope of the Bible

Hobbes declares that though there have been a variety of writers of Scripture (although he has lessened their number by collapsing much of the Bible into the work of Esdras), "yet it is manifest the writers were all imbued with one and the same spirit, in that they conspire to one and the same end, which is setting forth the rights of the kingdom of God, the Father, Son, and Holy Ghost" (EW III, 376 [424]). This is the aim of the Bible, Hobbes says.

But *is* the end of Scripture setting forth the *rights* of the kingdom of God? Hobbes's use of the term "rights" has a genealogy. In the first paragraph of chapter 32—the introduction to the third part of *Leviathan*—Hobbes said that his theme now is to be the "rights of a Christian Commonwealth." He intimates there, as well, that his work in the first two parts of *Leviathan* has been to derive "the rights of sovereign power, and duty of subjects . . . from the principles of nature only" (EW III, 357 [409]). But this notion of rights is strictly derived from Hobbes's analysis of nature and the word of God according to nature. It is heavily laden with the meanings of chapters 13, 14, and 15, meanings based in naturalistic understandings. By speaking of the right of the kingdom of God, he is introducing the essentially naturalistic understanding of parts 1 and 2 into his effort to interpret the prophetic word of God in part 3. Thus Hobbes seems to be reducing the end or purpose of the Bible to what may be comprehended by what he calls the natural word of God, that is, by "political reason."

Hobbes declares the Bible has one purpose or end, the "setting forth the rights of the kingdom of God," and one scope, "to convert men to the obedience of God" (EW III, 376 [424], 377 [425]). In the term "obedience," we see again Hobbes's concern for the Bible as law and his interest in law-abidingness for the sake of peace in this world. But we also see an understanding that does not concern itself with some grander purpose of human life described in traditional readings of Scripture. Is there some further *end* of obedience than the peace and the right to peace that Hobbes's "natural word of God" intends? The implicitly heterodox—not to say exclusively worldly—goals of human existence set forth in *Leviathan* were emphatically condemned by nearly all of Hobbes's contemporaries who commented on *Leviathan* in print, and have been noted by at least some modern critics. These old and new critics gathered from *Leviathan* that Hobbes slights what might be called "the transcendent." There is little notion in Hobbes's work, as one of the modern writers put it, of "the possibility of experiencing in this life the fullness of meaning and happiness which could make it possible to formulate analogically a conception of the blessed condition insured by faith in the future life" (Campodonico 1982, 113–23).

A traditional biblical notion of obedience to God is that it emerges out of an experience of the goodness and power of God (Rom. 2:4; Heb. 11:1–3). Hobbes does not speak approvingly of the sort of experience that transforms human lives and creates a supreme loyalty to a rule of action based in faith in another king and in a redemption that is not essentially political. Hobbes's aim is to strengthen a rule based on natural freedom or "right," which means, first of all, the right of self-preservation. Hobbes indicates he understands only too well that human beings do not lack the capacity for the sort of experience that transforms them into religious enthusiasts willing to give their lives for their beliefs. They have this ability to excess, and *too much* of it makes them susceptible to notions of resistance to civil power and to thinking they are called to a higher standard than that of the civil law. Hobbes attributed the English Civil War to such excess (Hobbes 1969, esp. Dialogue I). Thus when he speaks of what is required for salvation, he speaks of obedience to law for the purpose of insuring civil peace, not of passionate love for a savior without concern for any sacrifice such love might require.

Thus we see that for Hobbes the right to peace and peace itself is the end and is not *for* anything beyond itself. It is not "the peace that passeth understanding," not the "Prince of Peace," but the peace that makes it possible to live to an old age, safe from the violence of man, and secure among all the good things civil life can bring, things that Hobbes lists in chapter 13 before he speaks of the nasty, brutish, and short life of man in the state of nature. Obedience for the sake of this peace is the goal, not obedience in response to the revelation of the nature of sin and the human neediness for divine redemption, which seventeenth-century Christians claimed characterized the experience of faith. Is it any surprise, then, that Hobbes does not dwell on the aspects of Christian faith that seem to touch most profoundly on the powerlessness of man, particularly on the Crucifixion or the Fall, since these ultimately reveal the inability of human beings to command a solution to their human predicament and make them the more willing to devote themselves wholly to a savior?

Hobbes's stressing of obedience for the sake of a peace human beings can create, in contrast to obedience arising out of a profound neediness for the divine in their lives, amounts to an emphasis of the notion that men and women themselves can make the pivotal difference in their situation. To downplay human neediness of divine help is to downplay the potential for human indebtedness to God. If the resulting religious life is one reduced to the obligation to obey the sovereign, then the traditional propensity of biblical religion to promote a "higher" loyalty that is ultimately dangerous to civil order is subverted. Thus when Hobbes teaches that the scope of the Bible is "to convert men to the obedience of God," he is not nearly as interested in the tenets of Christian faith as the words make him seem.

Tensions between Hobbes's View and Generally Accepted Christian Belief

To escape Hobbes's state of nature, human beings authorize and empower a legislator whom they must *obey* if they wish to preserve themselves and to maximize their natural freedom in the presence of many others seeking to fully enjoy *their* own natural freedom. All this is done because they are obeying the law of nature, the law of their own desire to maximize their natural freedom, and, more immediately, the law of their desire to survive. Hobbes manages to identify this law of nature, this law of natural desire, with the law of God—and this is a most remarkable feature of his treatment of the Bible. But for man as he is depicted in the Scriptures, though the essential issue of obedience is undeniable in the story of the Fall, a story about the result of disobedience, the Bible according to the theologians we have been surveying in our study is not primarily about getting human beings to obey God in the sense of obeying the law of nature. That is, the Bible is not primarily about freeing human beings from the world embodied in Hobbes's fearful state of nature and securing their peace and safety. Obeying God is certainly part of the meaning of the Bible according to theologians like Augustine or Hooker and according to the evident meaning of varied biblical texts, but obedience to law is the *means* to unite God and man, not an end in itself (Rom. 3:9–31, 7:15–25; Eph. 2:13–18; Gal. 3:19–29). The New Testament writers John and Paul both seem to say that obedience is not possible without redemption, which latter is often considered the first purpose and end of the Scriptures, since there is no true freedom, no eternal life, and no fellowship with God, according to the Bible, without it (John 8:31–42; Rom. 8:1–21).

On the surface Hobbes's argument that the Bible's scope is to convert human beings to the obedience of God might be construed as a traditionally Christian view. It would be orthodox if one assumed Hobbes postulates the same reasons for obedience as have such varied makers of broadly accepted Christian belief as Augustine and Hooker. These two agree in their acceptance of the idea that a fundamental alteration in the human capacity to lead a moral life occurred at the same point very early in human history. They also agree that human beings are essentially helpless concerning a fundamental weakness in themselves and that escape from the consequences of this weakness must come from outside of themselves. Finally, Augustine and Hooker would agree that this way of escape comes through the grace of God and is not associated with human efforts to make things right. They agree, then, in acknowledging a power that transcends natural human capacities. Though Augustine and Hooker might argue about the role of human efforts in finding God's help or grace, both see human beings as finally unable to change the world or themselves; divine help is essential.

But Hobbes's postulates for obedience are not the same as those of Augustine or Luther or Hooker or Hobbes's contemporary critics. Hobbes demonstrates clearly his own purposes by dividing the Scriptures into three topical sections—one headed by Moses, one by Christ, and one by the apostles—all relating to the notion that the aim of the Scripture is to promote man's obedience to God. Even this might seem a traditionally sound interpretation of the prophetic word of God if Hobbes's final exposition of the point did not betray him:

> For these three at several times did represent the person of God: Moses, and his successors the High Priests, and Kings of Judah, in the Old Testament: Christ himself, in the time he lived on earth: and the Apostles, and their successors, from the day of Pentecost, when the Holy Ghost descended on them, to this day. (EW III, 377 [425])

What gives Hobbes away is that he fails here to distinguish the exceptional nature of Christ and Christ's work, a person and a work for whom and for which Moses, much less the high priests and kings of Judah, only set the stage, again according to traditional Christian understandings held by all the notable theological thinkers we have been discussing, and of which person and work the apostles only gave an explanation. Here, in Hobbes's passing over the unique nature of Christ and Christ's death, lies the great tension between biblical Christianity and his project of appropriating that religion for the cause of earthly peace.

If human beings, by means of reasoned self-interest, can set up their own means of escape from that which makes life and liberty not only difficult, but essentially impossible, what need is there for the biblical Christ of divine redemption? If Christ is only the chief of many voices, one added to those of Moses and a succession of high priests and kings and later followed by the voices of the apostles, Christ no longer constitutes a phenomenon significantly distinct to make him the redeemer of mankind. All of these persons, Hobbes argues, were ordained for the singular purpose of commending men to the obedience of God's natural word, a word that is based on the principle of the right to self-preservation. By treating Christ so, Hobbes transforms the Christ of the Crucifixion into the figurehead of a religion that gives good advice to human beings so that they can help themselves. Thus Christ becomes the way to escape not sin, which term also implies a definition of the individual with eternal repercussions, but rather to escape the anarchy of the state of nature, implying a definition of man that considers him as something only while he lives in this world. In Hobbes's teaching, Christ is transformed from great redeemer to bestower of natural rights, making the rights of human beings the great divine law. Thus Christ no longer is the manifestation of the essential divine help Augustine or Luther or Hooker or Christian critics of Hobbes in his own time understood him to be.

To insist on one's rights is to insist, first and foremost, on one's autonomy from any law higher than self-interest. Thus, to insist on one's rights is to turn away from the message of Christ, who is rather explicit on this point: "Except a corn of wheat fall into the ground and die, it abideth alone: but if it die, it bringeth forth much fruit . . . He that loveth his life shall lose it; and he that hateth his life in this world shall keep it unto life eternal" (John 12:24–26). But Hobbes turns the traditional gospel into a defense of natural rights.

Let us offer a specific example in one of Hobbes's critics of the distinction between Hobbes's view of the purpose of the Bible and the traditional understanding. George Lawson, among the most articulate of Hobbes's contemporary critics, in his criticism of Hobbes's treatment of the aim and scope of the Bible, argued that the true vision of the Scriptures is "to direct sinful man unto eternal life" (Lawson 1657, 162). He goes on, contradicting Hobbes's notion that the goal or purpose of the books of the Bible is "setting forth the rights of the Kingdom of God," saying instead that the principal subject is Christ himself, not first of all as king to be obeyed— though that is surely part of it and comes in time—but as redeemer of the sinful and guilty and as giver of eternal life. Lawson emphasizes that the essence of redemption is Christ's death on the cross, which takes precedence over all notions of Christ as reigning king. The Bible certainly speaks of Christ subjecting all things to himself as a conquering king, but the Scripture indicates that his incarnation was not so that he might first become a king, but that he might first sacrifice himself for the sins of mankind (Mark 10:45; 1 Tim. 2:5–6; Heb. 9 and 10).

Thus we have the idea that Christ's death was the ultimate purpose for which he was born according to traditional exegeses of the New Testament. Christ's purpose was to reconcile human beings to God and make them "fellow citizens" with the saints in the "household of God"—a polity open only to those who believe in Christ's death as an act of redemption. This view of Christ has nothing to do with what Moses or any of the kings of Judah did, nor with the works of the apostles (Matt. 27:51; John 10:9, 14:6; Rom. 5:1,2; Eph. 2:18,19; Heb. 9:8, 10:19,20; 1 Pet. 3:18).

In contrast to this view, Hobbes adds Christ to a list of biblical characters, all of whom contributed to the work of bringing human beings to the obedience of God. Hobbes emphasizes the notion that all three represented the same thing—a set of rules that men must obey—and he passes over the notion that Christianity centers on something located *in* Christ. Hobbes says "these three [Moses, Christ, the apostles] at several times did *represent* the person of God." Augustine, Lawson, Hooker, and other traditional interpreters of Scripture view the Bible as saying *not* that Christ *represented* God, but that he *was* and *is* God.

Why does Hobbes find it necessary to devalue the traditional view of the uniqueness of Christ as the sole solution to the human predicament, the only "door" to peace and safety, as the Bible would have it (John 10:1,9; 14:5)? I suggest the necessity is because of the connection of that "door" to the "household of God," and the special role of "fellow citizenship" implicit in that idea: the gospel and life of Christ suggest a kingdom that rivals the kingdoms of this world in a way that neither Moses nor the apostles does. The person and the life and death of Christ appeal to the same human loyalties that Hobbes wants to restrict to the kingdoms of this world. Hobbes wants to convert human beings to the obedience of the natural word of God—an obedience distinct from the notions of obedience associated with the specialness of Christ.

However, Hobbes's interpretive project does not proceed in a manner that encourages us to perceive, much less dwell on, the tension between his exegesis of the Bible and generally accepted Christian belief. He pushes us to remain concerned with the question he stated at the outset of chapter 33: what makes the Bible authoritative in the first place? Hobbes's argument turns us from concern about the aim of the Bible to the question of whose authority finally stands behind it. Thus we turn to Hobbes's discussion of how the Scriptures become authoritative.

Settling What the Word of God Says

Near the end of chapter 33, Hobbes presents the question of how the Bible becomes authoritative. He states this in three different formulations, one after the other in the same short passage: "It is a question much disputed between divers sects of the Christian religion, *from whence the Scriptures derive their authority*, which question is also propounded in other terms, as, *how we know them to be the word of God*, or, *why we believe them to be so*" (EW III, 377 [425], the emphasis is Hobbes's). This tripartite question is related to what Hobbes wrote at the very beginning of the chapter, "The question of the Scripture, is the question of what is law throughout all Christendom, both natural and civil" (EW III, 366 [415]). Hobbes answers on the same page, "Seeing therefore I have already proved, that sovereigns in their own dominions are the sole legislators; those books are only canonical, that is, law, in every nation, which are established by sovereign authority."

Since Hobbes has answered "the question of the Scripture" at the beginning of chapter 33, his rephrasing of the question a dozen pages later merits attention. By applying Hobbes's previous answer to the newly formulated tripartite question—"from whence [do] the Scriptures derive their authority?" or, "how do we know them to be the word of God?" or, "why do we believe them to be so?"—we see that the Scriptures derive their authority from the sovereign, who is empowered, according to the laws of nature to make all such determinations.

Hobbes is saying that we know the Bible to be God's word—that it is authoritative—because the sovereign says it is. Having disposed of this question once, Hobbes begins again some eleven pages later in the Molesworth edition with preparatory remarks such as, "it is a question of much dispute" and "the difficulty of resolving it, ariseth chiefly from the improperness of the words wherein the question itself is couched." His remarks, furthermore, seem to be responses to anticipated objections, for he says, "For it is believed on all hands, that the first and original *author* of them is God; and consequently the question disputed is not that" (EW III, 377–78 [425]).

But this is precisely what is in dispute. For it would seem that Hobbes, in making the word of God depend upon the word of the sovereign, ultimately makes the sovereign the author of the prophetic word (EW III, 164–65 [233], 252–57 [312–17]). Hobbes would like his readers to remain convinced that God is the direct author of the word of God, but he wants it understood as well that the sovereign, created by human beings on the basis of natural rights, political reason, and human passions, is to be the final judge of any question to do with God's word. But what if there is some lack of agreement between an already extant divine revelation and a civil sovereign of relatively new institution? Hobbes backs away from the potential tension, approaching the question with which we began this section once more to clarify matters: "Again, it is manifest, that none can know they [the Scriptures] are God's word, (though all true Christians believe it,) but those *to whom God himself hath revealed it supernaturally*, and therefore the question is not rightly moved, of our knowledge of it" (EW III, 378 [425], my emphasis).

We cannot *know* the Bible is God's word and is authoritative by *natural* knowledge. And that we cannot know *supernaturally* was shown in chapter 32 (EW III, 362–63 [411–12]). Hobbes also adds in that chapter that since one of the necessary two proofs of true supernatural revelation—the miracle—has ceased, we have no way left to know what is God's will other than by judging it according to the Holy Scriptures, from which, "by wise and learned interpretation, and careful ratiocination, all rules and precepts necessary to the *knowledge* of our duty both to God and man, without enthusiasm or supernatural inspiration, may easily be deduced" (EW III, 365 [414], my emphasis).

This leaves us to find God's will by applying our natural reason to the Bible. But we are still faced with the principal problem: how can someone know that the Scriptures are God's word (EW III, 378 [425])? Hobbes says none can *know* "but those to whom God himself hath revealed it supernaturally," but that alternative is no good to us at all now. Hobbes thus says "none can know" the Scriptures are God's word, but "all true Christians *believe* it."[8] *Belief* is the way, then, and thus Hobbes concludes that we should not ask how we *know* Scripture to be God's word, but rather how it is that we *believe* it to be.

Now Hobbes turns to the problem of the notion of belief (EW III, 378 [425–26]). Hobbes says that if we say men do not *know* the

Scriptures are the word of God, but they believe it, we are faced with the fact that human beings believe for all sorts of reasons. We cannot give a certain answer concerning how or why they believe. Thus, according to Hobbes, we cannot ask how men know the Bible is God's word because of the uncertainties forever implicit in knowing such a thing, *nor* can we ask why men believe the Bible, for there is no general answer that suffices for all persons.[9]

And that is all Hobbes has to say in response to the question, "From whence [do] the Scriptures derive their authority" or, as Hobbes otherwise states it, "How do we know them to be the word of God?" or "Why [do] we believe them to be so?" He equates the three forms of this question, and then proceeds to dismiss the second form (How do we *know* them to be the word of God?—We cannot know) and the third (Why do we *believe* them to be so?—We cannot speak of the source of belief because human beings believe for a multitude of reasons). After dismissing these forms of the question, Hobbes states the query one last time: "The question truly stated is, *by what authority they are made law*" (EW III, 378 [425], Hobbes's emphasis).

The correct way to state the question, then, is *not* "From whence do the Scriptures derive their authority?" (since that could mean, How do human beings *know* God? or Why do they believe in Him?), but "By what authority *are they made law*?"

This rephrasing of the question makes us again recall the opening sentences of chapter 33, where the question of Scripture is reduced to "the question of what is law throughout Christendom, both natural and civil" (EW III, 366 [415]).

So the tripartite question stated near the end of chapter 33, "from whence [do] the Scriptures derive their authority?" is transformed into "by what authority are [the Scriptures] made law?" Why does Hobbes do this? He says the former question is "much disputed between divers sects of Christian religion" (EW III, 377 [425]). The question is transformed because the first form is the cause of "much dispute," and, in fact, suggests the whole gamut of problems that the other two phrasings reveal, problems stemming from issues of knowledge and belief in God that often put human beings in contention with each other and civil authority and lead to the division of men's loyalties between worldly orders and heavenly ones. For Hobbes, the resolution of the problem is in transforming the question in order to clearly settle what the word of God says. A *settled* word of God is necessary for peace and this peace will be possible when the authority that makes the Scripture law is settled first. Thus, in the last two pages of chapter 33, Hobbes asks how the Scriptures are made law.

Making the Scriptures Law

Hobbes begins his treatment of how the Bible is made law by reminding us that "as far as they [the Scriptures] differ not from the law of nature, there is no doubt, but they are the law of God, and carry their authority with them, legible to all men that have the use of natural reason; the dictates whereof are laws, not made, but eternal" (EW III, 378 [425–26]). Thus the Scriptures are law in the same way the laws of nature are law: they are precepts found out by reason and carry their authority with them. But how? Why are the laws of nature an authority to us?

Hobbes tells us in chapter 14: "A LAW OF NATURE, lex naturalis, is a precept or general rule, found out by reason, by which a man is forbidden to do that, which is destructive of his life, or taketh away the means of preserving the same" (EW III, 116–17 [189]). The laws of nature are law in that our preservation demands we follow them: we are, in a sense, obliged to obey by our desire to continue living. So, as we still consider the quotation with which we began this section, Hobbes sees the Scriptures as a law to us because they carry in themselves their own authority, based in our self-interest, in our fear of death. But this sense of the Scriptures is applicable to us for Hobbes only insofar as they are the same as the natural word of God—precepts built solely on human reason. Hobbes says, as far as the Scriptures "differ not from the law of nature, there is no doubt but they are the law of God" (EW III, 378 [425–26]). But what if the Scriptures do differ from the laws of nature as Hobbes understands them? What if the Scriptures do differ from the "articles of peace" based in the passion for self-preservation, as we have tried to indicate the Scriptures appear to do (EW III, 115–16 [188]; Ruth 1; Daniel 3 and 6; Matt. 10:37–39, 13:44–45; Mark 8:34–38; Luke 11:25–37, 14:25–35; John 14:24–26)? Once a rift is discovered between the natural and the prophetic word, if something in the Bible cannot be reconciled with our self-interest, this view of the Scriptures as a law for us is completely erased.

Hobbes next turns specifically to the notion of God's law as written law, as something separate from natural law. These laws are not "legible to all men that have the use of natural reason," but are "laws only to whom God hath so sufficiently published them, as no man can excuse himself, by saying he knew not they were his" (EW III, 378 [426]). He continues,

> He therefore to whom God hath not supernaturally revealed that they are his, nor that those who published them were sent by him, is not obliged to obey them *by any authority, but his, whose commands have already the force of laws; that is to say, by any other authority, than that of the commonwealth, residing in the sovereign, who only has legislative power.* (EW III, 378 [426], emphasis mine)

Since Hobbes has already made his case against contemporary supernatural revelation, this is ultimately a reiteration of Hobbes's authorization of the law of God as the law of nature, since the law of nature, as Hobbes makes clear in parts 1 and 2 of *Leviathan*, is ultimately what authorizes the power of the sovereign (*Leviathan*, chapters 13 through 17 and 26).

Hobbes goes on, "Again, if it be not the legislative authority of the commonwealth, that giveth them the force of laws, it must be some other authority derived from God, either private or public" (EW III, 378–79 [426]). He then turns to a discussion of what these other private and public sources of authorization of the Scripture as law might be. As regards a private authority, Hobbes again reminds us of the untrustworthiness of "private revelation": "men . . . out of pride and ignorance, take their own dreams, and extravagant fancies, and madness, for testimonies of God's spirit; or out of ambition, pretend to such divine testimonies, falsely, and contrary to their own conscience" (EW III, 379 [426]). This being the case, Hobbes argues, no human beings could be obliged to take for divine law what particular persons say—the ultimate situation would be such confusion and uncertainty that it would be "impossible that any divine law should be acknowledged" (ibid.).

As for some other public authorization of God's word as law—by which Hobbes means the church as separate from the sovereign—he says that "if the Church be not one person, then it hath no authority at all: it can neither command, nor do any action at all" (EW III, 379 [426–27]). If the church is not united with that sovereign person called the Leviathan, Hobbes argues, it has no right, nor power, nor reason, nor voice—"for all these qualities are personal," that is, these are the qualities that by right can belong *only* to the sovereign according to the theory established in the first half of *Leviathan.*

Hobbes then turns even more specifically to the Catholic Church, the public body that claims it authorizes the word of God as law. Only a commonwealth, according to Hobbes's derivation of civil association through covenant, can make law, only a commonwealth can authorize the Scriptures as law, and, therefore, the Catholic Church cannot be a universal church unless there exists a universal commonwealth to which that church is joined (EW III, 379 [426–27]). If the whole of Christendom *were* one commonwealth, Hobbes says, "then all Christian monarchs and states are private persons, and subject to be judged, deposed and punished by an universal sovereign of all Christendom" (ibid.). Thus Hobbes concludes,

> So that the question of the authority of the Scriptures, is reduced to this, *whether Christian kings, and the sovereign assemblies in Christian commonwealths, be absolute in their own territories, immediately under God; or subject to one vicar of Christ, constituted over the universal church; to be judged, condemned, deposed, and put to death, as he shall think expedient, or necessary for the common good.* (EW III, 379–80 [427])

We thus understand from Hobbes's work—from the arguments of all of parts 1 and 2, and from chapters 32 and 33 of *Leviathan,* that the first possibility in the quotation immediately above is the one Hobbes insists upon: the sovereign has absolute authority in his own territory, and such authority is what makes the Scriptures divine law. Let the reader now understand what we have just painstakingly demonstrated in chapter 33, and what much else in *Leviathan* supports: Hobbes's attempt to establish the absolute authority of the sovereign over the meaning of revelation. The supremacy of political reasoning in the interpretation of Scripture was perhaps the most provocative of all his exegetical innovations and his contemporary critics dwelled on it. It was the basis upon which Hobbes received the severest reproofs and accusations.

A Representative Objection to Hobbes

The resolution of the problem of divided loyalties is a principal motivation of Hobbes's efforts to place the product of natural rights and natural reason in a position of authority over the Bible. Hobbes worried about the multiplicity of interpretations of the Scriptures, about the lack of a unitary orthodoxy, and about claims to power and right by those who said they were the church, since all these tended to oppose the voice, power, and right of the sovereign Hobbes established by means of his "political reasoning," his "science of natural justice."

Hobbes's *Leviathan*, from its first pages, attempts to comprise a complete system chiefly in order to substantiate the authority of the sovereign and to subordinate the church, which is to be joined to the sovereign power. The whole work, then, stands as an indictment of all other claims—particularly religious claims—to supreme authority, or, to use Hobbes's terms, of all other claims to "authority derived from God, either public or private" (EW III, 378–79 [427]).

But critics ranging from the Puritan George Lawson to men of more liberal religious inclinations, such as Edward Hyde, earl of Clarendon, or men whose thought extended to even more rationalistic views, such as the Cambridge Platonists—all differing among themselves—also would all put Hobbes's conclusions beyond the pale of accepted Christian belief.

George Lawson will serve as a representative critic. Lawson opposed Hobbes's dismissal of all other claims of sovereign authority and spoke instead in the strongest terms of the supremacy of God's prophetic word. Lawson argued there was a "two-fold law": "The one is Divine, and binds the conscience immediately; the other is humane and Civil, and cannot bind the conscience, but per accidens" (Lawson 1657, 163–64). He said the laws of civil sovereigns bind their subjects by the fear of civil and temporal punishments. They may even bind their subjects "to receive [the Scriptures] as authentick." But Lawson then added concerning the Bible: "laws they are and bind to obedience and belief, though there be no civil government in the world. The State and Church may declare them to be Divine, but no wayes make them to be such."

Lawson argued with passion that if people believe Hobbes's account of the authority of the Bible, then they believe in an authority that does not have the power to redeem the soul of a human being. Thus his indictment of Hobbes's project is an indictment of Hobbes's notion of the human situation—a notion separated from the idea of souls lost and fallen, needing Christ. It is true that salvation means something to Hobbes, too, but it is linked to the predicament of the state of nature. Christ is viewed as a means to be suited to the priority of rescuing human beings from this situation, but only so far as the natural rights of man—most notably the right of peace and safety—are served by him. Hobbes's universe is that of nature, and nature is all. The God of the Bible figures into Hobbes's formulations, but since God is converted into the supporter and legitimizer of the natural rights of man, God is there finally only to justify human freedom. But for Lawson, the universe is governed first by biblical tenets that posit an active God above nature and above human notions of rights.

The successful creation of a world where human beings are safest from the threat of violent death requires the limiting of those things that most inflame human passions. Hobbes's political thought is antagonistic to Christianity such as Lawson's—and to that of a wide range of other serious Christians who differ from Lawson in various ways—because the tenets of such sorts of faith place experience of, and loyalty to, the divine above other principles, including that of worldly self-preservation, thus potentially leading to a division of loyalties that Hobbes fears make for the civil war he calls "the state of nature." The meaning of life for men like Lawson is such that self-preservation and fear of death cannot be the first priority, but for Hobbes this kind of accounting, if allowed to take supremacy over a whole society, leads to the disaster the British Isles experienced in the 1640s. Thus in place of the old view of deity, whose authority too often leads to division of loyalties and strife, Hobbes offers a new God of nature who endows men and women with rights and does not prompt human beings to any other goal than obedience to Leviathan and whose highest will is peace.

Chapter Nine

Leviathan Chapter 34:
Hobbes's Naturalization of God

Two Diseases of Commonwealth

To establish the reasoning that makes peace and safety the chief goal of civil association, Hobbes wants to turn men's eyes from beholding other worlds to the consideration of their situation in this one. With this understanding in mind, we examine further Hobbes's reinterpretation of the Bible, turning now to the thirty-fourth chapter of *Leviathan*. But first, some context supplied from elsewhere in *Leviathan* will be helpful.

In *Leviathan*, chapter 29, Hobbes writes of the things that weaken and tend to dissolve a commonwealth, and to treat this subject he takes up the metaphor of the commonwealth as a human body. Setting up the authority of the commonwealth on a spiritual, or, as he calls it, a "ghostly" basis, is comparable in Hobbes's language to this body's contracting the disease of epilepsy.

He writes that a "ghostly authority," when established as superior to civil authority, "work[s] on men's minds, with words and distinctions, that by themselves signify nothing, but betray by their obscurity; that there walketh, as some think, invisibly another kingdom" (EW III, 316 [370]). This, Hobbes says, divides a commonwealth and makes every person subject to two masters. By challenging "the right to declare what is sin," the ghostly power, as he puts it, "challengeth by consequence to declare what is law, sin being nothing but the transgression of the law." Thus, two powers would coexist in the commonwealth, each having its commands "observed as law," which, Hobbes concludes, "is impossible."

At the end of chapter 39, Hobbes mentions a complaint related to this "epilepsy": "*Temporal* and *spiritual* government, are but two words brought into the world to make men see double, and mistake their *lawful sovereign*" (EW III, 460 [498]). He then adds, "the governor must be one; or else there must needs follow faction and civil war in the commonwealth, between the *Church* and *State* . . . and, which is more, in every Christian man's own breast, between the *Christian* and the *man*" (EW III, 460–61 [499]). Hobbes aimed to resolve this division of loyalties. He taught that civil sovereigns are pastors as well and that since, as in the church, some pastors are subordinate to others, there must necessarily be a chief among them. He thus declares, concerning the whole commonwealth, "Who that one chief pastor is, according to the law of nature, hath already been shown," and he adds that the Scripture confirms this. He refers here to the civil sovereign established through the covenant described in *Leviathan*, chapter 17.

Diagnosing the threat to the health of the commonwealth, Hobbes writes, "When therefore these two powers [the temporal and the ghostly] oppose one another, the commonwealth cannot but be in great danger of civil war and dissolution." He explains that the civil authority, being more visible, and more rationally understandable, always draws a large number of partisans, but because of human fears of the unknown and the religious rhetoric that encourages "fear of darkness and ghosts," spiritual authorities always draw to themselves a sufficient number of followers "to trouble, and sometimes to destroy a commonwealth" (EW III, 317 [371]).

Hobbes says the ancient Jews believed epilepsy to be one kind of possession by spirits. Hobbes explains the disease as "an unnatural spirit, or wind in the head" that "taketh away the motion which naturally [one] should have." This causes violent convulsions, so that—and here he draws on a story from the Gospels—"he that is seized therewith, falleth down sometimes into the water, and sometimes into the fire, as a man deprived of his senses" (Mark 9:17–29; Luke 9:39–43).

Hobbes applies this biblical passage to political things, comparing the spiritual powers in a commonwealth to a form of possession that "moveth the members of a commonwealth, by the terror of punishments, and the hope of rewards." This terror and this hope are "the nerves of the commonwealth," as Hobbes puts it, which ought to be moved by the civil (which is a synonym here for "natural") power, "which is the soul of the commonwealth." The political disease strikes through the use of "strange, and hard words" and then "suffocates" men's understanding and distracts the people, "either overwhelming the commonwealth with oppression" (that is, casting it into the water) or else casting it "into the fire of a civil war."

The spiritual power—those who teach a Christianity that represents a sovereign above the earthly one—is thus understood by Hobbes's use of Scripture to be like an evil spirit. As Christ casts out the devil in the gospel story, so Hobbes would have him also defend Leviathan, the defense of which requires the devil of religious authority to be exorcised. Thus certain Christians—notably Christian leaders—become evil spirits that Hobbes's Christ must cast out for the sake of the peace and safety of civil society (EW III, 317–18 [371–72]).

The source of the "epilepsy" of the body politic is, as Hobbes puts it, "the darkness of School distinctions, and hard words." Human beings are made susceptible through fears, but the actual disease only enters in through the use of Scholastic distinctions and hard words presided over by the Schoolmen and other religionists. What foments these distinctions—what allows this malady to take hold—are the works of Aristotle, by means of which human beings are made to "see double" and the body politic develops political "epilepsy." Though Aristotle never speaks of the most significant of these distinctions, "incorporeal substance," he does speak of the natural world in such a way as enables those who have married his works to Christian theology to use such a term.

The Revolt against Aristotle

Hobbes argues in several places in the second half of *Leviathan* that "all that is is body" and that the term "spirit" means nothing other than a very subtle form of matter. In arguing this, Hobbes contradicts the medieval synthesis of Aristotle and Christianity, which had been the foundation for most thinking about man and nature in Europe since the twelfth century. Hobbes's opposition to Aristotle took form in both an explicit criticism of Aristotelianism and in offering an alternative system integrating the Bible, modern natural science, and a new view of man. Hobbes's system, apparently comprehensive, was to take the place of the old system based on what Hobbes terms Aristotle's "absurd" *Metaphysics*, "repugnant" *Politics*, and "ignorant" *Ethics* (EW III, 669 [687]).

While Aristotle's natural philosophy was only one among several aspects of the Aristotelian *corpus* that Hobbes attacked, Aristotelian natural science, including the notion of the earth-centered solar system and Aristotle's teaching of "separated essences" and "substance," represented the heart of the world view against which Hobbes opposed his political thought. The mix of Aristotle and Christianity known as Scholasticism represented bad science for Hobbes. More importantly, he wanted to attack the whole set of theological and ultimately political notions based on the physical science of the medieval world.

For Hobbes, the revolt against Aristotle was especially a revolt against the Scholastic language that the Aristotelian model required and, indeed, was founded upon, and that mediated the filing of all natural phenomena into what C. S. Lewis has termed the "card catalogue" of the medieval worldview (Lewis 1964, 10–11). The abuse of language in order to create bridges between Christian tenets and notions of physical phenomena is central to Hobbes's complaint against Aristotelianism. He thought that such bridges were contentless imaginings, and more to the point, extremely dangerous in their potential for arousing the passions of human beings and dividing their loyalties. Finally, it is the political implications of Scholastic Aristotelianism that Hobbes seeks to countermand.

Hobbes's Anti-Aristotelian Prescription for Two Diseases of Commonwealth

Aristotle speaks in his *Metaphysics*, especially in Book VII, of the notion of "substance." Substance, in Aristotle's thought, is what stays when all else in a species of thing changes—it is its essence. It is, to use our own vernacular, what "goes *through* changes" while itself remaining unchanged. That is, it is that *something* that goes *through* and comes out the other side, as it were, fundamentally unchanged and still itself. It is the unchanging subject *to which* things happen. It is the *this* at the heart of a thing that comprises its individuality. Aristotle says that the substance of a thing is *not* material, though it is *in* matter. This leaves us to understand that substance is the immaterial essence of a thing and that essence is separable from matter. When we translate this to our thinking about human beings and Christian theology, the substance of a person becomes his or her soul; it is the essence of a human being and it is separable and has a separate existence when such a separation occurs. Thus to this substance is attached all the things the Scriptures say about the human soul, as, for example, Mark 8:36—"For what shall it profit a man if he gain the whole world and lose his own soul?" or Matthew 10:28—"And fear not them which kill the body, but are not able to kill the soul: but rather fear him which is able to destroy soul and body in hell." Since Hobbes sought to equate the kingdom of God rather with civil associations founded on natural reason than with a separate spiritual world and the "incorporeal substances" inhabiting it, the notion of separate essences was bound to lead astray.

Thus it was by means of Aristotle's physics and metaphysics that human beings were made to "see double" and civil associations contracted political "epilepsy." Hobbes, the physician for the ailments of civil association, makes his diagnosis: both ills can be cured finally only by healing the break between matter and substance, that is, between matter and spirit. Spirit must be understood as matter and the notion of substance fostered by Aristotle must be fully and irrevocably discredited.

This is the context, then, in which to begin to understand *Leviathan* chapter 34 and Hobbes's treatment of "incorporeal substance" and, indeed, his materialism throughout *Leviathan*. Thus Hobbes states: "The world, (I mean not the earth only, but the *universe*, that is, the whole mass of all things that are), is corporeal, that is to say, body . . . and because the universe is all, that which is no part of it is *nothing*; and consequently *no where*." To establish that there can be no "incorporeal body," Hobbes turns from the Aristotelian view of the cosmos to an entirely different understanding of nature—a mechanistic one. Hobbes speaks of this alternative view in the early chapters of *Leviathan*, though it is in his *De Corpore* that Hobbes develops an account of the very basis of philosophy, which takes aim at the notion of the natural world held by the Aristotelian Schoolmen.

He begins *De Corpore* by declaring the necessity of reasoning correctly, saying that each person brings "Natural Reason, into the world with him," since everyone has some ability to reason. He continues, "but where there is need of a long series of reasons, there most men wander out of the way, and fall into error for want of method" (EW I, 1). Reasoning, Hobbes goes on to say, is the clear definition of terms enabling a reasoner to add or subtract, that is, reach a right conclusion. This all begins with an understanding of names based on the distinction between that which truly is body or matter, and that which is only name (EW I, chapter 2, "Of Names").

Hobbes is very much concerned to show that names, which are the foundation of speech, when joined together can have consequences blurring the distinction between body and mere name. It is this blurring that leads to the greatest errors in reasoning. He says in *Leviathan*, as well as in *De Corpore*, that "true and false are attributes of speech" and not things. "Where speech is not," he says, "there is neither *truth* nor *falsehood*; error there may be" (EW III, 23 [105]). He says that, since "truth consisteth in the right ordering of names in our affirmations," each person who seeks truth needs "to remember what every name he uses stands for, and to place it accordingly, or else he will find himself entangled in words" (ibid.). And then he adds, "By this it appears how necessary it is for any man that aspires to true knowledge, to examine the definitions of former authors." Thus when Hobbes attacks what he calls "vain philosophy," he attacks the misuse of speech—of names—which runs contrary to his very first principle of philosophy: "All philosophy ought to depend . . . in right limiting of the significance of names . . . which limitations serve to avoid ambiguity . . . and are . . . called definitions" (EW III, 671 [688]).

Hobbes says the Schoolmen used Aristotle's metaphysics in a manner that promoted erroneous and ambiguous conceptions and in the process gave such names as "essence" to notions that "are the names of nothing" as though they were real things (EW III, 671–72 [688–89], 674 [691]). His aim in attacking such "vain philosophy" is to prevent human beings from being deceived and led into controversy "by them, that by this doctrine of *separated essences*, built on the vain philosophy of Aristotle, would fright them from obeying the laws of their country, with empty names" (EW III, 674 [691], 680 [696]). Aristotle's physics and metaphysics are vain because while those who follow these teachings are imagining what is not truly there, they are distracted from a very real consideration—their safety in this world.

Hobbes writes in *Behemoth* of the situation of most people in England in the seventeenth century, "as much as eternal torture is more terrible than death, so much they would fear the clergy more than the King" (EW VI, 182). Aristotle in the hands of the clergy and

Aristotle in the curriculum of the universities is the root of that which causes the dangerous disease of commonwealth Hobbes describes whereby human beings fearing the "ghostly" realm are divided from the civil sovereign who is their rightful ruler. Aristotle's physics and metaphysics underlie the notion of eternal torture that is more terrible than death and thus underlie the power given to the clergy because of this notion. Debunking Aristotle clears the way for the institution of Hobbes's new science of politics that promises lasting health for political bodies.

The Spirit of God—Corporeal or Not?

Chapter 34 begins Hobbes's effort to reinterpret key Christian concepts in order to move the religion of the Bible from the Aristotelian moorings, to which Scholasticism had anchored it, to a new basis as *natural* religion. Thus he turns specifically to the meaning of important biblical terms such as body, spirit, angel, inspiration, hell, miracle, redemption, and the kingdom of God and proceeds to naturalize them.

Hobbes begins chapter 34 by saying that it is necessary "to determine out of the Bible, the meaning of such words, as, by their ambiguity, may render what I am to infer upon them, obscure, or disputable." He says he will begin "with the words Body and Spirit, which, in the language of the Schools are termed *substances, corporeal* and *incorporeal*" (EW III, 380 [428]). Hobbes argues that *body* "signifieth that which filleth some certain room, or imagined place; and dependeth not on the imagination, but is a real part of what we call the *Universe.*" He says that the universe is "the aggregate of all bodies, there is no real part thereof that is not also body" (EW III, 381 [428]). Thus, apart from what is *imagined* (which Hobbes treats mechanically and materialistically in chapter 2 of *Leviathan*), all that is, is body.

He next explains that since bodies are subject to change (which is defined subjectively, that is, he says it is a "variety of appearances to the sense of living creatures"), they are called *substance* (which he defines as "*subject* to various accidents: as sometimes to be moved; sometimes to stand still; and to seem to our senses sometimes hot, sometimes cold," etc.). "This diversity of seeming," he says, "produced by the diversity of the operation of bodies on the organs of our sense, we attribute to alterations of the bodies that operate, and call them *accidents* of those bodies" (EW III, 381 [428]). That is, our *perception* of bodies changes, and we then attribute this change to some alteration in the body itself.

Since the changes we perceive in matter are to be understood ultimately as a variation of appearances to the senses, our understanding of change has more to do with the workings of our senses upon our minds than it has to do with our objective knowledge of matter. That is, the changes that matter *appears to undergo* actually tell us as much about ourselves as they do about matter itself. Seeming as perceived by "the organs of sense" indicates no alteration in the nature of matter itself.

Our sensory subjectivity is such that sometimes we think we notice changes in the consistency of body and so may be inclined to conceive of it at times as changing in and out of matter—and thus we may develop the idea of incorporeal body, and from that the belief in ghosts, spirits, and so forth. Hobbes's argument opposes such notions in order to allow him then to conclude that "*substance* and *body* signify the same thing." This is not the Aristotelian notion of the meaning of substance, but rather a radical departure. Substance is no longer the essence of something, the fundamental *this-ness* of a thing that makes it what it is; it is now simply another word for the corporeality of a thing, and the idea of a separate essence is lost. It is assumed that mechanical laws will explain how and why a thing is what it is; the notion of *essence* is seen as an illusion.

This passage on the meaning of body and substance at the beginning of chapter 34 represents no mere clarification of what may seem to us a small issue. It is, rather, a direct challenge to the Scholastic contention that behind all body and all matter stands another dimension or world. And Scholasticism is Hobbes's target when he writes, "therefore *substance* and *incorporeal* are words, which when joined together, destroy one another, as if a man should say, an *incorporeal body*" (EW III, 381 [428]).

For Hobbes's seventeenth-century critics, the implication of repudiating the notions of "substance" and "incorporeal body" as late-medieval philosophical-theological obfuscations was clear: Hobbes was denying the existence of the God of the Bible.[1] These critics understood that if Hobbes's equation of body with "substance" were allowed to stand, the traditionally understood Christian notion of spirit and God would be threatened. This is the point that underlies Bishop Bramhall's and other seventeenth-century critics' objections to Hobbes's treatment of substance. These critics were not all deep-dyed Aristotelians, nor were they alarmists reacting to a variation from their particular versions of strict orthodoxy; rather, their concern is that Hobbes has left no place for the God of the Bible, transforming the deity of the Scriptures into a name to explain the beginning for the natural causes of things.

The Meaning of the Term "Spirit of God" in Scripture

When the writers of the Hebrew canon wanted to speak of the spirit of God, they used the term *ruach*, a term rooted in an earlier Near Eastern culture—the Ugaritic—meaning "wind." But "when Israel spoke of the *ruach* of God they were using a *concept* that was found nowhere else in the Ancient Near East. . . . no other nation in the Ancient Near East spoke of its gods as having a spirit" (Neve 1972, 1).[2] The aspect of the divine nature most often expressed by *ruach* is the power of God in relation to his creation (as in Isa. 31:3: "Now the Egyptians are men, and not God; and their horses flesh, and not *spirit*"). The wrath of Yahweh, directed either against Israel, or taking the side of Israel against an enemy, was also referred to as *ruach*, as in Isaiah 30:28, where the word in the King James Version is translated as "breath": "And his *breath*, as an overflowing stream, shall reach to the midst of the neck, to sift the nations with the sieve of vanity." However, the Old Testament writers gave the term *ruach* a wide range of meanings: it continued to mean the original phenomena for which it stood—the wind—and it also was understood to mean the *human* spirit. The life that God created was called *ruach* since it was given by the God who has life in himself (as in Isa. 32:15: "Until the *spirit* be poured upon us from on high, and the wilderness be a fruitful field").

As Lloyd Neve's biblical exegesis indicates, there is a real distinction between *ruach* as wind and *ruach* as spirit of God. Citing Exodus 15:1–18 in which Moses thanks God for the deliverance of Israel from Pharoah at the Red Sea, Neve explains that *ruach* in verses 8–10 should be translated as "breath," not wind, explaining that the Old Testament does not speak of God "blowing" the wind in any other place, as if the blowing of the wind were equivalent to Yahweh's breathing:

(vs. 8) And with *the blast of thy nostrils* (*ruach*) the waters were gathered together, the floods stood upright as a heap, and the depths were congealed in the heart of the sea. (vs. 9) The enemy said, I will pursue, I will overtake, I will divide the spoil; my lust shall be satisfied upon them . . . (vs. 10) Thou didst blow with thy *wind* (*ruach*), the sea covered them; they sank as lead in the mighty waters.

The implication here is that it is not the wind that saves Israel in Exodus 15:8–10, not even a wind sent by God, though there is such a thing as a divine wind in Scripture in Exodus 14:21. In Exodus 15:8–10, what is meant is God himself. Neve explains that the term "breath" in verses 8 and 10 is not separable from God, but that "it is Yahweh himself acting alone" to give victory in order that the glory may be all God's (this is emphasized in Exod. 15: 1, 3, 4, 6, 7, 12, 16, 19). Thus we begin to see that God's breath—*ruach*—is not something the Bible allows to be naturalized; it is not a wind. It is something other, something transcendent, something above nature.

Hobbes and the Meaning of Spirit

Hobbes argues that human beings do not commonly attribute substance to what they cannot sense; thus they think they perceive "spirit" when they actually encounter matter: "Therefore in the common language of men, *air*, and *aerial substances*, use not to be taken for *bodies*, but (as often as men are sensible of their effects) are called *wind*, or *breath*, or (because the same are called in the Latin *spiritus*) *spirits*" (EW III, 381–82 [429]). Hobbes introduces the term "spirit" by equating it with substance, by which latter term he means materiality or substantialness as those notions are presently understood. The world of Scholasticism where substance could mean "essence" is left behind; substance is now body, and spirit is body, as well. For Hobbes, any other notion of spirit than that which teaches that spirit is corporeal, that is, *body*, is "an idol of the brain" (EW III, 382 [429]).

The perceptions that represent bodies to our minds are not always understood by their proper causes; sometimes by sight human beings may think they see corporeal things, when the sense of touch is able "to discover nothing in the place they appear, to resist their fingers." Such perceptions come, Hobbes says, in dreams or "distempered brains waking," yet through too much devotion to Aristotle and his Scholastic followers, men can be made to think that spirits are "made of air compacted by a power supernatural."

By receiving instruction from authority, rather than by studying nature, human beings take for ghosts images conveyed to them by "overly agitated" senses. Hobbes is willing to concede spirits exist, though "the proper signification of *spirit* in common speech, is either a subtle, fluid, invisible body, or a ghost, or other idol phantasm of the imagination" (EW III, 382 [429–30]; EW IV, 313).

The first definition of "spirit" as "subtle, fluid, invisible body" in the quotation above is the one Hobbes favors; the second meaning, "ghosts, or other idol phantasms," are notions he attributes to errors brought into Christianity from Greek philosophy and religion. Hobbes will insist again and again that spirit is invisible to the eye, but is nonetheless matter. The significance of this insistence becomes increasingly apparent when we see how Hobbes's definition of spirit—"subtle, fluid, invisible body"—differs from the meaning we receive of *spirit* from Scripture.

Hobbes and the Spirit of God in Genesis

In chapter 34, Hobbes has designated seven different groupings of meanings for the term "spirit." The first category is "the Spirit of God taken in Scripture sometimes for a wind, or breath." Hobbes's example for this is Genesis 1:1–2: "In the beginning God created the heaven and the earth. And the earth was without form, and void; and darkness was upon the face of the deep. And the Spirit of God moved upon the face of the waters." Hobbes wants "Spirit of God" here to mean wind, but the term *ruach* in this passage is employed in the same way as it is in Exodus 15:8–10—as the figurative breath of God; it is not wind at all, but the breath or power of Yahweh (Neve 1972, 10).

Yet Hobbes argues that if the spirit of God meant God himself in Genesis 1:2, then motion would be attributed to God, and consequently place, "which are intelligible only of bodies, and not of substances incorporeal" (EW III, 383 [430]). Hobbes does not acknowledge that the Bible speaks in these terms figuratively, so that God is repeatedly said to act locally. It is well known, and Hobbes knew, too, that anthropocentric phraseology is used to represent God throughout Scripture, as, for example, in Psalms 33:6, "By the word of the Lord were the heavens made; and all the host of them by the breath of his mouth." Hobbes's critics would agree that the anthropological phraseology of Genesis 1:2 indicates that while it is difficult to understand how the spirit of God "moving upon the face of the waters" might be understood, the verse need not at all be interpreted as establishing the corporeality or materiality of God.

Hobbes wants to understand Genesis 1:2 to mean "wind" because he is engaged in naturalizing the Bible. Hobbes argues that the *spirit of God* cannot mean God himself because that would contradict the materialistic, naturalistic, rationalistic basis he has established. The spirit of God, according to Hobbes's reasoning, must be body— that is, corporeal or substantial. Spirit is not incorporeal substance since Hobbes, by establishing his terms at the beginning, like a geometer with his axioms, has dismissed such a conjunction of terms as meaningless.

Instead, Hobbes wants to insist that Genesis 1:2 may best be understood by applying to it the meaning of Genesis 8:1:

> But the meaning of those words is best understood by the like place, (Gen. 8:1) where when the earth was covered with waters, as in the beginning, God intending to abate them, and again to discover the dry land, useth the like words, *I will bring my Spirit upon the earth, and the waters shall be diminished*: in which place, by *Spirit* is understood a wind, that is an air or *spirit moved*, which might be called, as in the former place, the *Spirit of God*, because it was God's work. (EW III, 383–84 [430–31])

Genesis 8:1, like Exodus 14:21 mentioned above, is a place in Scripture where *ruach* is understood actually to be wind; it is, indeed, understood to be sent by God, but the implication of this passage is quite different from that of Genesis 1:2, where the actual presence of God is indicated by the term. The use of *ruach* in Genesis 1:2 is similar to its use in other creation tradition texts, such as Psalms 104:30: "Thou sendest forth thy spirit [*ruach*], they are created: and thou renewest the face of the earth" (Neve 1972, 62).[3]

Neve writes that the *ruach* of Genesis 1:2 could not mean "wind" because "wind in the Old Testament is never allowed to participate in the creative process. On the contrary, by the time of the exile, the wind has been demoted and naturalized, perhaps as a reaction against just such a divine wind concept" (68). If the term *ruach elohim* (or the *ruach* of God) in Genesis 1:2 were translated to mean "wind of God," it would be unique in the whole Old Testament and

Neve concludes that "this argument alone seems decisive against the translation of wind" for *ruach* in the verse (ibid.).

The view we have taken here from Neve is confirmed by Hobbes's contemporary, Alexander Rosse. Rosse expressed the conviction that Hobbes was following Tertullian's opinion in his interpretation of Genesis 1:2, adding that the church had opposed Tertullian's view and "constantly held that there is meant, not a winde, but the spirit of God" (Rosse 1653, 36–37). In Rosse's view, the spirit of God of Genesis 1:2 represented an understanding of divine power that was not to be naturally explained.[4]

In the creation story in the second chapter of Genesis, the term *ruach* is not mentioned at all. The absence of the use of *ruach* in a passage describing God's breathing life into man is a further indication of the "otherness" of God. There is no naturalistic link between man and God in which the very spirit of God is converted into the human spirit. The absence of the term *ruach* in Genesis 2:7, then, is still another argument against naturalizing the spirit of God, in this case by identifying it with the spirit of man. Thus the notion of "the unique spirit of God is not present" in the text of Genesis 2:7, though the idea of God as creator and originator of life is. The life of man is through creation—not emanation—and "the divine breath, the spirit of Yahweh, does not pervade the universe as wind in the natural world or as breath in the nostrils of every creature" (Neve 1972, 12).

The religion of the Old Testament, then, stresses this unbreachable divide between God and his creation. Any attempt to comprehend God and man "in the same breath," as it were, is contrary to the original meaning of Scripture; Hobbes attempts to do this, however, because he seeks the naturalization of the biblical term "spirit of God."[5]

Hobbes's Treatment of Spirit and the Criticism of His Contemporaries

Concerning his exegesis of the term "spirit" in chapter 34, Hobbes's contemporary, the Puritan George Lawson, wrote, "he hath observed seven distinct senses of the word *Spirit* in the Scripture. But he fearfully abuseth some of those places alledged by him" (Lawson 1657, 167). Lawson especially criticizes Hobbes's statement that the notion of God as spirit is beyond human understanding. He argues, for example, that Christ's saying, "God is Spirit," *can* be understood:

> We may know something of the thing by some measure of knowledge, though we do not perfectly know it with the most perfect knowledge. Christ by these words did teach us something; and if he did, how can it be said that the place falleth not under our understanding? For there is nothing teachable that is not intelligible. And by that place we may easily understand that God is a far more perfect and excellent substance or being, than any inanimate or irrational body can possibly be. (Lawson 1657, 169; John 4:24)

Lawson contends that matter cannot possess the divine attributes that Hobbes wishes to give it, arguing that Hobbes's campaign against incorporeal substance is not against a usage of words but actually against the supremacy of God over human reason. Yet Lawson argues that the Scriptures speak of God's spirit in the way they do so that human beings will understand this supremacy, even if a full understanding is not possible. Faith, then, for Lawson, must be in the mysterious *otherness* of God. Hobbes, on the other hand, has offered us an explanation of spirit that is so thorough that, if followed, cannot help yield the impression that God is body—which is to say, brought down to the natural world and made into the stuff, in the most fundamental sense, that all things are made of. Hobbes's stress is not on the God who created all things out of nothing, but on the God who is ultimately matter, and, at least in the sense that matter is comprehensible, that much the less mysterious.

Leviathan, chapter 34, Lawson says, is the commencement of Hobbes's "Scripture-lexicon" and the words "body" and "spirit" are the terms Hobbes treats first in this lexicon (Lawson 1657, 166). There follows in chapters 34, 35, 38, and 39, a Hobbesian exposition on the meaning of twelve more terms. Hobbes returns to the meaning of spirit several times in these subsequent chapters, and in others of his works, as well, both to reassert his position and to defend himself from the reaction to his views, a further indication of the importance of this particular definition.[6]

Lawson takes issue with Hobbes's treatment of these first terms by criticizing Hobbes's claim that "incorporeal substance" is a contradiction. Words, he says, are used to signify our minds to others and he thus implies that when we wish to relate matters to do with Scripture and to understand the notion of spirit, the term "substance" may have a significance that does not mean "corporeal" or "body." He writes,

> We find some of the antient Divines affirming Angels to be bodies and bodily creatures; yet by body they mean substance, and yet did acknowledge them to be Spirits. And for my part, I cannot be persuaded that either Angels or Souls are rational pure forms, as some, nay many Peripateticks do affirm. *Yet they may be Spirits, and this nature better expressed by the word Spirits than the word Bodies.* (Lawson 1657, 166, emphasis added; also 168–69)

For Lawson the words used to signify these phenomena may represent *the principle* of a thing, though the nature of its consistency may be unknown to us. The term "incorporeal substance" represents that unknown quality, while for Hobbes everything that is is corporeal, even God (Lawson 1657, 167–69).[7]

The importance of the nature of God becomes increasingly apparent when we see it is an issue discussed repeatedly in Hobbes's writings and in the criticism *Leviathan* received from his contemporaries. It is important because the argument about the nature of God is actually an argument about God's existence. Hobbes became involved in answering one of these critics, John Bramhall, the bishop of Derry. Bramhall's book, *The Catching of Leviathan*, prompted Hobbes's own *Answer to Bishop Bramhall* (EW IV, 281–384).[8]

The form of Hobbes's *Answer* is to present Bramhall's charges one by one, quoting them, and then to give an answer. One of Bramhall's charges, quoted by Hobbes, is as follows:

> he destroys the very being of God, and leaves nothing in his place, but an empty name. For by taking away all incorporeal substances, he taketh away God himself. The very name, saith he, of an incorporeal substance, is a *contradiction*. And *to say that an angel or spirit, is an incorporeal substance, is to say in effect, that there is no angel or spirit at all.* By the same reason to say, that God is an incorporeal substance, is to say there is no God at all. Either God is incorporeal; or he is finite, and consists in parts, and consequently is no God. This, that there is no incorporeal spirit, is the main root of atheism. (EW IV, 301–2)

Hobbes's answer to this charge includes a discussion of the indivisibility of God, a reiteration of his argument denying incorporeal substance, declaring the absurdity of the term "essence," and a mocking criticism of the Schoolmen for their slavish subscription to ancient authority. While insisting that God is corporeal and at the same time defending himself as a Christian, Hobbes attributes qualities to that corporeality that no other sort of matter possesses. This "matter" of God differs so from all other forms of matter that the term "materiality"—or corporeality—seems inappropriate. The "matter" of God becomes omniscient, it is pure, perfect—and a host of other terms that Hobbes says ought to be applied to the perfect deity. But if God is matter, does this divine matter obey natural laws of motion, as does more mundane corporeal substance? What *is* the divine if God is matter (EW IV, 302–5)? The sense of God one is left with is weak and vulnerable to such questions, yet Hobbes's argument does not consider them. Despite Hobbes's lengthy and sarcastic response to Bramhall's accusations of atheism, the deepest implications of the charges finally go unanswered.

Lawson and Bramhall both suggest that the term "incorporeal substance" accounts for what the Bible teaches about the divine that cannot be wholly explained *naturally*. The term has a naturalistic sense, but it speaks of what must be considered *supernatural*. This helps explain why Aristotle was originally thought to be helpful by the doctors of the church, since Aristotle's terminology seemed to bridge the gap between human knowledge of the natural world and the teachings of Scripture. Aristotle made biblical principles more understandable to human reason and experience—and the Aristotelian notion concerning substance is a chief example of this. The Scholastic point was not one of devotion to Aristotle, but to what Aristotle helped explain, that is, the mystery of God. Aristotle was brought in in the first place not to supplant Christian theology, but to serve it. Scholasticism and Aristotle did not create the idea that God is *incorporeal spirit*; the term was only an attempt to express that which was already there in Scripture.

Hobbes is aware that his position in denying incorporeal substance exposes him to charges of atheism, but he defends himself quite boldly, not only arguing that the early father, Tertullian, also taught there was no incorporeal substance—and no one was calling *him* an atheist—but also declaring that in his *De Cive*, as well as in *Leviathan*, he has attributed to God expressions only of the highest reverence (see also EW IV, 426). Hobbes states that he is not diminishing the reverence due to God, but only dispelling Scholastic myths originating from errors imported from the Greeks. He explicitly leaves a place for the resurrection of the dead and the existence of miracles, angels, and true prophets. Yet Hobbes makes every effort to reinterpret these phenomena, by either converting them into metaphors, casting doubt on the authority of those who reported seeing these things, subordinating the interpretation of the meaning of such phenomena to the sovereign power, or, finally, providing a new exegesis of Scripture to render the supernatural more purely natural in order to counter the effects of the supernatural view of the divine. For Hobbes, the biblical and supernatural apprehension of God is extremely volatile—it is dangerous to political stability since the appeal of such a God to human loyalties that might be politically devisive can be enormously strong (EW III, 317 [371]; EW IV, 182). Thus, in all cases Hobbes circumscribes the supernatural with rationalistic cavils, attempting to control that which is most threatening to civil peace and safety.[9]

The effect—and intention—of Hobbes's treatment of spirit, miracles, angels, and other such biblical terms is to lessen susceptibility to supernatural ideas while maintaining reverence for a more naturally conceived understanding of the divine. He aims to neutralize the more politically dangerous (and traditionally orthodox) interpretations to allow his argument from the natural word of God, that is, from human reason, to take the place formerly occupied by the more generally accepted Christian position.

Disguising Hostility toward Christianity: Hobbes's Recourse to the Incomprehensibility of God

While Hobbes seeks out naturalistic interpretations of Scripture whenever possible, such meaning cannot always be given. For example, Christ says "God is a Spirit" (John 4:24), but one cannot find this description of God in *Leviathan*, chapter 34, among Hobbes's seven naturalistic categories of meaning for the term "spirit" in the Bible. However, Hobbes has another meaning beyond these seven; it is the category that "falleth not under human understanding" (EW III, 383 [430]).

This phrase finally means that whatever it is applied to is incomprehensible. Hobbes thus concedes *incomprehensibility* in regard to the biblical term "God is a Spirit" while still not conceding the existence of incorporeal substance. Since he repeatedly affirmed that nothing exists that is not material, Hobbes's notion of incomprehensibility—that which "falleth not under human understanding"—renders the text, "God is a Spirit," meaningless; Hobbes does not fit it under one of his seven categories, and nothing exists that is not corporeal. "Falleth not under human understanding" in this case can only mean that the text means nothing.

Hobbes is aware that his argument has not touched on certain difficult passages concerning the spirit of God, and therefore, after his repeated efforts to establish the "materialization" of spirit, he concedes that his treatment of "spirit" still leaves some passages in the Bible unaccounted for. He says that if none of his other definitions of spirit are adequate for a biblical use of the term—if spirit does not mean a wind, breath, "gifts of understanding," "life," "aerial body," or "metaphorical dispositions," then the place "falleth not under human understanding" and *our faith therein consisteth not in our opinion, but in our submission"* (EW III, 383 [430], emphasis added). Thus, where the Bible says God is a spirit, we cannot know what it means, but we ought to submit. But to what?

Traditional Christian faith teaches that a believer should always submit his or her will to the word of God, but this is not what Hobbes has in mind; rather, men and women should submit not simply to the Bible, but to what the supreme civil authority established by natural reason says the Bible means. By turning at this point to argue that the authority of Leviathan is supreme and that the duty of subjects is to submit, Hobbes is changing the subject. He thus *hides* the implications of his radical interpretation of the meaning of spirit by returning to his argument that believers should submit to sovereign authority concerning the meaning of the Bible. Thus Hobbes instructs believers to submit not only to the sovereign, but also to Hobbes's own interpretations of the term "spirit." Meanwhile, the matter immediately at hand—the notion of "incomprehensibility"—is left as a loophole to help readers "over the hump" in accepting Hobbes's interpretation.

What, then, do we make of Hobbes's recourse to "incomprehensibility"? Hobbes uses the notion as a means of preserving something of the mystery of God in order to better secure the safety of civil association from the passions of human beings whose fear of death—which often leads to the problem of divided loyalties—can only be quenched in the belief that a God above nature exists and is concerned with their fates. He uses "incomprehensibility" as a way to preserve those elements of revealed religion that are important to securing peace. Hobbes resorts to this loophole to dissipate whatever might nourish disloyalty to Leviathan. The idea of incomprehensibility thus plays an important part in his treatment of the Bible, helping him to convert Scripture into a means of promoting equivalence between loyalty to God and loyalty to Leviathan. Hobbes's efforts to equate "substance" with "body" and "body" with "spirit" are in the service of this conversion of the Bible; incomprehensibility, "that which falleth not under human understanding," is a catchall category for whatever cannot be included successfully in such an equation.

In seeing this, we must understand that Hobbes is making a great effort to transform religion while not destroying it. For Hobbes it was essential that religion be safely maintained, since its seeds are always present, ineradicable in human nature, and are often ready to spring up into passions that potentially threaten civil order. Passions arising from human anxieties about mortality are intractable, but if they can at least be channeled safely into a religion that is subordinated to civil power, their dangerous potential will not be realized. Hobbes attempts this "channeling" through skillfully engineering the meaning of the Bible in the second half of *Leviathan*, retaining the reassuring familiarity of Christianity while unloading its potential for conflict. Thus, the second half of his masterpiece not only represents the harnessing of religious passions for the sake of civil, worldly peace, but also proclaims the vital importance of religion to Hobbes's teaching: it must be preserved for the interests of man, but it must be made politically safe for those same interests.

By using the idea of incomprehensibility, Hobbes can still refer to the idea that God could be in some locality and move about while not occupying a certain space and having a certain dimension in that space. He writes, "and so the place is above our understanding, that can conceive nothing moved that changes not place, or that has not dimension" (EW III, 383 [430]). Though Hobbes argued that in Genesis 1:1–2 the words "spirit of God" must refer to some *body*, to some form of matter—a wind—he also mentions that if this explanation is insufficient, then we may regard the meaning of the passage as incomprehensible. The notion of incomprehensibility— "a place above our understanding"—Hobbes holds in reserve as his last recourse, by means of which he avoids becoming utterly explicit in his destruction of an essential ingredient of Christian faith.

To make civil authority safe, religion must be rendered politically safe, which means doing damage to the meaning of Christianity.

But Hobbes did not openly display the full extent of his antipathy toward biblical religion; he carefully designed and placed limits on his own reinterpretation of Christianity in order to preserve a form of faith for the sake of the Leviathan—the civil association it finally serves.

Through his treatment of Scripture, Hobbes allows the authority of natural rights to emerge triumphant. By reinterpreting Christianity to weaken the links between human beings and a kingdom beyond this world and to establish the idea that God's kingdom is in harmony with the kingdom built on the natural rights of man on this earth, Hobbes inaugurated a form of faith that would serve rights-based civil association and not seriously disrupt civil life. At the same time he established a view of deity that has become familiar to secular liberal societies—the Nature's God who is the justifier of rights-based political association and the defender of the inalienable rights of man.

Hobbes's reinterpretation of Christianity to make it support his natural-rights teaching provides a clue to the meaning of the religious language employed by all subsequent rights-based, that is, liberal civil association. The greatest of all the documents of liberalism, the Declaration of Independence, speaks of a God not in tension with the principle of natural rights, but who rather *endows* human beings with "inalienable rights" and blesses civil associations of all those who dedicate themselves to their preservation. The language of the declaration shares with Hobbes's philosophy an apparent reconciliation of the biblical deity and the natural rights of man, while revealing none of the tensions Hobbes's work sought to eliminate by his reinterpretation of Christianity.

Chapter Ten

The Purpose of the Last Half of *Leviathan*

Why the First Half of *Leviathan* Is Not Enough

At the end of chapter 31, Hobbes states that he is "at the point of believing these, my labors, are as useless, as the commonwealth of Plato" (EW III, 357 [407]). He says there was a moment when he feared his work of moral philosophy might be as useless as he believes those of the ancients have been, for he judges that the learning of Athens and Rome regarding moral philosophy has never had any real practical application; the writings of Plato and Aristotle never brought the peace and safety that would change the world. But Hobbes then observes how different his doctrine is from the practice of politics everywhere else in the West, places that have received their learning from Athens and Rome.

Then, reminding his readers that Plato, greatest of the ancient moral philosophers, held the opinion that it was impossible for disorders of states and civil wars ever to be taken away unless sovereigns become philosophers, Hobbes retreats from his apprehensions and says he takes hope, reiterating his confidence in the principles of natural right, the "science of natural justice," as he calls them, that he has established over the first thirty-one chapters. Hobbes declares that Plato did not set down the "theorems of moral doctrine," but he writes that if any sovereign—and he need be no philosopher—will apply the teachings found in these thirty-one chapters of *Leviathan*, he will find them true, that they work, that they will change things as none of the works of the ancients were ever able to do. Though Hobbes intimates that all those who argued

203

about moral philosophy and the establishment of justice before *him* were failures and gave men no hope, he, ultimately, has better hope for his work.

Hobbes thus concludes the first half of *Leviathan* as though he were concluding the work and writes on the final page of the last chapter of part 2 of his hope that "one time or other, this writing of mine may fall into the hands of a sovereign [who will apply it]" (EW III, 357–58 [408]). *Leviathan* stands ready at the end of chapter 31 for application, for use, awaiting only some governor who will but take it up. Hobbes's teaching on the foundation of justice in the natural rights of man appears finished.

Yet Hobbes embarks on a new part of the work, which he entitles "Of Christian Commonwealth," beginning a treatment of the Bible and Christianity that continues for sixteen more chapters, doubling the size of the book. We see, then, that *Leviathan* is not fully completed after all at the end of chapter 31, and we should wonder at this. Why are we given the second half? It is as though Hobbes is saying something has been left out, something important has been neglected up to this point, and now the work must begin again in order to include it. But why does Hobbes begin again?

I believe that Hobbes may be understood in the second half of *Leviathan* to be addressing unseen interlocutors among his audience who might be willing to embrace his science of natural justice, but who first demand a defense for what he is doing that takes their Christian concerns into consideration or leaves their religious predispositions intact. But we can neither hear nor see them—we only see the evidence of their complaint in the form of parts 3 and 4 of *Leviathan*. We can only hear their voices if we understand the second half of *Leviathan* to be an answer to their objections, fears, and resistance, though we do see their existence implied in Hobbes's "Review and Conclusion" (EW III 710–14 [725–29]). To what objection, then, are parts 3 and 4 a response?

The persons to whom *Leviathan* is principally addressed are the educated readers for whom faith in God remains a real possibility and yet whose understanding of religion is susceptible to transformation (see chapter 2). Hobbes's understanding of these persons is revealed in his chapter 12—they are persons who come to religion ultimately because of anxiety about death. In Hobbes's teaching, *politics* comes into being, at least in part, to secure human beings from fear of violent death at the hands of men, but *religion* comes into being because of fear of what lies beyond death, fear that transcends those matters to which politics in Hobbes's teaching first address themselves, for Hobbes's politics in his science of natural justice can save a person from violent death at the hands of human beings, but not from the fact that he or she must ultimately die.

Unless these persons' concerns are addressed, the effort to secure a remedy from the disorders of commonwealth cannot succeed. These sorts of private concerns about death or fate force Hobbes in *Leviathan* to pause and make a second beginning in order to defend his teaching from objections generated in some of his audience by the yearnings that make human beings attempt to comprehend the whole of being and their own fate. Hobbes knows his project cannot succeed without his dealing with the view of man based on a yearning for a fuller understanding of the meaning of life, and thus a further reassurance concerning the meaning of death; Hobbes knows his project must address a yearning for transcendence. Such yearnings, all representing the desire to transcend death, often are manifested through ambition for honor or glory or nobility or knowledge of the whole of existence, and these all find their most powerful and potentially politically dangerous focus in religion. Hobbes's argument "stops," or rather, starts again, when the cause of natural justice threatens to eclipse these private yearnings in man concerning his end, and this is what prompts his new beginning in chapter 32.

The pause and new beginning we have perceived in the movement of Hobbes's work are caused by the understanding that all public considerations of the whole outside of the sanctions of political authority are potentially dangerous speculation; Christianity was just such a consideration of the whole of being. Hobbes sees Christianity as it was most often understood as likely to provide the grounds for division of loyalties between those who wish to "take men as they are" and those who wish for men to be something else than they are.

The first half of *Leviathan* ends, then, with the presuppositon (related, as we have noted, to an explicit mention of Plato) that genuinely to obtain what human beings wish for concerning a comprehensive knowledge of the whole, is impossible; it is a dream.[1] But Hobbes's teaching is that the science of natural justice cannot relieve the disorders of political life until it addresses this dream—that is, until it addresses the question of religion.

Hobbes's teaching is that political philosophy, if it is to constitute a true science of natural justice, should not look at what human beings *ought* to be. It should not seek to understand justice in terms of speculation about the purpose of human life, for that is to aim at what no one can be sure of. But he also teaches that political philosophy can never forget that a large number of human beings in any polity will incorrigibly return to the question of what *ought* to be, and therefore the religious "question" must always be a central one to political thought. The second half of *Leviathan* is Hobbes's teaching concerning how to deal with this question.

The Second Half of *Leviathan* As Instruction on How to "Tame" Religion

Let us review what Hobbes teaches in order to make our explanation of the second half of *Leviathan* as clear as possible. As Hobbes writes in *Leviathan*, chapter 17, the end of political society is our own preservation and a happier life thereby. For Hobbes, human passions are generally reducible to the passion for avoiding death—and if political philosophy aims at such a low end, it can succeed in establishing principles of justice upon which the most just and enduring regimes might be founded.

How can this be? In his state of nature, Hobbes sees human beings as atoms: individuals understood to be fundamentally alone and unattached to any community or family. They possess naturally freedom to consider themselves first and to preserve themselves first—which is to say they possess natural *rights*. Human beings so conceived willingly forfeit certain freedoms or rights when they enter into political society, so long as the sovereign power they trust to ensure their preservation is able to do its job. We may thus conclude that Hobbes does not picture the human condition as naturally political, but rather solitary or individualistic, based on rights that are prepolitical. All politics exist, in Hobbes's view, for the protection of prepolitical human rights. All politics exist for the preservation of life and freedom—to help the human individual survive and maximize his or her liberty. Thus human beings must be understood in terms of their vulnerability, not in terms of ends which are conceived on the basis of speculation about the meaning of life. It is not the meaning of life that is most important, according to Hobbes, but rather the preservation of it—for that is, at least, something we can all agree upon.

The purpose of the second half of *Leviathan* is to add a justification for commmunity, for purposeful life, and, consequently, for virtue, back into a formula that fundamentally lacks such motivations for cohesion. Principles of self-preservation, self-interest—the Hobbesian political glue—go a long way, but not all the way all the time. The second half of *Leviathan*, then, may be understood in part as a response to invisible interlocutors who demand a protection for the most private yearnings beyond mere protection of their lives and safety, even while they have been persuaded of the primary importance of worldly peace and safety. The second half of *Leviathan* is addressed, first of all, to the private yearnings for transcendence, for living *beyond* the arrangements politics provide. It is not, finally, always enough to be safe and live peaceably in this world—perhaps because such safety is never as sure as human beings would like. Anxieties about safety can never be fully relieved. Human beings seem to want assurance, then, based on concerns not only about this world, but about a world they imagine to be beyond this one. Perhaps we may also say, then, that the second half of *Leviathan* shows what tends to be lacking in regimes based on the rights Hobbes first discovered—the absence of a sense of what peace and safety are finally for.

What does the first half of *Leviathan not* say about the human need for religion that makes it necessary for the second half to be as important as we here claim it is? Is not the importance of religion made plain in many places in the first thirty-one chapters? Why isn't the first half of *Leviathan* enough to establish this importance?

The first half is not enough because, though it contains enough evidence to suggest a role for religion in the formation of rights-based regimes, indeed, enough to provide a modern interpreter such as Howard Warrender with grounds to argue Hobbes's political theory is dependent on faith in God to oblige human beings to obey *Leviathan*'s sovereign, it does *not* contain a guide for the right understanding of that species of religion dangerously capable of challenging the rights of man. The first half of *Leviathan* does not teach how to circumvent the potential threat to peace posed by authentic Christianity.

While the first half of *Leviathan* does indicate that Leviathan's rights-based society needs to be concerned about religion, it does not clearly demonstrate how the Leviathan regime is to "domesticate" religion to deprive it of the capacity to disturb peace and safety. The first half of *Leviathan* contains no instruction regarding how a religion may be "tamed" to serve human freedom based solely on man's good in this world. Christianity, for Hobbes, is potentially an unpredictable force that can destroy the peaceful order of a society based on human rights; parts 3 and 4 of Leviathan provide the lessons required to harness it, to tame it, to provide a pattern to demonstrate how it ought to behave to provide the sense of purpose or meaning that will make Hobbes's science of natural justice produce as long-lived a regime as possible.

Fear of violent death at the hands of men cannot be the foundation of all political life if there is a God we ought to fear, and so after making plain how to deal with this first fear as though fear of God were not an issue, Hobbes then turns in the second half of Leviathan to the problem of the fear of God. He transforms this great potential claim on human loyalties so that God does not interfere with the peace provided by civil association that is based on human anxiety about the violence of man towards man. Hobbes does not so much attack Christianity, then, as reformulate it so that the biblical God does not destabilize the solution his political science establishes in the first half of Leviathan.

For Hobbes, human beings are isolated and estranged from nature and threatened by it, and they must make whatever arrangements they can to protect themselves in their natural vulnerability expressed by the state of nature. The second half of Leviathan reminds us that beneath the surface the threat posed by man's natural condition allows very little room for the virtue of self-denial or self-sacrifice because the problem of survival, or self-preservation, is too pervasive for that. But this problem or threat is to be veiled, and thus softened somewhat, by the religion that Hobbes formulates out of biblical texts, which seems to indicate a place for the virtues the Christian religion addresses. Yet close inspection reveals that religion actually serves the realm dedicated to self-preservation; it points to matters of transcendence only for the sake of secular security.

The second half of the work is designed to appease the strongest human passions in order to harness them to the greatest ambitions for the political realm. By basing politics on what may be termed the lowest common denominator, on what almost all human beings can agree upon—self-preservation—Hobbes indicates how very much politics ought to accomplish; his hopes for it are very great precisely because he asks so little of it. Yet he cannot be candid about how little he believes human beings must concern themselves about (that is, about how little he believes human beings must concern themselves about God), since men and women do not easily accept their independence from all authority when such independence also testifies of their infinite smallness in the universe. Thus he marries a reinterpretation of Christianity to what is essentially secular salvation.

Fear As the Seed of Religion

The capacity of religion to aggravate civil strife is introduced early in *Leviathan*, when Hobbes addresses what he calls the "seed of religion" (EW III, 94 [168]). Hobbes writes that human beings are by nature continually anxious about the future and hence try to find some solace and haven from this unceasing anxiety:

> This perpetual fear, always accompanying mankind in the ignorance of causes, as it were in the dark, must needs have for object something. And therefore when there is nothing to be seen, there is nothing to accuse, either of their good, or evil fortune, but some *power*, or agent invisible: in which sense perhaps it was, that some of the old poets said, that the gods were at first created by human fear.

Human beings invent gods, then, as a means of dealing with anxiety about death. Fear of gods or God leads men and women to listen more to the voices that tell them of eternal rewards and punishments—things that pertain to the divine—than to the voices of civil authority. The "seed" of religion can divide loyalties and therefore divide kingdoms into warring camps. Furthermore, Hobbes understands this seed of religion to be part of the human constitution, though it grows better in some soil than in others. It is born of anxiety about what is to become of one's life. As Hobbes says:

> It is impossible for a man, who continually endeavoureth to secure himself against the evil he fears, and procure the good he desireth, not to be in a perpetual solicitude of the time to come; So that every man, especially those that are over provident, are in an estate like to that of Prometheus. (EW III, 95 [169])

Seeking relief from these "torments of Prometheus," human beings will turn to "some power or agent invisible." As long as human beings are anxious and fear the future, there will be men and women in whom the seed of religion will grow. To this extent, then, religion cannot be eradicated and so must therefore be controlled if any plan for peace is to prevail.

This is not to say that Hobbes does not consider it possible for one form or another of institutional or private faith to fail. But even if one "formed" religion, as Hobbes puts it, fails, the religious inclination is permanent: "[it] can never be so abolished out of human nature, but that new religions may again be made to spring up out of them, by the culture of such men, as for such purpose are in reputation" (EW III, 105 [179]). A specific religion may come or go, and Hobbes offers reasons for such things, but the continuing rise of new religions or new formulations of old religions is permanent, because human beings will always be anxious about the future and there will always be men and women ready to cultivate this anxiety and nurture the seeds of religion to satisfy their own desire for power.

The Great Danger

The fear of what may befall human beings in time to come, especially after death, which Hobbes seeks to diminish and regulate in *Leviathan*, is the enemy of rights-based civil association, because it separates human beings from their worldly interests; it leads to a division of loyalties between those who trust in this world and those who believe in a world to come. The greatest enemy of rights-based civil association and of the natural freedom of man appears to be whatever allows fear of death and the hereafter to be exploited, leading to this problem of divided loyalties.

For Hobbes, the problem of the division of allegiance is fundamentally the fruit of the wedding of the teachings of Christianity to the erroneous teachings of those who use religion to further their own ambitions for power. The edifice these sorts of persons may constitute presents a powerful and attractive picture of the human situation able to sustain human beings even in the presence of their strongest fears, but which combination also comprises, through the problem of divided loyalties, a potent threat to the peace and safety of man in the world.

Thus in part 4 of *Leviathan*, the final four chapters of the work, Hobbes launches his greatest attack on the enemies of natural reason and of the civil association built upon such reason. Hobbes's aim is to govern the course taken by the fear of what lies after death, a fear that arises from natural consequences, but which is then aggravated and exploited by powerful religionists who draw on the Bible. Chapter 47, the last chapter of part 4 and of *Leviathan,* treats those who spread, defend, and generate all the errors of reasoning that blind human beings to their best interests in this world. These are persons who exploit the natural fears of human beings in order to further their own power at the expense of what natural reason teaches concerning the law of nature and human well-being.[2]

In chapter 47, Hobbes lists the doctrines that keep such people in power and keep human beings more fearful of invisible worlds where they might meet God, than fearful of disobeying their civil sovereign, even if this choice leads to war and death. As the first half of *Leviathan* constitutes an attempt to diminish the dangers represented by the universal *fear of violent death* at the hands of men, so the second half endeavors to bring under control the *fear of unknown worlds,* which finally also means to deprive those persons of power who foster such fears. Hobbes goes to the source of the strength these people have in the masterful concluding chapter in *Leviathan* in order to destroy their power, for it is these ambitious persons who seek political power by means of religion, that are the great danger.[3]

Through a clearing away of Aristotle's teachings, as we saw in the preceding chapter, and through a reinterpretation of the Bible to preclude its being used to threaten his vision of civil order, Hobbes teaches that "diseases" of commonwealth may be prevented. Hobbes's aim in the last half of *Leviathan* is prescriptive: he indicates two chief threats to the peace—that is, the health—of civil association, by which means those who would use religion to further their own power destabilize civil association; his intention is to show how these instruments or weapons in the hands of ambitious religionists may be neutralized. These twin threats are the notion that the soul is immortal and the doctrine that the church of Christian believers now on earth constitutes the biblical kingdom of God. To meet the great danger presented by those who appeal, by means of these notions, to the religious susceptibility of anxious men and women, Hobbes reinterprets the Bible to render these instruments less able to prompt the division of loyalties.

The Exaltation of Peace As Antidote
to the Greatest Danger

If it happens that human beings care more for the realm presented to them through belief in God than they fear what men may do to them—even more than they fear that men may kill them—then there exists a ground from which they may dare to deny the supremacy of their physical well-being to all other considerations. Thus they will be supplied with the rationale or understanding of the world that allows them to object to authorities that bear the sword and are able to bring death. The realm of religious faith, with its roots in the unseen and the unknown, the fear of which Hobbes says originally brings men and women to conceive of God, prompts human beings also to think of the possibility of living beyond physical death. The notion of outlasting death is manifest in the idea that men and women have souls or an immortal essence that can somehow escape the fate of the body and that these souls may live happily in another world—a kingdom of God.

There is great potential force against worldly power in biblical sayings, such as the passage from the Gospel of Matthew, "And fear not them which kill the body but are not able to kill the soul, but rather fear him which is able to destroy both soul and body in hell" (Matt. 10:28). Those who object to worldly powers may then see them as unable to kill wholly; the soul, the Resurrection, and the notion of the possibility of immortality thus become political issues as they give human beings a ground from which to resist civil authority, to disagree with one another as partisans of differing views of the divine will, or to attempt to seize civil power in the name of divine power.

For Hobbes the idea of the immortal soul ultimately arises out of the fear of death, but when it serves as a means of inspiration by which human beings defy the princes and powers of this world, it only makes the actual possibility of violent death more probable by making it all too possible for there to be no peace. If human beings are persuaded that their greatest good lies beyond this world, Hobbes has little doubt that they will be easier prey both to their own dangerous passions and to the passions of ambitious persons who would lead them, in the name of a higher loyalty, to resist the order that maintains safety in this world. Hobbes cannot defeat the passions of ambition and of hunger for power by eliminating them, but he can deprive them of their most dangerous potential by showing human beings that the greatest human interest is, above all, worldly peace. However, to find agreement on this most important matter, the ground upon which it is based must be controlled through an argument that does not grant rival bases for authority. The Aristotelian gloss on the biblical teaching about the soul, as well as the notion of the biblical kingdom of God to which the soul may be joined through "citizenship" in heaven, must be altered through a new biblical interpretation. In part 3 of *Leviathan*, then, Hobbes alters this teaching.

For Hobbes the greatest irony—an irony his political philosophy aims to eliminate—occurs when human beings, who grasp the idea of a future life in response to fear of the very fact of death, bring violent, unnatural death closer to themselves by believing their ultimate good demands they oppose the sovereign political authority—that which is most directly able to keep them safe from death. Hobbes reinterprets the Bible, then, to deprive passionate human beings of their principal means for disrupting civil order; that is, he undermines such predominant biblical notions as the immortality of the soul and the kingdom of God, for the sake of peace, and this requires a new view of peace, one limited to the earth.

The exaltation of peace in Hobbes's work over traditional notions of biblical godliness was problematic for some of his orthodox religious readers from the beginning. Hobbes begins part 2 of *Leviathan* by speaking of the great end men have in mind in instituting civil society: "the introduction of that restraint upon themselves [in] the foresight of their own preservation" (EW III, 153 [223]). In *Leviathan*, chapter 18, Hobbes clarifies this further, writing that the "conservation of peace and justice [is] the end for which all commonwealths are instituted" (EW III, 168 [236]). But Hobbes's contemporary critics faulted him for this, pointing out that peace was not the most important thing, that human beings had a higher end, communion with God. George Lawson, again one of the most eloquent of Hobbes's contemporary critics, wrote,

There is a twofold end of regular civil Government; The first is Peace; the second is Godliness and Honesty, to which Peace is subordinate. For the Apostle exhorts us *to pray for kings, and all that are in authority, that we may lead a quiet and peaceable life in all Godliness and Honesty*: I Tim 2:1 [and 2:2]. Government is for Peace, Peace for Godliness, and the performance of our duty towards God. . . . earthly states are erected, and subordinated to an higher end than peace and plenty here on earth: they should be so ordered as to prepare men for eternity. (Lawson 1657, 11–12; Matt. 10:34; John 14:27)

Hobbes's treatment of Christian commonwealth emerged out of a concern that thinking like Lawson's exacerbated the problem of divided loyalties and endangered civil peace; his treatment of Christianity appears as a design to explain a new understanding of peace. Thus, in *Leviathan* Hobbes is interested in treating the notion of the soul and the kingdom of God in a way that will defuse the potenial of this understanding to disturb this world's peace.

The Notion of the Immortality of the Soul As a Threat to Hobbes's Plan for Peace

Hobbes wrote in *Leviathan* that at death the soul dies and is only revived later, at the general resurrection (EW III, 443 [483–84]). He said, furthermore, that he saw nothing in Scripture to persuade him that there is any existence of the soul without the body: "that the soul of man is in its own nature eternal, and a living creature independent on the body, or that any mere man is immortal, otherwise than by the resurrection on the last day, except Enoch and Elias, is a doctrine not apparent in Scripture" (EW III, 443 [483]; see also 626 [647–48]).

But in the *Elements of Law* of 1640, Hobbes wrote that belief in the Scriptures is a fundamental point of faith, "by which we believe those points and the immortality of the soul, without which we cannot believe he [Christ] is a Saviour" (EW IV, 175). In *De Cive* (1642), Hobbes says that the "Saviour's Office" is to teach all those things that cannot be understood by natural reason, but only by revelation, such as "that he was Christ; that his kingdom was not terrestrial, but celestial . . . [and] that the soul is immortal" (Hobbes 1983, 230). These indicate that between 1642 and 1651 Hobbes's view of the soul changed. Why did this change occur? It is my belief that Hobbes found this heterodox view useful as he sought to subordinate traditional theological teachings to his new political tenets to further the peace of this world.

In *Leviathan*, soul and body are one; there are no "separated essences." Now, in the final version of Hobbes's political philosophy, death means complete death—the soul, merely another word for life, or breath, ceases at the death of the body. This view of the soul is known as Christian mortalism—a heterodox view held, indeed, by sincere believers and not unique to Hobbes, who appropriates it for his own purposes.

It must be stated, however, that the term "Christian mortalism" is misleading. The teaching takes its name in reaction to the notion of the soul's immortality, the view held by Augustine, Calvin, and, in general, by orthodox Christianity. But the meaning of the soul's immortality is not a unitary one, that is, there are different ways of viewing it. Some theologians held that the soul is by nature immortal, while many of the early church fathers understood the Scriptures to teach that the soul is by nature mortal and only becomes immortal by God's grace. Norman T. Burns makes this clear in his *Christian Mortalism from Tyndale to Milton* (Burns 1972, 12). The Reformers appear to have agreed with these early Fathers. Since they held man's position in relation to God was one of the most humble and utter dependence, the notion of the soul's natural immortality seemed inappropriate. Thus they, too, understood the soul to be immortal only as a gift from God. Thus, as Burns puts it, this view provided "an orthodox gloss on 1 Tim. 6:16, which refers to God 'who only hath immortality' " (Burns 1972, 12). This view, as held by Reformed theologians, does not suggest that the soul actually ever dies.

The term "mortalism," on the other hand, suggests death and annihilation; the views of Tyndale and Luther, which some have included under the mortalist heading, are not of the mortalist kind at all and it is a mistake to call them mortalists. As Burns points out, these pillars of the Reformation believed the souls of the dead "sleep" when the body dies; they do not die. Passages from Scripture in support of this view were found in 1 Corinthians 15:51 and 1 Thessalonians 4:14–15.

Burns cites the respected historian of Christianity, George H. Williams, who "complains of 'the ineptness of nemenclature' with which discussion of the heresy has been burdened" (Burns 1972, 10n1). Burns further explains that the term "mortalism" actually involves at least three different views: (1) the belief that soul and body are annihilated at death and that neither soul nor body is ever resurrected; (2) the belief that the soul dies temporarily until the Resurrection, when God restores life to the bodies of the dead; and (3) the belief that the soul becomes unconscious or asleep upon the death of the body until the Resurrection. Hobbes, Burns asserts, was of the second view—not of the "soul-sleeper" view he associates with Tyndale and Luther. Thus Burns classes Hobbes with Milton, whose views on the matter he found in Milton's work, "The Christian Doctrine" (Milton 1931–38, 15:37–53, 215–51). Though Burns's work is very helpful on this theme, he believes Hobbes to have sincerely held the view he attributes to him; he is unprepared to suspect Hobbes of anything but candidness.[4]

Arguing for the mortality of the soul in *Leviathan*, Hobbes surveys verses from the Bible that seem to contradict his view and then proceeds to reinterpret them, using as his tool a naturalistic argument based in mechanistic materialism, so that these verses confirm his naturalistic orientation. He does not, however, deal thoroughly with all of these passages and ignores others that might be more problematic for his view (EW III, 616–36 [639–57]).

He states in one place, for example, referring to the place where the church has generally held the souls of the dead to be, that "the doctors of the Church doubted for a long time, what was the place, which they were to abide in, till they should be reunited with their bodies in the resurrection; supposing for a while, they lay under the altars" (EW III, 616 [639]). Here Hobbes makes an oblique reference to Revelation 6:9–10: "And when he had opened the fifth seal, I saw under the altar the souls of them that were slain for the word of God . . . And they cried with a loud voice, How long, O Lord, holy and true, dost thou not judge and avenge our blood on them that dwell on the earth?" But rather than dealing directly with the challenge these verses pose for the mortalist position he has embraced, Hobbes instead refers the reader both back to his extensive argument against incorporeal substance and forward to the purpose to which the Catholic Church put this text—generating the doctrine of purgatory, seeming by this latter to suggest the doctrine was tainted by the worldly ends to which the Catholic Church had put this teaching. In other words, Hobbes fails to address directly the challenge the passage of Scripture in Revelation 6 presents. Other passages that might lend authority to the traditional Christian views concerning the immortality of the soul are also ignored in this extensive "proof" for his new position—such as the story Christ tells in Luke 16:19–31, or the passages in 1 Corinthians 15:51 and 1 Thessalonians 4:13–15 concerning "soul-sleeping" (as opposed to soul-dying). Hobbes argues instead by reiterating his argument from chapter 34, that "soul" in Scripture means either the life of the creature, or the body and soul jointly. The term "soul" does not mean the existence of some "incorporeal substance" apart from the body (EW III, 614–17 [637–38]; 622–25 [644–47]).

At the Resurrection, Hobbes says, the souls of the faithful are to be recreated by God's grace, to be joined to their bodies for eternity. If there are at present, then, no "incorporeal souls" and no "spiritual" dimension to which such souls could belong, there is no concomitant authority belonging to that dimension to which human allegiance may be diverted.

Hobbes's treatment of the Scripture here ought not to be divorced from his skepticism about the authority of the Bible indicated by his treatment of incorporeal substance in chapter 34 of *Leviathan*, nor from what we have learned of that skepticism through our examination of chapters 32 and 33, nor from his insistence on the human inability to know anything of the divine by means of natural reason, nor from the priority of human reason and earthly aims over any other ends as he gives signs of in chapters 12 and 13 of *Leviathan*. If Hobbes is to maintain any semblance of Christian faith he must not disallow such essential tenets of faith as the Resurrection or eternal life, but he appropriates arguments for these things in a manner that always places Christianity under the guidance of natural reason and under political power that is based on the rights of man over all other authority. These arguments may reach conclusions that jibe with various doctrines held by sincere believers—orthodox or heterodox—but they are generated not out of faith, but from Hobbes's "political reasoning."

As for the unsaved, that is, the souls that do not belong to Christ, they have less to fear in Hobbes's reinterpretation since Hobbes teaches there are no eternal torments. The souls of the unsaved will perish, and there will be no ceaseless punishment to fear (EW III, 449–51 [489–90]). Death is not such a terrible fact if the alternative for a life of unrighteous unbelief is eternal punishment. Hobbes leaves the souls of men and women in peace by abolishing the idea of separated souls living apart from their bodies, so when all is done, even God shall not disturb them.

Chapter 38, in which Hobbes introduces his Christian mortalism, begins:

The maintenance of civil society, depending on justice; and justice on the power of life and death, and other less rewards and punishments, residing in them that have the sovereignty of the commonwealth; it is impossible a commonwealth should stand, where any other than the sovereign, hath a power of giving greater rewards than life; and of inflicting greater punishments than death. Now seeing *eternal life* is a greater reward, than the *life present*; and *eternal torment* a greater punishment than the *death of nature*; it is a thing worthy to be well considered, of all men that desire, by obeying authority, to avoid the calamities of confusion, and civil war, what is meant in holy Scripture by *life eternal*, and *torment eternal*. (EW III, 437 [478], Hobbes's emphasis)

Since the argument of the first half of *Leviathan* is none other than the establishment of the civil sovereign as the sole possessor of the capacity to give the greatest rewards and punishments, it is fitting, but still deserving of our surprise, that Hobbes brings to the fore a doctrine he has heretofore specifically rejected and now installs it prominently in his biblical exegesis. Of course, his utilization of the doctrine that most Christians in the seventeenth century considered heresy, *could* represent Hobbes's sincere belief in an interpretation of Scripture most Christians have never accepted. However, considering the argument set forth above, I believe Hobbes found this heterodox doctrine useful given the circumstances he describes in the first paragraph of the chapter in which it is introduced: the concept of another realm, by means of which greater rewards and punishments may be dispensed, needed to be distanced from the world of Leviathan.

Hobbes's rejection of "non-corporeal substance" demonstrated by his materialism makes his Christian mortalism unsurprising; indeed, his political teaching concerning the supremacy of the sovereign established on the basis of the state of nature, natural rights, and mathematical learning, makes this unorthodox concept of the death and resurrection of the soul almost necessary. If men and women believe God will punish their everlasting souls with eternal punishments at the end of a life of disobedience to him, they will be more likely to obey the divine authorities than the civil ones if the two should come into conflict. Hobbes's Christian mortalism aims to eliminate or minimize this danger (EW III, 437, 448–52 [478, 488–91]).

What should remain surprising is the coincidence of Hobbes's appropriation of these things in a manner that places Christianity under the guidance of natural reason and under political power that is fundamentally autonomous from the authority of Scripture. It is more than coincidence that Hobbes's materialism necessitates a view of the soul that so nicely aides resolution of the problem of divided loyalties, exalts his view of peace, and confirms the principles upon which the first half of *Leviathan* is based. The introductory paragraph of chapter 38 indicates where Hobbes's true loyalties lie; they are to the science of natural justice, and not Christian theology.

The principles of the Hobbesian project that we have introduced in this study will also guide us if we seek to understand who, according to Hobbes, the redeemed for eternal life shall be. Hobbes declares they will be those who believe in Christ, but Hobbes's declaration is problematic. Hobbes says that their faith consists in obedience to the commandments of God and Christ, those commandments that are the very laws of nature found out by reason:

> Our Saviour Christ hath not given us new laws, but counsel to observe those we are subject to; that is to say, the laws of nature, and the laws of our several sovereigns. . . . the laws of God therefore are none but the laws of nature, whereof the principal is, that we should not violate our faith, that is, a commandment to obey our civil sovereigns, which we constituted over us by mutual pact with one another. (EW III, 586–87 [611–12])[5]

The meaning of salvation here is greatly altered: the redeemed become those who are good citizens in Leviathan's state, those who support the principles based on mathematical learning and the axiomatic state of nature. To trust in Christ thus means to rely on reasoning founded upon the principles of self-preservation and the peace and safety of human beings in this world. Authentic Christianity, manifest in believers who put their trust in the person of Christ above any other authority, is supplanted.

Christian mortalism is thus a convenient "middle ground," which, by not departing wholly from possibly genuine Christian faith, manages to constitute a prudent disguise for Hobbes's true attachment, which is wholly to this world. The advantage Hobbes's change to Christian mortalism appears to bring to his teaching is that it attenuates the cord that ties human beings to the world to come. Without explicitly destroying the hope of the Resurrection and the promises of heaven, Christian mortalism serves to remove them as far as possible from the realm of human freedom in this world.

The "Erroneous Doctrine" That Threatens Hobbes's Plan for Peace: The Church Now on Earth Is the Kingdom of God of the Bible

There is another biblical issue beyond the question of the soul, Hobbes says, that is troublesome to the effort to secure human beings from the fear that may undo the civil association (see Peters 1956, 254–55). To this one issue, Hobbes says, almost all other biblical problems are subordinate:

> The greatest and main abuse of Scripture, and to which almost all the rest are either consequent or subservient, is the wresting of it to prove that the kingdom of God, mentioned so often in Scripture, is the present Church, or multitude of Christian men now living, or that being dead, are to rise again at the last day. (EW III, 605 [629])

Hobbes says that all the dangerous authors of spiritual darkness, against which part 4 of his *Leviathan* is written, seek "to settle in the minds of men this erroneous doctrine, that the Church now on earth, is that kingdom of God mentioned in the Old and New Testaments" (EW III, 693 [708]).

If the kingdom of God exists here and now in a parallel "dimension," so to speak, and is represented on earth by believers in Christ, it poses a threat to the peace of this world. To again cite the beginning of chapter 38, if civil power depends on justice, Hobbes writes, and if justice depends

> on the power of life and death, as well as in lesser rewards and punishments, residing in them that have the sovereignty of the commonwealth, it is impossible a commonwealth should stand, where any other than the sovereign hath a power of giving greater rewards than life, and of inflicting greater punishment than death. (EW III, 437 [478])

Hobbes observes that since eternal life is a greater reward than life in the present world, and because eternal torments are a greater punishment than natural death, human beings may all too easily be led to obey voices that instruct them how to avoid the greatest punishments, which same voices may then lead them away from obedience to civil authority. This is why, Hobbes writes, all men should consider "what is meant by Holy Scripture, by *life eternal*, and *torments eternal*; and for what offences, and against whom committed, men are to be eternally tormented; and for what actions they are to obtain *eternal life"* (EW III, 437 [478–79]).

Hobbes will explain the meaning of these things in such a way as to prevent them from being appropriated for purposes of attaching human beings to another, rival kingdom than that of Leviathan. Thus, Hobbes's considerations of eternal life and eternal torments, how to obtain the former and escape the latter, are dedicated thoroughly to naturalizing or rationalizing Christian teaching. Hobbes tends to regard these teachings as metaphors, or else aims in other ways to equivocate about their traditional Christian meaning. But his primary means of undermining the power of these key aspects of Christian theology is to undermine the realm they pertain to, that is, to undermine the traditional meaning of the kingdom of God and fill the place formerly held by it with the kingdom of nature's God, in which "there is no other way to know anything, but by natural reason, that is, from the principles of natural science" (EW III, 353–54 [404]).

Hobbes stresses that loyalty to the way of natural reason—which produces the Leviathan, the kingdom of nature's God—is demonstrated by obedience to God's laws, that is, to the laws of nature. It is obedience to these laws, catalogued in chapters 14 and 15, "that is the greatest worship of all" (EW III, 355–56 [405]). In *Leviathan*, as we have seen, Hobbes aims to confirm that the Scriptures support these laws. Thus biblically justified, the rights of sovereigns and the duties of subjects, based on "the natural inclinations of mankind and upon the articles of the law of nature, now constitute the kingdom of God" (EW III, 710 [725]). The church is to reside underneath the authority of Leviathan then, not because Scripture teaches Christians to be subject to the civil powers of this world, which it does, but because the church is subject to the conclusions of Hobbes's science of natural justice, that is, to the conclusions of the project based in natural reason alone established in parts 1 and 2 of *Leviathan*.

Hobbes's conclusion that the church should be subject to civil authority, was not, in itself, so unique; its distinction was in how Hobbes arrived at his teaching, in how he transforms the meaning of the Bible to support his conclusions, and in the nature of the consequent subordination of biblical meaning—and thus of believers—to civil authority. When Christians argued in Hobbes's time for royal supremacy in ecclesiastical matters, they did not argue for the subordination of the church by naturalizing God, questioning the Bible, and exalting human ends and the autonomous individual above all else.[6]

The Effect of Hobbes's Reinterpretation:
A New Notion of Redemption

The gospel asks, "For what shall it profit a man, if he shall gain the whole world and lose his own soul" (Mark 8:36)? The Bible thus appears to be concerned with preventing the "loss" of souls, that is, with "saving" them. By lessening the awesome expectations associated with death by altering the meaning of the soul and the kingdom of God, Hobbes effectively transforms the meaning of Christian redemption, that is, the meaning of the salvation of the soul.

In Hobbes's political theory, the Scriptures are no longer concerned chiefly with a redemption that consists in reconciling God and man through Christ's death; instead, the focus of Scripture becomes the lessening of the division between man and God by radically minimizing the division between civil authority—that is, Leviathan—and God. Thus, while the great sin was formerly understood to be human disobedience to God, Hobbes's reinterpretation makes the great "sin" disobedience to a worldly sovereign. Hobbes puts God on the side of Leviathan by means of his teaching that natural reason is the word of God, so that the great divide requiring atonement—the making of peace between man and the divine will—is no longer chiefly between God and all mankind, but between Leviathan and those who would rise against the Leviathan's power. Hobbes teaches that God is now firmly allied with civil power by means of his argument from reason in parts 1 and 2 of *Leviathan* as it is applied to interpreting divine revelation in parts 3 and 4.

Thus Hobbes can write, "Lastly, obedience to his laws, that is, in this case, to the laws of nature, is the greatest worship of all" (EW III, 355 [405]). This ultimately means that obedience to the end established by such laws—Leviathan and his ultimate purpose—is the greatest worship of all, while teaching that disobedience to the laws of nature is the greatest sin of all. In Hobbes's new reading of the Scriptures, the great "sin" is rejection of the laws of nature, for such a sin, when it is finished, will produce the state of nature and war, promising a nasty, brutish, and short life ending in sudden and violent death for all men.

When human beings obey the sovereign, what do they do? The sovereign exists only because human beings have willed this sovereign power exist, and it exists to serve their natural liberty, which they minimize when they come into civil association under Leviathan that they might maximize it. We may say that Leviathan serves human rights—human freedom—especially the right to self-preservation expressed as the right to peace. Thus, the greatest worship of all turns out to be the worship of peace and freedom, that is, the worship of human rights, a notion that would not seem foreign in liberal societies today. Hobbes's resolution of the problem posed by the state of nature is a new kind of redemption or salvation effected by a transformation of that biblical doctrine.[7]

Hobbes's teaching is designed to protect human beings from the ubiquitous threat of physical death in their natural state, but only one "man," Leviathan, the artificial man, is to be preserved, if not forever, then at least for the longest possible time, or, let us call it, for an "artificial eternal life." It is he, the civil power as personated by the sovereign, who will be "redeemed" by Hobbes's great work. Hobbes's political theory provides for an everlasting sovereign—not a person, but an institution or creation. Perhaps this, beyond his godlike power, explains in part why Hobbes can call Leviathan the mortal god: civil authority's longevity, while still subject to the diseases that cause the dissolution of the commonwealth, is now to be longer than human beings heretofore thought possible—a godlike longevity. Hobbes's interpretation of the Bible, in causing the traditional understanding of the biblical teaching of eternal life for all who believe in the sacrifice of one man, Christ, to pale (though he does this behind the veil of continual ambiguities), instead teaches that one "man," Leviathan, the artificial man embodying the power of civil government, shall "live" almost forever. Curiously, this reverses the biblical notion that one man died so that many could live forever; instead we see the traditional Christian teaching of eternal life of many in another world delicately subverted for the sake of the greater longevity of the one. And yet this one is to live so long for only one purpose: that the many may have a safe and long *physical* life in this world.[8]

The traditional Christian idea of the soul gives way in *Leviathan* in order that peace, safety, and the natural rights of man may reign. By Hobbes's reinterpretation of the Bible, the kingdom where the civil power can endure forever based upon, and serving, the natural rights of all the members—rights that are developed around the self-preservation of the individual—triumphs over the traditional Christian view of God's kingdom. We may even say that with Hobbes's reinterpretation of the Bible, the kingdom of nature's God, erected for the same purpose as the modern liberal polity—the protection of natural human rights—first appeared on the earth.

Hobbes's "Conspiracy" against Christianity

Hobbes's teaching about the soul and the biblical kingdom of God are key elements of his conspiracy against Christianity. The term "conspiracy" indicates the judgment that while Hobbes's treatment of the Bible is actually motivated by another end than that of Christian faith, his teachings are presented as though motivated by a genuine desire to interpret the Scriptures rightly because the interpreter is a genuine believer. Hobbes "plays" the theologian in order to establish, covertly, the independence of unassisted human reason and the supremacy of the rights of man over all authorities.

Concerning conspiracy, let us consider Hobbes and his work by using a biblical metaphor: Hobbes's efforts are like those of Laban in Genesis 29. There we find Laban, Jacob's future father-in-law, about to see his youngest daughter Rachel married to Jacob, who has long been in love with her. On the night Jacob is to wed Rachel, Laban tricks the young suitor into believing his other daughter, Leah, is the wife to be. In the dark, veiled, in the passion of the moment, Jacob mistakes the silent Leah for Rachel, only to discover in the light of the next morning that he is with Leah and not with his beloved Rachel. Leaving the rest of the story aside—especially the revelation of true identity the following morning—we see that Laban is the father of a conspiracy to deceive Jacob.

Hobbes is a clever matchmaker, like Laban, and he deals with Christianity in *Leviathan* as Laban deals with Rachel and Jacob in Genesis. The commonwealth, or rather, its individual members are a suitor, a man, looking for a maid—a religion to be married to. The expected bride is not the bride the matchmaker thinks is best for him, so, as Laban does with Leah and Rachel, Hobbes switches the expected woman for another one—someone who, in the dark and veiled, looks like "Rachel," the expected and beloved bride. This expected bride—if I may be forgiven the metaphor—is authentic

Christianity; the bride Hobbes provides appears to be her in many ways, but the two ladies are not the same.

This study is the story of why Hobbes conspired to make this match and of how the maids were switched. It is also the story of how at least some of Hobbes's readers did not notice the change—that part of his readership whom he was most interested in affecting. Hobbes, like the Bible's Laban, is the artful father of a conspiracy. Laban's efforts were for the sake of his eldest child, and, perhaps most of all, to keep Jacob in his employ. Hobbes's efforts were for the sake of his science of natural justice, and they were meant to keep Hobbes's intended audience from rejecting his project.

We have discussed Hobbes's argument against Aristotle, against the doctrine of the immortality of the soul, and against the teaching that the church on earth is the kingdom of God, in order to show more clearly the territory Hobbes sought to conquer. But Hobbes's battle against the chief enemy to his political reasoning was fought in a conspiratorial manner. He aimed to deprive the greatest enemies of his project and, in his view, of civil peace—that is, the authors of spiritual darkness (EW III, 693 [708])—of their great power not by frontal assault upon them, but by undermining their capacity to affect their listeners. He aimed to do this by instituting a new understanding of Christianity that would redefine civic responsibility principally as obedience to Leviathan. He hoped to betroth a most educable audience, including especially university students (EW III, 713 [728]), to this religious understanding, thus depriving the "authors of spiritual darkness," who would divide men from their principal civic duties, of the primary means of winning their hearers' attention.

We have shown that the primary means of dividing human beings from their worldly civic duties is the claim that there is another realm apart from Leviathan and it is attached to the deity to which human beings owe their chief allegiance. A frontal assault on this dangerous aspect of religious power would have been counterproductive both for Hobbes and his project—to say the least; furthermore, it was Hobbes's intent to preserve the form or shape of the enemy kingdom he wished to conquer, the better to take it over and use it for the interests of this world. Hobbes had no wish to destroy all religious authority—he could not have done so even if he had wished to; he wanted only to subordinate it to Leviathan. In order to do this, Hobbes wished to create a counterfeit Christianity, one that would serve the rights of man based on the principles derived from Hobbes's discovery—the state of nature. The extent to which some of the elements Hobbes fought to defeat are still alive and at-large should in no way blind us to the truth: Hobbes won the war he fought. Biblical religion is no longer a serious threat to peace and safety within societies based on the principles developed from the natural rights Hobbes discovered.

The Christian religion, over time, was rationalized into an attenu-ated form for many believers, a shadow of its former self, by the victorious march of reason Hobbes did much to initiate, that the rights of man might rule according to the interests of man. But even that attenuated form is now presumed to be unessential to the continuing and enduring victory of rights by many men and women living today in the greatest society governed by the principles of rights. Yet I believe Hobbes would have thought otherwise; he took great care to preserve the form or shape of biblical religion because he recognized the religious passion not only as a threat, but as a much-needed guarantor to the success of rights-based polities.

We spoke earlier in this chapter of the greatest danger addressed by Hobbes's treatment of the Bible and Christianity, the problem of divided loyalties and the importance of "domesticating" Christian-ity to prevent it from doing harm to the interests of man on earth (which is to say, first of all, the interest of self-preservation). But the second half of *Leviathan* suggests that Hobbes was also aware of another danger: the concern that human beings, not more deeply attached to the civil association he presents than the behavior the principles of self-preservation would tend to encourage, will not give such an association the support it needs to succeed. Thus we now turn from his concern in reinterpreting the Bible for the purpose of preventing the problem of divided loyalties to the im-plicit demonstration in his work of the necessity of religion to help make human beings loyal to Leviathan, thus insuring the success of political associations based on the rights of man.

For the Sake of Peace and Safety: The Need for Transcendence

Hobbes's reinterpretation of the Bible appropriates elements of the Christian religion to make secure the great principles of liberty and self-preservation that we have discussed under the rubric of natural rights. He makes these principles secure, in great part, by hiding or covering their starkness, especially the starkness of the principle of self-preservation, a principle that is central to Hobbes's human-rights teaching, but which also reveals the dangerous, provocative, and unattractive nakedness of the human passions and which is thus in need of the shielding or covering or beautification only religion can provide.

Hobbes's natural-rights teaching needs the covering of religion because the civil association based on self-preservation cannot always easily find the moral authority to secure the devotion required for its preservation without supplying the grounds for attachment to such a society. The natural-rights basis in the autonomy of the individual seems to need not only the means to prevent the division of loyalties over matters of the greatest questions of human existence, but also the means by which to stir citizens to do deeds that eclipse their rationalistic and self-interested calculus, deeds involving sacrifice for others, giving one's life for the polity, or deferring one's rights for some common concern. How else, for example, can such a society defend itself from an attack by a foreign power? Are the principles of self-interest and self-preservation enough to engender the required sacrifices? In Hobbes's hands, the Bible hides the coarse and stark truth of the foundations of his political thought, the law of self-preservation, and acts to make it seem holy and transcendent. Hobbes, by his appropriation of the Bible, gives to the principles of his science and to the rights of man an authority we associate with the law of the divine.

Hobbes uses religion to attach men's hearts to the polity based on rights, regulating it to supply a controlled form of transcendence in order to rescue human beings from the fear of death and imaginations concerning death when death itself can no longer be averted by their self-preserving works. Thus Hobbes reinterprets the Bible not only to reckon with the problem of divided loyalties, but also to supply a seeming transcendence to foster devotion to civil order and to regulate the fear of death that can otherwise lead to a division of loyalties. Hobbes would not have fear become so inordinate that human beings become all the more susceptible to subversion by religionists who would divide them from their civic duties, but at the same time, Hobbes is aware that fear is what keeps human beings "in check." It is the passion that generates and preserves Leviathan. Hobbes is aware that fear of unseen powers, harnessed to the authority of Leviathan, can provide an enormous support to the peace-preserving task of civil power. The Bible, then, is the raw material from which Hobbes extracts this sense of transcendence; he reinterprets it and appropriates this refashioned religious authority in order to regulate fears and to complete his plan for peace. Hobbes's appropriation of the Bible to supply this sense of transcendence is done for the sake of Leviathan; to suggest Hobbes marries authentic Christianity to his project is to misunderstand both his project and Christianity.

Hobbes understood that holding death at bay, even for the longest time possible through political arrangements guaranteeing preservation against the violence of men, is not enough; human beings need a further sense of overcoming (a means of meeting the inevitable fact of death when it can no longer be thwarted in its principally threatening form, in the form of the violence of men) lest the finality of death be too overwhelming and they seek another foundation than the one that Hobbes outlined in the explicitly political first half of Leviathan.

Hobbes fears human beings will revert to the pure products of fearful imagination, abandoning the reason he has exalted and with it the worldly kind of salvation characterized by safety from the fearful state of nature. The dangerous, politically subversive comforts human beings find in imaginings of the supernatural to which their fear of death leads them, are the little sins against the laws of natural reason that lead them to fall back into the state of nature. A religious, transcendent account of the world must be brought in if human beings are to be saved from such a state—the truest hell the reason based on the fear of death can know. The Bible is such an account, ready at hand, but as understood in the world of the seventeenth century, and, indeed, in the meaning its various books plainly claim for it, the Bible represents a world that is no friendlier to unassisted, independent natural reason than the wildest of superstitious imaginings; indeed, to such reason, unusual as it was in seventeenth-century Europe, that is exactly what the Scriptures often were, and, as such, they were a threat to peace.

The most explicitly political half of Leviathan—the first half—aims to secure human beings against the violence implicit in man represented by the state of nature. But it is the fact of this latter fear—the problem of mortality, generally—that is always breeding imaginations in the minds of human beings concerning the ends of their individual lives and creating a susceptibility in them to questions concerning whom they ought to obey. Even though reducing the possibility of violent death is the foundation for civil association, the general fact of death—of human mortality—remains *the* threat to the stability of civil association. Hobbes's response to this great threat is to appropriate the Bible as the substantiation for a new theology that is intended to reassure men across the entire range of their fears while at the same time instructing them concerning where their loyalties must finally lie.

The entire enterprise of civil association founded on rights is connected by Hobbes to God. Hobbes found it extremely important to betroth religion to his science of natural justice and the natural rights of man, but only after he had made religion fit for the marriage by his reinterpretion of Scripture. One chief question that arises is whether, or how much, a divorce of the foundation of Hobbes's thought from even such a modest bride as Hobbes has supplied is one that will threaten the posterity of the match. Hobbes seems to teach that the well-being of both the polity based on natural rights and its bride, as it were, depend on their remaining together. This is why Leviathan has two parts that are meant to be connected. Political association based in self-preservation needs the support of religion for the purpose of governing human fear; only in this way can peace and safety be guaranteed.

The Danger of Irreligiousness

In *Leviathan*, chapters 11 and 12, Hobbes teaches that as long as human beings fear death, such fear will give birth to religion. But it appears that there is also a possibility that some human beings may not always fear death or be anxious about the future, and these sorts of persons fall into two categories: those who have "confronted" the biggest questions and met them with religious or philosophical resolve, so that we could say they do not fear death, or do not fear it as much as the many do; and those who have no fear of death—or too little—because they are unthinking. The former category represents those who are the source of problems to do with the division of loyalties—the proud fathers of "spiritual darkness," as Hobbes would call them. But our concern at present is with the second category.

What about those whose capacity for anxiety about the future has been weakened through a life of too easy circumstances, or too desperate ones, leading to lives characterized by habits of immediate self-gratification? Would such persons forget to think soberly about the long view, about mortality, about self-preservation, and thus about how they ought to live? If human beings do not exercise their capacity for calculation concerning the beginning and end of things, will they cease in some measure to be led by the passions Hobbes counts on most (EW III, 94–95 [168–70])?[9] Perhaps what is required to put a human being in such a state is only sufficient compulsion or opportunity to indulge the passions that lead away from thinking about the future; perhaps only too many amusements are required for such an effect (inasmuch as the word amuse may be defined as "away from thinking"). Such attitudes may not affect a majority, but may produce a number significant enough to then affect the health of a society. Would "formed religion," to use Hobbes's term (EW III, 105 [179]), curtail the problem these kinds of human beings pose for civil association?

Hobbes's project depends on the sobriety of human beings concerning fear of death, both violent death at the hands of men and the general fact of death that faces all human beings. Hobbes indicates that so long as men and women are not led away from sober anxiousness about the future, they can be counted on, generally, to fear death (as Hobbes implicitly prescribes in *Leviathan*, chapter 13) and thus to follow the principles of the laws of nature described in *Leviathan*, chapters 14 and 15. (It seems noteworthy that the importance of religion to the generation and control of fear is the subject of chapters 11 and 12.)

This fear, then, is the foundation that will lead men and women to the prudent conduct that makes good subjects or citizens, the conduct that Hobbes demonstates "gets men out" of the state of nature in the first place. Such persons, generally governed by self-interest alone, will be confirmed in their good behavior by the additional incentive of belief in a deity who will judge them and reward them for it. But those whose self-indulgence leads them to forgetfulness are even more in need of being reminded of sanctions for bad behavior, even if the sanctions are constituted only by fear of the bad opinions of others for one's failure to subscribe to the religious principles that define good behavior. And what if such persons believe there is no divine master at all? Will such convictions of masterlessness lead to socially destructive behavior? Since religion may serve as a regulator for the fears that are so important in helping to prompt human beings to follow the prudential laws of nature (*Leviathan*, chapters 11 through 13), rules that lead to civil association and thus to peace and safety, the regulation of this "regulator," that is, the regulation of religion, must be very important, indeed. To undervalue its importance is to despise a primary mechanism for the preservation of civil order, and this is why Hobbes dedicates half of his *Leviathan* to it.[10]

Hobbes's teaching suggests both that religion is a permanent fixture that no human society can expel completely, and that there will always be some persons, who, susceptible to the allures that make them socially irresponsible, will be dangerous ultimately to civil peace and safety. This class of individuals, unwilling to be mindful of the need to defer gratification or think about tomorrow, acting as masterless men and women, are especially in need of some "checking" authority capable at least of making them pause before acting in ways that may threaten peace and safety. Fear of Leviathan's sword can do much of this, but a religion based on a deity who beholds all things, even the most secret ones, must be more effective; thus Leviathan must employ religion.[11] But if there is no "formed" religion provided that is effective on a societal scale, how will a society based on rights and the autonomy of the individual fare?

A Veil Cast over the Masterlessness of Man

If we remove the veil, the religious covering Hobbes provides in the last two parts of his treatise, we find that the implication of his teaching is that human beings are fully free from God and thus wholly free from any kind of natural master. This is never explicit, since it was not Hobbes's purpose to undermine all faith in something above man.

Let us give one indication of this. What is the meaning of Hobbes's insistence on the materiality of spirit in *Leviathan*, particularly in chapter 34? Hobbes suggests that what men commonly consider as body or matter are those things that, by sensing, they may perceive as obstacles to their power. This implies the potential for mastering such obstacles—indeed, whatever "body" is perceived by sense is potentially "body" that may be controlled by man, but whatever escapes such sensing is not understood, is not subject to control. Thus Hobbes, by making the mysterious notion the Schoolmen called "substance" into body, removes a vast category of uncontrolled territory from the human mental map of the universe and puts it into the realm of human understanding—the realm of the possibility of human mastery. The removal of the mystery of "incorporeal substance" is thus a liberation. If human beings use reason to reduce all things to matter, to what Hobbes calls "body," and to that which is susceptible to natural laws, have they not willed to make the whole of being into something they can come closer to controlling? Have they not attempted to subject all things that exist to that which they may measure and categorize and, to some degree, master? By reducing all things to body, Hobbes lays the foundation of uniformity upon which human beings may re-make what they treat after their own design. Such a process may be understood even to take place in Hobbes's reconceptualization of the God of the Bible as "the God of nature" in *Leviathan*, chapter 34, and elsewhere in the work.

If we argue that "body" is what human beings can potentially control, Hobbes's work may be seen as an attempt to understand the kingdom of the biblical God by rendering it as "body," as material and natural, bringing it into the realm of human sense and human reason and thus human control. Hobbes is capturing the traditional Christian realm of spirit and planting upon it the flag of the naturalistic kingdom generated through the science of natural justice described in *Leviathan*. But in all the new power Hobbes implicitly gives to human beings by asserting the primacy of reason, his work nevertheless preserves an apparently miraculous realm pertinent to the aspects of the Bible least susceptible to naturalistic understandings. For his broader audience, educated, but still reli-gious, Hobbes covers up the deeper implications of human auton-omy in *Leviathan* with ample arguments to show the religiosity of his project. But apart from the broad audience among the educated Hobbes desired to influence (EW III, 710–14 [725–29]), I believe a smaller audience, constituted by two different parts understood him as we have understood him here, that is, in terms of his declaration of independence from all traditional authorities, from the Bible as well as Aristotle. To one part of this audience, Hobbes's teaching was barely disguised atheism. To another part of Hobbes's reader-ship, his teaching appeared as a "revelation" of man's masterless-ness. His intention was to cover this implicit revelation, not only to protect himself, but because it was necessary to make his project workable.

What characterizes this masterlessness? Hobbes teaches that un-less human beings dispel all authorities that the study of nature does not itself authenticate, and that without a method based in reducing and reconstituting all things to constitute a science, there can be no true knowledge. For Hobbes, final causes can never be known, and thus the only true knowledge has to do with the *how* of things, rather than the ultimate *why*. Hobbes teaches that human beings can only truly know what they can wholly take apart and put together, only what they make—that is, what they limit and define by naming, and what they construct from such strict processes. This is exactly what takes place in the forming of axioms and constructing of proofs in the science of geometry, which is why Hobbes praises geometry above all other studies as the first and foundational science. The application of the principles of the science of geometry—principles of naming to control one's field of work and to enable reason to work without the interference of the passions—for governing nature in general and for the sake of human interests, is thus understood by Hobbes to be the only true knowledge. This means that true knowledge can finally only be based on what human beings can make and control.

For Hobbes, the real excitement of the day was that of liberation from all the past through the discovery of a new way; his real motive was liberation—to be free of all authorities and all fears. Basil Willey sums up the spirit of the revolt against the medieval tradition of which Hobbes was a foremost example: "to be rid of fear—fear of the unknown, fear of the gods, fear of the stars and fear of the devil—to be released from the necessity of reverencing what was not understood" (Willey 1934, 5). This was only possible through the notion of true knowledge we are speaking of here.

Thus, instead of the fate of the eternal soul and the relationship of human beings to a transcendent God serving as the focus of political life, the independent human mind, based in this world and claiming rights for itself from a nature distinct from any notion of the biblical God, becomes the centerpiece of political existence.

The Implications for Human Self-understanding of Hobbes's Science of Natural Justice

Hobbes was a pioneer of a great project: the liberation of the human mind to permit the extension of the independence of man over all nature, over his own nature, over all things. But does not his view—based on mathematical learning that ignores questions the answers to which human beings cannot be certain about (the province of dogmatic learning]—finally leave one vast field of human concerns aside? Hobbes's mechanistic, materialistic conception of nature, his account of human emotions and human psychology in the state of nature, his discussion of the generation of commonwealth on the basis of laws of nature or articles of peace, and his treatment of the Bible in parts 3 and 4 to confirm his findings in the first half of *Leviathan*, all work together to establish his science of natural justice, knowledge that will enable human beings to make themselves safer than ever before. This science will free them of those forces that have tended to master them against their best interests in this world.

But this project, which we have characterized as motivated by a yearning for liberation—to be free of fears and free of masters—leaves aside a kind of comprehensive account of the world that some would say is finally required for the fullest sense of security and freedom since it does not address the question of first causes or the question of "Why?" about the whole of being. If Hobbes's treatment of the biblical account is as skeptical as we have argued it is here, and if his understanding of the human capacity to know is as limited as we have seen, then we are left with the fact that Hobbes does not appear to account for the gap between the origin of things and "the way things go on." We know only this—that his *Leviathan* is fully dedicated to the latter—though, of course, his use of Christianity disguises this, one of its most important functions.

The problem Hobbes avoids—if we see beneath the disguise of religion in which he clothes his political philosophy—may be understood in part as the matter of deciding between some notion of a creation and a view of the world as being in continuous process without beginning or end. But finally the problem Hobbes does not deal with is the problem of life itself: he does not tell us where and how the inorganic becomes organic; he must tell us where life comes from if he wants to be truly comprehensive, and not merely provide an account that will persuade those whom he persuades. What, for example, would he say to those who understand him as we have claimed to do here? He appears to teach that human beings simply cannot know the problem of origins or the question of "Why?" We can know how to make this world safe—let us do what we can do.

In the second sentence of the introduction to *Leviathan*, Hobbes writes, "For seeing life is but a motion of limbs, the beginning whereof is in some principal part within." This "principal part within" is clearly the heart, but where does the beating heart come from? Hobbes does not tell us how organic matter comes from inorganic, and this is the first problem that the materialist must deal with—apart from answering the question of the origin of all things, of matter itself.[12]

This is a topic that reaches to the heart of the innovations of modernity, for in neglecting it, Hobbes reveals the modern propensity to ask the "how" of things to the exclusion of the "why." The overlooking of "the problem of life"—the question of origins and of what man ultimately is—represents the tendency toward conscious exclusion of this realm of thought in the debates concerned with political and moral life in the West. The origins of life, having been rendered an issue that at best can only be a matter for speculation, seem a matter better left untended since such questions contain the seeds for the sort of passionate divisions that may destroy peaceful civil association. But the "problem of life" remains *the* real question behind a great part of moral discussion.

Hobbes implies that he accepts the biblical account, and he does refer to God and the biblical account of creation in various places, and thus seems to appropriate building materials from divine science to bridge the gaps he does not overtly tackle through natural science. His materialism is made to conform, at least in appearance, with the orthodox religious account of the beginnings of things. So Hobbes rather successfully obscures this issue.[13]

It has been the argument of this study that Hobbes finds the biblical account only instrumental for purposes of his political reasoning; the greater context of Hobbes's thought makes us suspect that biblical references appended to Hobbes's science of natural justice do not indicate his fundamental reliance on these accounts. How, then, does Hobbes deal with the questions that religion addresses, his conclusion that religion is born out of fear of death notwithstanding? How, then, does Hobbes deal with the question of what life is *for*, his teaching concerning its preservation having been brought to perfection? He does not and, indeed, he cannot, for to attempt to do so is to plunge human beings back into dogmatic learning concerning which there is no agreement and over which human beings all too often go to war. Thus his teaching has very great implications for human self-understanding. We can see the great implications of his project when we compare his picture of human independence with the biblical view: "What is man, that thou art mindful of him? and the son of man, that thou visitest him? For Thou hast made him a little lower than the angels, and hast crowned him with glory and honor. Thou madest him to have dominion over the works of thy hands; thou hast put all things under his feet" (Ps. 8:4–6).

The biblical view leaves something still above man, who is "a little lower than the angels"—a God "who is mindful of him"; this Hobbes ultimately (though not explicitly) does not do. Man is no longer the being *between* God above and the creation below. Once he may have been crowded in between, responsible for nature but still responsible to God, but such a universe is no longer a possibility for Hobbes. Man is now alone here. He knows nothing beyond this of any higher purpose or any "place" where he may belong. He only knows he must conquer nature, beginning with the state of nature, in order to survive. The universe is not naturally a home for him, then. He has no comfortable niche, no God to care for him, only a jungle or a cosmos out of which he must wrest a spot for himself. The universe is hostile to him; he must defeat nature to make a place for his own restless, insecure, masterless nature.

Yet even while this understanding stands behind the teaching he bequeathed to us, Hobbes hid this "nakedness," the exposure of autonomous and also unprotected man to an impersonal, masterless universe, by means of his appropriation of religion. This is how Hobbes deals with the question of what life is for—he hides his conviction of the fundamental absence of an answer to this question behind his appropriation of a transformed Christianity. The truth of man's masterlessness and solitude in the universe was never to be explicit; indeed, it was carefully disguised, and the disguise stood Hobbes in good stead, in spite of the trouble he had from his religious opponents, for though they accused him, they could never indict him.

Hobbes's appropriation of religion was finally for the purpose of reaching the audience whose approval was most necessary for the advancement of his project. These were persons who might accept Hobbes's political teaching if he could demonstrate to them that their religious needs were not being slighted—needs that included some response to the question of origins and meaning that could satisfy the human hunger for a comprehensive account of being. *Leviathan* had such readers as these, who would accept his political reasoning and who would not be inclined to fault his theology if it could suitably clothe man with enough meaning to allow the individual the right to pursue personal peace and safety first in good conscience. Their approbation was not published, of course, in a time and place dominated by traditional and orthodox Christian views, but when an era more congenial to Hobbes's intentions and theology—or less concerned and acquainted with authentic Christianity generally—arrived, Hobbes's theology could be approved in print, and even accepted as true Christianity. Such persons would not suspect that behind Hobbes's astute use of religion lay another revelation entirely—one of man's masterlessness and utter solitude in the universe.

Hobbes's attention to religion for the support of the rights of man seems to indicate that *something* was necessary to elevate human considerations above the basis of rights-based society in the rather low "common denominator" of individual self-preservation. Hobbes understood deeply the utility of religion for this purpose, though he does not seem at all to have admired it as something beautiful.

Hobbes, with no misgivings, irreligiously appropriated religion as an instrument to preserve order and liberty for the sake of a very low conception of man. By "aiming low" he hoped to achieve what he aimed for: a civil association in which the physical peace and safety of human beings would be guaranteed more fully, and for greater duration, than ever before. Hobbes thought that by creating the conditions for extended peace, that all the productive energy so often dissipated by frequent human recurrence to the condition approaching the state of nature, would finally be allowed to develop its greatest potential to benefit mankind; human beings would know security and prosperity as never before. Hobbes's treatment of religion is strictly for the sake of his project, a project with the rights of man at its center. His treatment of religion in *Leviathan* is the original warning to those who believe in rights that, while religion must be controlled, it must not be lost.

By making rights transcendent, that is, by suggesting that God stands above human freedom, licensing it, Hobbes understood that the eyes of human beings would be lifted a little above the goals of self-interest and comfortable self-preservation and from the temptations of amusements and the anxieties of freedom. Thus Hobbes used God to sanctify and justify the freedom to pursue fundamentally self-interested lives, contrary to the teachings of Christianity. Hobbes's profound skepticism—not to say antipathy—about the Christian religion did not blind him to the assistance it could give to the principles of his science of natural justice by underwriting them with a transcendence that would make men and women devoted to the commonwealth that exists to maximize the principles of self-interest. Neither was he unaware that religion served as a veil required to prevent men and women from seeing the true human situation that lay behind his state of nature and the science of natural justice he discovered in order to provide a way of escape from it.

John Hunt and those Hobbes scholars mentioned in the second chapter who have followed him in believing Hobbes's treatment of the Bible and Christianity are ingenuous, are wrong when they say that the second half of *Leviathan* confirms that Hobbes's project is based in Christian belief. Hunt and these others do not see that the basis of Hobbes's teaching does not allow any true harmony between that teaching and biblical Christianity. Hobbes added the second half of *Leviathan* to govern what civil associations cannot long survive without, and so had to leave the biblical story enough intact to make it serviceable. For Hobbes, a serviceable religion is one that meets the demand of human beings for some account of existence that gives life meaning and is responsive to the deepest human anxieties, and which, at the same time, does not divide them from the primary concern of peace and safety in this world.

Hunt and those who have followed him, who think Hobbes's original critics were in error, mistake Hobbes's appropriation of the Christian religion for his genuine embrace of it. His understanding of reason as, essentially, the servant of the passions, when brought to bear upon the teachings of Scripture, reveals to us that man's freedom and autonomy and not man's responsibility to God, rules in the teaching of *Leviathan*. Hunt and a growing number of modern scholars who have come after him cannot believe that the enormous biblical erudition in *Leviathan* could be less than ingenuous, but Hobbes's early critics and men of earlier eras knew better.

Notes

Chapter 1
Introduction: Human Rights
and Biblical Religion in *Leviathan*

1. Hobbes's view of the divine as the power that sanctifies the principles of rights is alive and well in contemporary American life. Examples of the appropriation of the divine in a manner completely free of biblical strictures in order to sanctify the idea of human rights may be seen in how sacrifices for the country, especially when they involve soldiers and sailors dying in service, are eulogized by the president. In such a context the stark basis of rights disappears behind the beautiful veil of biblical allusion. Such speeches may include allusion to the cause they fought for—freedom, equality, and the rights of man—and conclude with references to the eternity where such martyrs go, a heaven in which all variants of belief are either forgotten or equalized. Thus, President Bush, in eulogizing the forty-seven dead crew members of the battleship *Iowa* could say, inattentive to whatever each man might have believed or not believed, "Your men are under a different command now, one that knows no rank, only love; knows no danger, only peace. May God bless them" (Bernard Weinraub, "Bush Joins the Grief over Iowa," *New York Times*, 25 April 1989, A-18).

2. In *Leviathan*, Hobbes does not appear to distinguish between the terms "freedom" and "liberty"; in fact, he uses them as synonyms repeatedly in the first two paragraphs of chapter 21. He does, however, distinguish between freedom/liberty and power. In reading Hobbes, some commentators—in order to make clear the distinction between liberty from obligation or other external impediments to a person's using his or her power to do what he or she wishes to do, and internal impediments associated with lack of power to do what one wills—assign the word "freedom" to designate the internal power to act, while allowing "liberty" to represent, as Hobbes tells us in the beginning of the fourteenth chapter, absence of external

239

impediments. Following Hobbes's usage, we shall treat liberty and freedom as synonyms.

3. On no natural knowledge of God, see EW III, 17 [99], 92–93 [167–68], 125–26 [197], 135 [206], 352 [403], 383 [430], 672 [688–89], 677–78 [693–94]; see also EW IV, 59; on God and religion as the invention of human anxiety, see *Leviathan* chapters 11 and 12.

4. Cowley's poem is quoted in this anonymous work, *The True Effigies of the Monster of Malmesbury, or Thomas Hobbes in His Proper Colours*, a brief publication printed to answer and criticize Cowley's praise of Hobbes.

5. Hobbes's mechanistic materialism is fully developed only in *De Corpore* or *Elements of Philosophy, The First Section, Concerning Body*, 1655 (EW I); in part 4 of that work, he turns to the principles he sees underlying human psychology. There, in chapter 25, Hobbes argues that sensation is a motion and that it is to be explained by rules of mechanics alone. Proceeding then from sensation, Hobbes argues that consciousness can be understood as mechanical, too. In short, Hobbes finds that man is mechanical, a machine (see EW III, 1 [85], where Hobbes also argues that man is a machine). In chapter 1 of *Leviathan*, entitled "Of Sense," before Hobbes launches into a mechanistic account of the senses, he writes, "To know the natural cause of sense, is not very necessary to the business now in hand; and I have *elsewhere* written of the same at large. Nevertheless, to fill each part of my present method, I will briefly deliver the same in this place (EW III, 1 [85], my emphasis). This "elsewhere" Hobbes refers to cannot have meant the *Elements of Law Natural and Political* (EW IV), published in 1640 (the first version of Hobbes's political theory), since he said no more there concerning that subject than he was to say in *Leviathan* (1651). The main sources for Hobbes's account of "the natural cause of sense," where Hobbes writes "at large" on this subject, would seem to be *De Corpore*, but this work was not published until 1655, four years after the publication of *Leviathan*. To what work, then, was Hobbes referring in chapter 1 of *Leviathan*? Frithiof Brandt's study of Hobbes's mechanism provides evidence of an early draft of *De Corpore*, which may be dated as early as 1644 (Brandt 1928, 177). This must be the work Hobbes refers to in the first chapter of *Leviathan*, but more importantly, here are grounds that suggest how early Hobbes was seriously working on a comprehensive philosophical system based on matter and motion, which, we may suppose, would then serve as the basis upon which a human psychology could be explained, and out of which, then, a social science based on natural mechanical laws could be developed. We see, then, the apparent interdependence of Hobbes's mechanism and his psychology. Hobbes's account of matter and motion, from which he wished to derive a psychology of man, is of great value to him in his biblical exegesis. Hobbes, by making a mechanistic conception of nature appear as the fundamental explanation of all things, has prepared the way to make it the key to understanding divine things as well.

6. In *The Iliad* XII: 1–120, Circe warns Odysseus concerning prowling rocks and the terrors of Scylla and Charybdis.

Chapter 2
The Controversy Concerning Hobbes and Christianity

1. I wish to thank David Foster and Daniel Gallagher who, in response to a paper I gave at the New England Political Science Association Annual Meeting in 1993, pointed out to me Hobbes's concern for this group of readers.

2. The term "conspiracy" implies the sharing of subversive knowledge among a select group. Inasmuch as Hobbes's most philosophically inclined readers understood his true attitude toward biblical religion, we might say a kind of conspiratorial understanding existed between them, but my intention is not really to suggest so precise a sense of conspiracy by using this term; I only want to convey what I believe to be the nature or character of Hobbes's own intent.

3. See also Maurice 1862, 235–89, and Maurice 1872, 235–90 and 438. As far as I have been able to determine, these were among the very first published interpretations of this kind in England, but assuming I am correct about Hobbes's chief audience, I presume a number of readers, even in Hobbes's own time—and ever since—were privately persuaded that Hobbes was a genuine believer. It is interesting to consider, however, why such interpretations were not published before they were.

4. For additional arguments in favor of Hobbes's theism from this period, see Dewey 1974 and Doyle 1927.

5. See also "Hobbes," in Strauss 1953, for the further development of Strauss's argument concerning these issues.

6. Other contemporary scholars who consider Hobbes to be in the Christian tradition include Henning Graf Reventlow, who sees Hobbes in the tradition extending from Erasmus to Chillingworth (Reventlow 1984, 206, 222). Hobbes's religious attitudes, according to Reventlow, make him "completely a child of his time" and connect him to "the Anglicanism of Laud." See also E. J. Eisenach, who writes, "To close students of Reformation theology . . . what is striking about Hobbes's formal theology is not its uniqueness or its virtuosity, but its orthodoxy within Reformation tradition, especially that articulated during the English Reformation a century earlier" (Eisenach 1982, 222ff). See also S. A. Lloyd (1992, 272): "Hobbes believed in the basic doctrine of the Judeo-Christian tradition."

7. A religion such as this—which we suggest Hobbes did a very great deal to inaugurate—now thrives in America. It is described at times by scholars as the American civil religion, and perhaps popularly regarded as "the American Creed." Herberg 1974, 76–88, speaks of this religious attitude as "The American Way of Life," in his essay "American Civil

Religion: What It Is and Whence It Comes." See also Bellah 1974, 21–44, and Mead 1963, 55–71.

Chapter 3
The Nontheistic Foundation of the First Half of *Leviathan*

1. A. E. Taylor's article, "The Ethical Doctrine of Hobbes" (Taylor 1965), first published some twenty years before Warrender's book, contains an argument similar to that of Warrender's. Our reason for treating Warrender is that he develops the Taylor thesis to a far greater extent than Taylor himself did, and thus represents the challenge of this view at its fullest strength.

2. See also Watkins 1965, 85–86, and Taylor 1965. At this point a fuller discussion of Hobbes's concept of the state of nature and its bearing on the question of the meaning of Hobbes's religious expression might have been applicable but would appear too much as a digression. Such a discussion will, however, follow in chapter 4, after further preparation in the continuing argument of this study makes it more appropriate.

3. On no natural knowledge of God, see (EW III, 17 [99], 92–93 [167–68], 125–26 [197], 135 [206], 352 [403], 383 [430], 672 [688–89], 677–78 [693–94]; see also EW IV, 59).

4. Note how Hobbes speaks in *Leviathan*, chapter 1: "The cause of sense, is the . . . object which presseth the organ proper to each sense . . . which pressure, by the mediation of the nerves . . . continued inwards to the brain, and heart, causeth there a resistance, or counter-pressure, or endeavor of the heart *to deliver itself*" (EW III, 1–2 [85]). The heart and brain of the individual subject seeks *deliverance* from the effects of material pressure as conveyed through the senses. This pressure is reconstituted, through much experience, into fear. The human subject seeks deliverance from this fear: there is a desire for physical security. We thus see deliverance on the level of physiology transferred to the level of human psychology. This desire for security becomes the primary element in the reasoning subject who seeks escape from the state of nature. Man, by means of reason which works by fear, as understood finally in a material and mechanistic way, must *deliver* himself from his situation. The need for deliverance leads human beings to reasonings that teach the benefits of obligations.

5. See Warrender 1957, 98–99, for his position that the laws of nature are the commands of God; 282, for Warrender's treatment of God's power to punish as the enforcing sanctions of the laws of nature; 299–302, for his notion that God's will alone is the obliging force—and it is a mystery. It is true that obligation may indeed exist between human beings in the Hobbesian state of nature—there can be obligation in the absence of a common power if obligation is based on Hobbes's definition of it in *Leviathan*, that

is, on men obliging themselves by laying down a right. If, however, obligation is defined in the way Warrender seeks to term it, that is, as the effect of laws of nature that are the commands of God obliging human beings, then I contend there is no such obligation. For further discussion in agreement with the view held here, see Barry 1968, 123–27.

6. For Hobbes, this is the case in the birth of both kinds of commonwealth, those inaugurated by either institution or acquisition.

7. A history of the state of nature might involve making connections from Hobbes's notions to the biblical account of the origins of things in Genesis. Hobbes does not do this, though at least one commentator has assumed it (Doyle 1927).

8. See Nagel 1959, 68–83. Nagel writes,

Warrender feels that there are in Hobbes two separate systems, a theory of motivation and a theory of obligation, the former having self-preservation as the supreme principle, based on the fact that all men will regard death as their greatest evil, and the latter based on the obligation to obey natural law regarded as the will of God. He explains the egoistic appearance of the theory of obligation on the grounds that it must be consistent with the theory of motivation, but he claims that self-preservation is a "validating condition" of obligation and not a ground of obligation. (70)

Chapter 4
A Curious Ambiguity: Hobbes's Departure from the Christian Natural Law Tradition

1. In his *Liberal Mind*, Kenneth Minogue wrote:

The seeking of peace, though it is for Hobbes the supreme command, is logically dependent upon the general rationale of the laws of nature—"Do not that to another which thou wouldst not have done to thyself" (*Leviathan* chapter fifteen). Here the communal bias of the Sermon on the Mount has been, by a negative reformulation, transformed into a kind of right of privacy, a freedom from the invasion of others. (Minogue 1963, 26)

2. I wish here to recall and reiterate my previous argument that right has an even more fundamental meaning in Hobbes's thought—the liberty to all things not only for self-preservation, but also, to use a term Hobbes uses, for "delectation" (EW III, 111 [184]).

3. I wish to note here the extent to which Warrender strains to find evidence that will give God a fundamental role in Hobbes's thought. Why he goes to such lengths will be considered further along in the chapter.

4. It is interesting to note that in *Leviathan*, to support his argument for a God who rules by natural right of irresistible power (though this

power, as we have noted, does not, in Hobbes's view, oblige), Hobbes gives us a view of who this God is. He uses four different examples, all from Scripture, but one of these is sufficient for our purposes (EW III, 346–47 [397–99]). Hobbes writes: "And Job, how earnestly doth he expostulate with God, for the many afflictions he suffers, notwithstanding his righteousness? This question in the case of Job, is decided by God Himself, not by arguments derived from Job's sin, but from his own power." Thus Hobbes gives an example of the "right of nature, whereby God reigneth over men . . . derived . . . from his irresistible power." What we see here is Hobbes assimilating God, the author of the laws of nature, to the God of the Bible. The God Hobbes is referring to when he speaks of a God who might exercise power in a state of nature and by that power persuade human beings, out of fear, to lay down their natural right and become obliged to him, is not some impersonal God who uses nature to do his will, but the God of Abraham, the God who personally allows Job to be afflicted. Thus we see Hobbes associating the God he has posited, who is both author of the laws of nature and the deity he associates with his notion of the state of nature, with a deity he plainly identifies as the God of Abraham, that is, the God of the Bible. Hobbes clearly associates them, thus leading his readers to think they are one and the same. Warrender, as we shall see, attempts to say the two need not be connected.

5. I am indebted to Barry and Orwin, in particular, for the argument of this and the preceding section of this chapter.

6. Liberty and right are associated in the first sentence of *Leviathan*, chapter 14: "The Right of Nature . . . is the liberty each man hath to use his own power." Liberty is explained further in the first sentence of both chapter 21 and chapter 31, which sentence in the latter chapter states, "That the condition of mere nature, that is to say, of absolute Liberty, such as is theirs, that neither are sovereigns nor subjects, is anarchy, and the condition of war." (EW III, 116 [189], 196 [261–62], 343 [396]).

7. Michael Oakeshott seems to have thought this was the case. In his essay, "The Moral Life in the Writings of Thomas Hobbes," he comments on the reading of this passage, which forms the basis for Warrender's argument:

> It is a loose way of talking to say that Hobbes anywhere said we are obliged by the Laws of Nature because they are the Laws of God; what he said is that we would be obliged by them if they were laws in the proper sense, and that they are laws in the proper sense only if they are known to have been made by God. And this means that they are laws in the proper sense only to those who know them to have been made by God. And who are these persons? Certainly not all mankind; and certainly only those of mankind who have acknowledged God to be maker of this law. The proposition, then, that Hobbes thought the Law of Nature to be law in the proper sense and to

bind all mankind to an endeavour for peace, cannot seriously be entertained, whatever detached expressions (most of them ambiguous) there may be in his writings to support it. (Oakeshott 1975a, 107)

Oakeshott goes on to say that "even God's so-called 'natural subjects' can have no natural knowledge of God as the author of a universally binding precept to endeavour peace." Oakeshott concludes that concerning *Leviathan* "only when the endeavour for peace is enjoined by a positive law does it become a duty, this law alone being law in the proper sense as having a known author; and this law is binding only upon those who know its author." I am entirely in agreement with Oakeshott on this point, but I am interested, beyond this, in why Hobbes is being ambiguous.

8. The passage is quoted in full at the beginning of the section of this chapter entitled "Warrender's Acceptance of Hobbes's Equation of the Word of God and the Laws of Nature," (p. 68).

9. Warrender writes,

In the present work, Hobbes's statements regarding the place of God will be taken as a necessary part of his theory, and it will be contended that this allows the most probable construction to be put upon his text. Thus it will be held that, with regard to natural law, the ground of obligation is always present as this derives from the commands of God in his natural kingdom, and does not depend in any way upon the covenant and consent of the individual or upon the command of a civil sovereign.

Few critics have failed to gather Warrender's insistence that Hobbes's theory depends on the necessary role of God. But see Warrender 1960, 48–57, where he appears to back away somewhat from his claim that God is necessary to Hobbes's theory in response to John Plamenatz's criticism (Plamenatz 1957, 295–308).

10. Thomas Nagel notices a tendency in Warrender to cling to a natural law view of God and a desire to read an old-fashioned morality into things, as does Harvey Mansfield, Jr. (Nagel 1959; Mansfield 1971, 97–110). See also Oakeshott 1975, 69–72.

11. See note 4, above. Michael Oakeshott wrote concerning this notion of natural religion in the context of Hobbes's thought:

To those of Hobbes's contemporaries for whom the authority of medieval Christianity was dead, there appeared to be two possible ways out of this chaos of religious belief. There was first the way of natural religion. It was conceived possible that, by the light of natural Reason, a religion, based upon "the unmovable foundations of truth" (Herbert of Cherbury, De Veritate), and supplanting the inferior religions of history, might be found in the human heart, and receiving universal recognition, become established among mankind. Though their inspiration was older than Descartes, those who took this way found their guide in Cartesian rationalism, which led them to the fairyland of Deism and the other fantasies of the saeculum rationalisticum, amid the dim ruins of which we now live. The other way was that of a civil religion, not the construction of reason but of authority . . . aiming not at undeniable truth but at peace. (1975, 71)

Concerning the sort of religion Hobbes wished to propagate, our argument is that Hobbes's treatment of the Bible takes both these ways into account—the first to help bring human beings to the second. For A. E. Taylor's description of Hobbes's religion, see Taylor 1965, 53–54. See also Peters 1956, 240ff.

12. Crane Brinton appears to summarize the "faith" Hobbes pioneered and Howard Warrender seems to have embraced:

The basic structure of Christian belief survived, however, not without heresies and schisms, until, roughly, the late seventeenth century when there arose in our society what seems to me clearly to be a new religion, certainly related to, descended from, and by many reconciled with, Christianity. I call this religion simply Enlightenment, with a capital E. Let me note here only that Enlightenment does have a theory of the structure of the universe, or a cosmology, which is certainly a thoroughgoing monism—all is Nature, and Nature is all. . . . There are in the West a great number . . . and especially among the educated and privileged classes, who cannot, even in its most recent and subtle theological forms . . . accept the basic Christian transcendental world view, cannot accept as real in any sense the Christian City of God, but do expect, long for, sometimes firmly believe in, a city of Earth transformed—usually by the grace of science and reason—into a City of God built of, for, and by human beings, Homo sapiens, a primate mammal. (Brinton 1964, 315–16)

Commenting much later on Brinton's remarks, Sidney Mead adds that "it was the theology of 'Enlightenment' in Brinton's sense that legitimated the thrust of the Declaration and the constitutional structures of 'the first new nation' in Christendom" (Mead 1977, 28–29). Note also the distinction in Butler 1990, 196, between the civil religion as represented in the Declaration, and orthodox faith:

The Declaration of Independence provides clear-cut evidence of the secondary role that religion and Christianity played in creating the Revolutionary struggle. The religious world involved in the Declaration was a deist's world, at best; at worst, the Declaration was simply indifferent to religious concerns and issues. The god who appears in the Declaration is the god of nature rather than the god of Christian scriptural revelation, as when Jefferson wrote of "the laws of nature and Nature's God."

Hobbes was the "prophet" of this new faith; Warrender's significance, in failing to get to the bottom of Hobbes's project in his *Political Philosophy of Hobbes*, is to point to its success.

13. This quotation was taken from Bishop Bramhall's "Epistle to the Reader" prefacing his responses to Hobbes in their debate; Hobbes reproduced them himself in order to answer them in his own work.

14. See note 4, above.

15. Hobbes states on many occasions that there can be no natural knowledge of God—all we can know of the divine by our unassisted reason is that there must be some origin of things, that is, a First Mover. See chapter 3, note 3, above.

Chapter 5
Hobbes's Sense of Reason

1. It should be noted that in *Leviathan*, chapter 9, in which all learning produced by reason—that is, all "mathematical learning"—is outlined on a chart, no place at all is found for religion. Mathematical learning, we recall, "is free from controversies and dispute, because it consisteth in comparing of figures and motions only" (EW IV, Epistle Dedicatory).

2. It is worth noticing the substance of this example—Hobbes's illustration of prudence: it deals with death at the hands of human beings, and fear, that is, with the passions that are most powerfully engaged in guiding reason for Hobbes. We should remember that both the human being guided by prudence and one guided by Hobbes's careful "method of seeking" that leads to science, are governed by the passion for self-preservation.

3. Since Hobbes uses the first term to summarize the first half of *Leviathan* in chapter 31 and the second to do this in chapter 32, the two terms may thus be understood as synonymous. In the early sentences of chapter 32, Hobbes also uses a third term, "the natural word of God," to describe and summarize the findings of the first half of the work.

4. Blake 1979, Colorplate No. 17. Blake's painting of the Ancient of Days with compass and plans provides us with an apt illustration for our point, but it is worth noting that Blake has the greatest antipathy toward the Hobbesian sense of reason, and it is no accident that he gives the name "Urizen" to a principal figure in his cosmology, a figure personifying the enormously powerful impulse in man to "figure things out," an impulse, Blake indicates, that limits human beings and makes them miserable.

Chapter 6
Hobbes's Departure from Orthodoxy

1. See the discussion in the section of chapter 2, "A Survey of the Controversy."

2. The most famous of Hobbes's early critics, Edward Hyde, earl of Clarendon, commented at length on Hobbes's disregard of his own advice:

It is to be wish'd that he had chosen rather to have acquiesce'd under the modest and prudent resolution of the third paragraph of this Chapter, that when any thing is written in the Scripture too hard for our examination, we are bidden to captivate our understanding to the words, and not to labour in sifting out a Philosophical truth by Logic of such mysteries as are not comprehensible, nor fall under any rule of natural Science; because he says very well "that it is with the mysteries of our religion, as with wholesome pills for the sick; which swallowed whole, have the virtue to cure; but chewed, are for the most part cast up again without effect." I say it is a great pitty that he had not rather rested under that sober consideration, then embarked himself . . . in a Sea of new and extravagant interpretations of several texts of Scripture, without any other authority then of his own ungovern'd fancy. . . . [He] exercised his unruly fancy and imagination, upon making it as doubtful what is Scripture, and the sense and meaning thereof as difficult, as he was able to do. (Clarendon 1676, 202–3)

3. For further discussion concerning this passage on the metaphor of pills for the sick, see Johnson 1974, 103–5, 123–25. Johnson cites opinions that differ from his own view in his endnotes on p. 134. Concerning this passage see also Lange 1881, 284. Lange's views are more in line with those of some of Hobbes's own contemporary critics who saw this metaphor concerning pills and sickness as an indication of Hobbes's unbelief.

4. This authority, it is important to remember, is the purest manifestation of human reasoning, as part 1 of *Leviathan*, culminating in the sixteenth chapter, brings out. There Hobbes shows that the sovereign is authorized by reasoning human beings; the sovereign "personates" or represents the interests of many men concerned with preserving themselves. This all flows out of the laws of nature found out by reason, which are themselves derived from the state of nature. Out of chapter 13 comes chapters 14 and 15 and out of these chapters comes the commonwealth, to whose shape and substance chapters 17 through 31 are dedicated. As Hobbes puts it,

The only way to erect such a common power as may be able . . . to secure them in such sort, as that by their own industry . . . they may . . . live contentedly . . . is to confer all their power and strength upon one man, or upon one assembly of men, that may reduce all their wills, by plurality of voices, unto one will . . . to bear their person. CEW III, 157 [227])

5. See Clarendon 1676, 197–98, concerning another critic's strong reaction to Hobbes's placing the sovereign above Scripture.

6. Rosse (1653) explains the distinction further:

God's word saith, that a Virgin did conceive and bear a Son; that God became a man; that our bodies shall rise again out of the dust; but our natural reason saith, this is impossible: therefore when St. Paul preached the resurrection to the Athenians, who wanted not natural reason enough, they thought he had been mad. How comes it that the Apostle saith, "The natural man understandeth not the things of God's Spirit"; And Christ tells Peter, "That flesh and blood," (that is) natural reason had not revealed the mystery of his Divinity to him, but his Father in Heaven; and that St. Paul saith, that he received not the Gospel of man, nor was he taught it, [but] by the revelation of Jesus Christ, Gal 1.12. And that he was not taught by man's wisdom, but by the Holy Ghost, I Cor 2.13. How comes it, I say, that the Scripture speaks thus in villifying natural reason, if it be the infallible word of God; yea, what need was there of any written word at all if our natural reason be that infallible word. (32–34)

Background for Rosse's criticism of Hobbes is given in Bowle 1969, 17–19, 61–71.

7. I am indebted to Hughes for his explanation of the Reformers' approach to Scripture (Hughes 1965, 21–29) which is summarized here.

8. I am indebted to Trevor-Roper's discussions of Laudism, Calvinist-Arminian controversies, and the Great Tew circle, which I draw upon in this essay.

9. I am indebted to Orr for his discussion of Chillingworth and Hooker.

10. See the argument in Hooker 1970, 1:327–36, 364–80 [Bk. II, vii, viii and Bk. III, viii].

11. See Mintz 1962 for discussion of the animosity toward Hobbes among the Cambridge Platonists such as Cudworth and More.

Chapter 7
Leviathan Chapter 32: The Biblical Prophets Are Not Trustworthy

1. For references in part 1 of *Leviathan* for Hobbes's rejection of supernatural notions concerning these phenomena, and for his naturalistic accounts of them, see: for dreams, EW III, 6–8 [90–91]; for visions, EW III, 8–10 [91–92]; for inspiration, EW III, 63–64 [140-41].

2. Hobbes's treatment of Scripture in chapter 32 refers the reader to the authority of the sovereign established by the principles of natural justice worked out in the first half of the work. This begins a pattern that occurs in chapters 33 and 34, and that is repeated through the rest of the second half of the book.

3. See the sections entitled "The Notion of God's Right" and "Why Hobbes Did Not Want to Make Absolute Power Oblige" in chapter 4.

4. See chapter 3, on the several uses of the term "oblige" in *Leviathan*.

Chapter 8
Leviathan Chapter 33: The Bible and Political Reasoning

1. "Seeing therefore I have already proved, that sovereigns in their own dominions are the sole legislators; those books are only canonical, that is, law, in every nation which are established for such by the sovereign authority" (EW III, 366 [415]). Hobbes's arguments in support of this conclusion are found in numerous places in *Leviathan*, but perhaps the most important passages relevant to this point are in chapter 17, on the generation of a commonwealth, and chapter 18, on the rights of sovereigns.

2. An example of contemporary reaction to Hobbes's argument of the extent of the supremacy of the sovereign can be found in Clarendon's *Review and Survey*:

Hobbes found it necessary to his purpose first to lessen the reverence that was accustom'd to be paid to the Scriptures themselves, and the authority thereof, before he could hope to have his interpretation hearken'd unto. . . . [Hobbes seeks] to allow them [the Scriptures] no other authority but what they receive from the Declaration of the King; so that in every Kingdom there may be several, and contrary Books of Scripture; which their Subjects must not look upon as Scripture, but as the Soveraign power declares it to be so; which is to shake or rather overthrow all the reverence and submission which we pay unto it, as the undoubted word of God. . . . [Christianity cannot be] preserved, when the Scriptures, from whence Christianity can only be prov'd and taught to the people, are to depend only for the validity thereof, upon the will, understanding, and authority of the Prince, which (with all possible submission, reverence, and resignation to that Earthly power, and which I do with all my heart acknowledge to be instituted by God himself, for the good of mankind) hath much greater dignity to it self, and more reverence due to it, then it can receive from the united Testimony and Declaration of all the Kings and Princes of the World. (Clarendon 1676, 197–99; see also Lawson 1657, 1–2, 163–64)

3. See Metzger 1965. Metzger explains that none of the fifteen books of the Apocrypha is in the Hebrew canon of the Bible, but fourteen are in the oldest Greek translation of the Old Testament, the Septuagint, completed about 285 B.C. at the request of Ptolemy II (309–247 B.C.), king of Egypt. The only book left out of the Septuagint was II Esdras. While endorsing

most of the Apocrypha as canonical, the Catholic Council of Trent (1546) was reacting against the Protestant antipathy toward the Apocrypha. Nevertheless, they denied canonical status to both books of Esdras. Metzger adds, "In the official edition of the Vulgate, published in 1592, [1 and 2 Esdras] are printed as an appendix after the New Testament, 'lest they should perish altogether' " (Metzger 1965, x, xiv–xv).

4. Smith 1954, 58–59:

[The phrase] "the Canaanite was then in the land" is no sign of post-Mosaic authorship, nor a later interpolation, as if the meaning were that the Canaanite was there at the time, but is so no longer. What really is meant is that Abram on his arrival found the country no longer in the hands of the old Semitic stock, but occupied by the Canaanites, who seem to have gained the ascendancy, not so much by conquest as by gradual and peaceful means. We gather from the Egyptian records that this had taken place not very long before Abram's time.

Alexander Rosse, Hobbes's contemporary, argued similarly that Hobbes was incorrect to infer that "the Canaanite was then in the land" must mean that Moses did not write Genesis (Rosse 1653, 34–35).

5. One scholar (Waller 1954, 103) writes concerning the issue of the authorship of the Pentateuch and Joshua, that Josh. 24:26, at the end of the book, is one of the "signature" passages which attribute biblical books to their authors. Another such passage is Deut. 31:24–27, which concerns Moses' authorship. These signature passages are each soon followed in the biblical narrative by accounts of the death of the writer: the Joshua passage is followed by the narrative of Joshua's death in 24:29–33; the story of the death of Moses is found in Deuteronomy 33 and 34. Both these death narratives are plainly the work of another than the one whose death is related, but the presence of such an addition to the works in no way need detract from the authenticity of the books, and may also help account for the presence of the "unto this day" passages in Joshua. There seems to be some tradition for accepting a limited editorial treatment regarding these passages. But, concerning the latter book, an equally plausible explanation makes Joshua himself the author of these phrases, since the last occurrence of the phrase (at 15:63) appears to refer to a time many years before Joshua's death at the age of 110. The passage in Joshua 15 treats the inability of the tribe of Judah to drive the Jebusites from Jerusalem and concludes with the words, "where they dwell unto this day." This interpretation thus makes Joshua's authorship of the phrasing plausible.

6. Richard Popkin (1982) writes,

As early as the twelfth century the Jewish scholar Ibn Ezra (1092–1167), indicated that there were some lines that weren't by Moses, because they dealt with matters after his death. Ibn Ezra did not use this to suggest any skepticism about the Bible, but rather to suggest that there might be something special in these non-Mosaic lines. (136)

7. Popkin (1982) writes,

During the outburst of Bible study in the sixteenth century, several scholars saw the difficulty in claiming Moses was the sole author. Suggestions were made that perhaps Ezra wrote some or all of the Pentateuch. From Hobbes onward, the actual denial that Moses was the author . . . was definitely a key issue in developing skepticism about revealed religion in the Jewish or Christian sense. (136–37)

8. George Lawson argued in his remarks concerning *Leviathan*, chapter 32, that such knowledge might be had, and he cited the Scriptures as his support (Lawson 1657, 160). The passage he chose was John 7:17–18: "Jesus answered them, and said, My doctrine is not mine, but his that sent me. If any man will do his will he shall *know* of the doctrine, whether it be of God, or whether I speak of myself" [my emphasis].

9. Though human beings do believe for many sorts of reasons, does this mean that they do not base their adherence to the Bible on belief? If they do not *know* (as Hobbes would have it) that the Bible is God's word, and thus cannot base their actions on such knowledge, can they not base their behavior on *belief*, regardless of the reasons for that belief? But Hobbes *asserts* that because all these reasons cannot be fitted under one general answer to the question, "Why do men believe the Scripture to be the word of God?," that belief therefore is no basis for determining where the Scriptures derive their authority. Seeing Hobbes's decided reluctance to pursue this question further, I suspect belief is not given a more considered examination because to do so would be contrary to Hobbes's naturalistic aims.

Chapter 9
Leviathan Chapter 34: Hobbes's Naturalization of God

1. Bishop John Bramhall and others of Hobbes's earliest critics discerned a pattern in all of Hobbes's exegeses which departs from orthodoxy as it aims toward transforming the God of the Bible into the God of nature:

They who deny all incorporeal substances can understand nothing by God, but either nature, (not *naturam naturantem*, that is, a real author of nature, but *naturam naturatam*, that is, the orderly concourse of natural causes, as T.H. seemeth to intimate,) or a fiction of the brain, without real being, cherished for advantage and political ends, as a profitable error, howsoever dignified with the glorious title of *the eternal cause of all things.* (EW IV, 312–13; Hobbes here quotes his opponent)

Bramhall sees Hobbes's position as either a reduction of God to natural causes or else an exploitation of a fiction for some other end—a political one.

2. I am indebted to Neve's study for my discussion of the spirit of God.

3. Neve adds, in favor of the translation of this term as *spirit of God,* "the strongest argument exists in those creation texts which date from approximately the same period: Isa. 40:13, Ps. 33:6, and Job 26:13. All of them use *ruach* not as a created element, but as a creating power." He explains that *ruach* in the first two of these three passages, "without question, cannot be translated as 'wind'," while the third, though somewhat ambiguous, should be translated as "breath" or "spirit" rather than "wind." Neve concludes, "arguments against the translation of 'wind' for *ruach elohim* in Gen. 1:2 leave as the only possibility for translation, 'spirit of God.' The *ruach elohim* is the life-giving power of God through which God works to bring into being his creation" (Neve 1972, 67–71).

4. John Whitehall, another of Hobbes's contemporaries, writes of Hobbes's argument (concerning Gen. 1:2, that motion implies body and thus God is body):

For mark the Argument, motion and place belong to Bodies, therefore nothing but a Body can have motion or place. [This] Suppose[s] . . . all things to be the same, to which one circumstance or qualification equally belongeth. But fully to answer Mr. Hobbes, motion in this place of Scripture is intended . . . the special and extraordinary operation of God's Spirit . . . upon the Waters, and not to denote God's moving from place to place as bodies do; for in that sense neither motion nor place can be attributed to God, who is every where, but in no place either circumscriptly or definitely, as Bodies are. But it follows not therefore, that God by his Spirit cannot extraordinarily act in one place more than another. (Whitehall 1679, 99–100)

Thus Whitehall agrees with his fellow critics George Lawson and Bishop Bramhall: God is something not corporeal; to these men the notion of incorporeal substance appears to be truly meaningful and not absurd, as Hobbes would have it.

5. When Hobbes asks Bramhall, "I would gladly know in what classes of entities the Bishop ranketh God?," after cornering him with only two possible options, one that favors Hobbes and the other that leaves God as nothing, Bramhall defends his own position:

Infinite being and participated being are not of the same nature. Yet to speak according to human apprehension, (apprehension and comprehension differ much: T. H. confesseth that natural reason doth dictate to us, that God is infinite, yet natural reason cannot comprehend the infiniteness of God) I place him among incorporeal substances or spirits, because he hath been pleased to place himself in that rank, *God is a Spirit*. Of which place T. H. giveth his opinion, that it is unintelligible . . . and fall[s] not under human understanding. (EW IV, 313)

Bramhall places God in another category of being entirely. He becomes "infinite being," while the world of human beings is "participated being." His point is to stress the otherness of God's existence—its complete distinction from the existence of that which is created.

6. Hobbes deals with and defends his position concerning the meaning of *spirit* in, among other places, his *Answer to Bishop Bramhall* (EW IV, 295–305); in his *Historical Narration Concerning Heresy* (EW IV, 393–94); in *Considerations upon the Reputation of Thomas Hobbes* (EW IV, 426–27; and elsewhere in *Leviathan* (EW III, 641–44 [661–64], 672–76 [689–93]).

7. Hobbes wrote,

The first principle of religion in all nations is, *that God is*, that is to say, that God really is something, and not a mere fancy; but that which is really something, is considerable alone by itself, as being *somewhere*. . . . whatsoever is real here, or there, or in any place, has dimensions, that is to say, magnitude, whether it be visible or invisible, finite or infinite, is called by all the learned a *body*. It followeth, that all real things, in that they are *somewhere*, are corporeal. (EW IV, 393–94)

8. *Castigation of Mr. Hobbes . . . Concerning Liberty and Universal Necessity* (1658) by John Bramhall, Bishop of Derry, contains an appendix entitled *The Catching of Leviathan* (1658). Bramhall's *Collected Works* appeared in Dublin in 1676; in the 1677 edition, *The Catching of Leviathan* is the third section of the third volume, pages 869–903.

9. In the conclusion of his *Answer to Bishop Bramhall*, Hobbes writes in his defense, quoting Scripture,

He accuses me first of destroying the existence of God; that is to say, he would make the world believe I were an atheist. But upon what ground? Because I say, that God is a spirit, but corporeal. But to say that, is allowed me by St. Paul, that says (I Cor. XV.44): There is a spiritual body, and there is an animal body. (EW IV, 383–84)

However, Hobbes's use of the biblical term "spiritual body" cannot be used to explain the notion that spirit is corporeal and thus God is, because the Scripture differentiates between the nature of human beings and the nature of God. St. Paul's use of the term "spiritual body" in 1 Corinthians 15 refers to human beings and is an attempt to explain the difference between human nature before and after the hoped-for resurrection. The distinction

Paul makes may be compared to the distinction between a chrysalis and a butterfly, and the discussion has to do entirely with human destiny. The term "spiritual body" in this passage, then, does nothing to advance the proposition that the "substance" of deity is material, as Hobbes would have it. This example of Hobbesian biblical exegesis represents the sort of misappropriation of Scripture that only confirmed the fears of Hobbes's contemporary critics. See also EW III, 361–63 [410–13], 375 [423]).

Chapter 10
The Purpose of the Last Half of *Leviathan*

1. It is curious that, at the apparent conclusion of his own work, which, it turns out, is but a pause between finishing and starting again, Hobbes mentions another work, also one concerning the establishment of a just political association, whose organization as a text is formed around precisely the same phenomenon—for all those familiar with Plato's *Republic* know that at the center of that work, in the fifth of the ten books, Plato, too, seems to stop, pause, and start all over again.

2. Hobbes's attack on these powerful religious elements, both priests and presbyters, is repeated in *Behemoth*, written in 1668, but not published until after his death. Hobbes places much of the blame for the English Civil War on churchmen. It is noteworthy that Hobbes's anger is not reserved for the Catholic clergy. In *Behemoth* it is quite plain that any institution claiming authority superior to that of the established civil government is to be condemned. His sentiments even in *Leviathan* ought not to be understood strictly as anti-Catholic; indeed, the emphasis on the Catholic manifestation may only be an indication of Hobbes's prudence, since his whole political theory bears out that he could not have been any less opposed to similar Protestant claims to authority in 1651, when *Leviathan* was published.

3. Hobbes . . . rejoiced . . . in the silencing of unworthy fears. . . . He came very near to proclaiming his complete emancipation, especially in the last and longest book of *Leviathan*, "Of the Kingdom of Darkness," where he piled learning upon irony, and irony upon invective, in a savage and magnificently incisive peroration. Here his governing assumption was that superstition was dangerous only when priest or presbyter fathered it. The kingdom of darkness was a confederacy of these deceivers . . . who had added the errors of Greek demonology and the vanity of Aristotelity to their own politically subversive enchantments. (Laird 1934, 236–37)

4. For a more traditional Christian view concerning the soul and the overcoming of physical death, see Augustine 1984, Books XIII, XX, XXI.

5. Concerning Hobbes's reduction of the meaning of Christ to the laws of nature, see Campodonico 1982, 114, 121–22. Campodonico writes,

Hobbes theologically justifies this position by asserting the perfect equality in the Scriptures between Christ and natural reason: "the same Christ is called the true light that lighteth every man that cometh into the world. All which are descriptions of right reason, whose dictates we have showed before, are the laws of nature" (EW II, 51). In Hobbes, the Christian event is brought to rest solely in "natural reason" of which true light is a symbol. Although Hobbes recognizes a supernatural revelation of God, in his outlook Christian faith is coherently reduced to the abstract statement, "Jesus is the Christ." All that remains then is for men to follow their natural reason as the "undoubted word of God" (EW III, 358).

6. I have argued that Hobbes does, indeed, do these things. The autonomy to the individual from all authority he does not establish himself and that might oblige him to obey law, may be seen by considering *Leviathan*, chapters 13 through 15, which I have treated in chapters 3 and 4. Hobbes's radical questioning of the Bible may be demonstrated through careful consideration of *Leviathan*, chapters 32 and 33, in my chapters 6 through 8. The naturalization of God takes place in *Leviathan*, chapter 34, the subject of my chapter 9. Together, these elements form the basis that constitutes Hobbes's unprecedented scheme of subordinating church to state.

7. Angelo Campodonico, in "Secularization in Thomas Hobbes's Anthropology" writes,

Hobbes, though never openly denying them, tries to rationalize and secularize those doctrines of Christianity which would oppose through their implications his idea of man and his positioning of faith as a matter of secondary importance. Primarily Hobbes seems to ignore the total unprecedentedness . . . incomparable to any pattern found in natural reason, peculiar to the Christian message, the "foolishness" of Christ's sacrifice of atonement. It is obvious, therefore, why Christ does not play any significant role in Hobbes's theology. (Campodonico 1982, 114ff)

8. In his famous "Introduction to *Leviathan*," Michael Oakeshott speaks of the political order as "salvation and deliverance." He writes that all political philosophy is an attempt at a type of salvation: "Each masterpiece of political philosophy springs from a new vision of the predicament, each is the glimpse of a *deliverance* or the suggestion of a remedy" [my emphasis], Oakeshott 1975, 5–7. See, too, "*Leviathan*: A Myth," Oakeshott 1975b, 150–54. Oakeshott compares Hobbes's work to the Christian story of beginnings, "the myth which no subsequent experi-

ence or reflection has succeeded in displacing from the minds of European peoples." Oakeshott also connects Hobbes's work to liberalism: "Hobbes, without being himself a liberal, had in him more of the philosophy of liberalism than most of his professed defenders" (Oakeshott 1975, 63). J. W. N. Watkins speaks of "the essence" of Hobbes's project as a turning from his predecessors, who appealed to extrahuman principles—God, God's laws, and God's punishments and rewards here and hereafter—to the resources that are within us: "Hobbes showed how men, although nature dissociates them and renders them apt to invade and destroy one another [(EW III, 113–14 [185–87])] are nevertheless able, without supernatural assistance, each proceeding under his own steam and using his own natural facilities, to build a peaceful society for themselves" (Watkins 1965, 98–99).

9. See Edward Banfield's "Present-Orientedness and Crime" (1991, 313–23), for an analysis of the social implications of a minority in a civil association whose lives are habituated to immediate self-gratification. Banfield begins his essay with a footnote reference to Hobbes.

10. See Tocqueville 1966, 442–43. Tocqueville appears to agree with Hobbes in regard to the social utility of religion. They seem to agree that without some grounding such as religion provides, the great freedom of masterlessness leads to restlessness and anxiousness, which, on a grand scale, can lead to great public disruptions, ripeness for panic, susceptibility to civil strife, and finally, openness to demagogues. Both Hobbes and Tocqueville seem to suggest that a human being cannot endure endless anxiety, searchings, and cares, and so either seeks, often desperately, for some authority to provide him with an anchor for his life or will fill his life with distractions—amusements—to take him away from thinking about his troubles and fears. In a society based on the implicit masterlessness of man, religion may still hide the truth that human beings face unlimited horizons for action—with all that this portends. Religion is so *useful* because it can activate the capacity in human beings to pause before acting in ways that may threaten peace and safety. The religion Hobbes preserves makes God the author and finisher of human autonomy, even while not disallowing a distant divine comfort, judgment, and reward. Believing in God reminds human beings that beyond the apparently limitless horizon there is yet a price to pay for their actions.

11. See Diulio 1995 for a contemporary view that scientific evidence from a variety of academic disciplines may indicate the capacity of religion to "curtail many severe socioeconomic ills," especially those related to the class of persons we have been discussing here.

12. See Lange 1881, I: sections 2 and 3; see also Smith 1976.

13. The current abortion debate in the United States, with the tension between rights-based arguments and biblical ones, reflects the fact that rights-based arguments are "untethered" to any argument concerning origins; that is, such arguments do not touch the matter of what human

beings ultimately are; these arguments are focused upon the liberty of the individual in this world and they do not ask further questions. The frustration of the biblical partisans with their opponents is a frustration with the unwillingness of the rights-based arguments to address "first causes." The biblical partisans have tried to bridge this gap by enlisting rights language themselves, but they have failed to carry the day. The divisiveness created over these matters has become apparent to all. My argument has been to stress the fundamental tension between the rights-based arguments upon which modern liberalism was founded, and the tenets of biblical faith. I have tried to show how Hobbes attempted to disguise this tension by adopting, as much as was necessary for the preservation of the peace of civil association, the forms and traditions of Christian faith.

Bibliography

All references to the Bible are from the King James Version. References to Hobbes's writings are from the *English Works of Thomas Hobbes*, edited by William Molesworth (London: John Bohn, 1839), and are cited as "EW," followed by the roman numeral volume number and the page number. Updated spelling and capitalization are Molesworth's emendations. References to *Leviathan* (EW III) are followed in brackets by page numbers from the more common edition of *Leviathan* edited by C. B. MacPherson (Harmondsworth, Middlesex: Penguin, 1968). Readers using the new edition of *Leviathan* edited by Edwin Curley (Indianapolis: Hackett, 1994) will find that volume keyed to the Molesworth edition by page numbers placed in brackets at the bottom of the right-hand page throughout the book. The second volume of the Molesworth edition of Hobbes's works (EW II) refers to his *De Cive*. The fourth volume (EW IV) contains his *Elements of Law* (1–228), *An Answer to Bishop Bramhall* (279–384), *Narration Concerning Heresy* (385–408), and *Considerations upon the Reputation, Loyalty, Manners and Religion of Thomas Hobbes* (409–40). The fifth volume (EW V) contains *The Questions Concerning Liberty, Necessity and Chance*, while in the sixth (EW VI) are *A Dialogue between a Philosopher and a Student of the Common Laws of England* and *Behemoth: The History of the Causes of the Civil War in England*.

Allen, J. W. 1941. *A History of Political Thought in the Sixteenth Century.* 2d ed. London: Methuen.

Aubrey, John. [1680] 1898. *Brief Lives.* Ed. Andrew Clark. Oxford: Clarendon Press.

Augustine. 1984. *Concerning the City of God Against the Pagans.* Trans. Henry Bettenson. Introd. John O'Meara. Harmondsworth: Penguin Books.

———. 1985. "Treatise on the Gospel of John." In *The Political Writings of St. Augustine.* Ed. Henry Paolucci. Chicago: Gateway Editions.

Banfield, Edward. 1991. *Here the People Rule.* 2d ed. Washington, D.C.: AEI Press.

Barker, Ernest. 1934. Introduction to *Natural Law and the Theory of Society, 1500–1800*. See Gierke 1934.

Barry, Brian. 1968. "Warrender and His Critics." *Philosophy* 43, no. 164:117–37.

Bellah, Robert. 1974. "Religion in America." In *American Civil Religion*. See Richey 1974.

Blake, William. 1979. *Blake's Poetry and Designs*. Eds. John Grant and Mary L. Johnson. New York: Norton Critical Editions.

Bloom, Allan. 1987. *The Closing of the American Mind*. New York: Simon and Schuster.

Boas, Marie. 1952. "The Establishment of Mechanical Philosophy." *Osiris* 10:412–541.

Bowle, John. 1969. *Hobbes and His Critics: A Study in Seventeenth Century Constitutionalism*. New York: Barnes and Noble.

Bramhall, John, Bishop of Derry. 1677. "The Catching of Leviathan." In *Collected Works*, III. Dublin.

Brandt, Frithiof. 1928. *Thomas Hobbes' Mechanical Conception of Nature*. London: Librairie Hachette.

Brinton, Crane. 1964. "Many Mansions." *American Historical Review* 69 (Jan.): 315ff.

Brown, K. C. 1962. "Hobbes's Grounds for Belief in a Deity." *Philosophy* 37, no. 142:336–44.

———, ed. 1965. *Hobbes Studies*. Cambridge: Harvard University Press.

Brown, Stuart M., Jr. 1965. "The Taylor Thesis: Some Objections." In *Hobbes Studies*. See K. C. Brown 1965.

Burns, N.T. 1972. *Christian Mortalism from Tyndale to Milton*. Cambridge: Harvard University Press.

Butler, Jon. 1990. *Awash in a Sea of Faith: Christianity and the American Republic*. Cambridge: Harvard University Press.

Campodonico, Angelo. 1982. "Secularization in Thomas Hobbes's Anthropology." In *Thomas Hobbes, His View of Man*. Ed. J. G. van der Bend. Amsterdam: Rodopi.

Carlyle, R.W. and A.J. Carlyle. 1928. *A History of Medieval Political Theory in the West*. Vol. V. New York: Barnes and Noble.

Caton, Hiram. 1985. "On the Basis of Hobbes's Political Philosophy." *Political Studies* 22, no. 4:414–31.

Chambers, Oswald. [1935] 1963. *My Utmost for His Highest*. Grand Rapids: Discovery House.

Clarendon, Edward, earl of [Edward Hyde]. 1676. *A Brief View and Survey of the Dangerous and Pernicious Errors to Church and State of Mr. Hobbes's Book, Entitled Leviathan*. Oxford: Printed at the Theater.

Curley, Edwin. 1996. "Calvin and Hobbes, or Hobbes as an orthodox Christian." *Journal of the History of Philosophy*. Forthcoming.

Dewey, John. [1918] 1974. "The Motivation of Hobbes's Political Philosophy." In *Thomas Hobbes in His Time*. See Ross, Schneider, Waldman 1974.

Diulio, John J., Jr. 1995. "The Coming of the Superpredators." *Weekly Standard* 1, no. 11 (27 Dec.): 23–28.

Doyle, Phyllis. 1927. "The Contemporary Background of Hobbes's State of Nature." *Economica* 7 (Dec.): 336–55.

Eisenach, Eldon. 1981. *Two Worlds of Liberalism: Religion and Politics in Hobbes, Locke and Mill.* Chicago: University of Chicago Press.

———. 1982. "Hobbes on Church, State, and Religion." In *History of Political Thought* 3, no. 2:222ff.

Ellicott, Charles John, ed. [1882] 1954. *Ellicott's Commentary on the Whole Bible: A Verse by Verse Explanation.* 8 vols. Grand Rapids: Zondervan.

Faulkner, Robert K. 1993. *Francis Bacon and the Project of Progress.* Lanham, Md.: Rowman & Littlefield.

Featley, Daniel. 1626. *Pelagius Redivivus, or Pelagius Raked Out of the Ashes by Arminius and his Schollers.*

Gauthier, David P. 1969. *The Logic of Leviathan: The Moral and Political Theory of Thomas Hobbes.* Oxford: Clarendon Press.

Gierke, Otto. 1934. *Natural Law and the Theory of Society, 1500–1800.* Vol. I. Cambridge: Cambridge University Press.

Glover, W. B. 1965. "God and Thomas Hobbes." In *Hobbes Studies.* See K. C. Brown 1965.

Goldsmith, M. M. 1966. *Hobbes's Science of Politics.* New York: Columbia University Press.

———. 1969. "Introduction." *The Elements of Law,* by Thomas Hobbes. Ed. Ferdinand Tonnies. London: Frank Cass.

Heath, Thomas L. ed. 1926. *The Thirteen Books of Euclid's Elements.* 2d ed. Vol. I. Cambridge: Cambridge University Press.

Herberg, Will. 1974. "American Civil Religion: What It Is and Whence It Comes." In *American Civil Religion.* See Richey 1974.

Hinnant, Charles H. 1980. *Thomas Hobbes: A Reference Guide.* Boston: G.K. Hall.

Hobbes, Thomas. [1839–1845] 1966. *The English Works.* Ed. Sir William Molesworth. 11 vols. London: John Bohn; rpt. Druck, Germany: Scientia Verlag Aalen.

———. 1968. *Leviathan.* Ed. C.B. Macpherson. Harmondsworth: Penguin Books.

———. 1969. *Behemoth or The Long Parliament.* Ed. Ferdinand Tonnies. London: Frank Cass.

———. 1969a. *The Elements of Law.* Ed. Ferdinand Tonnies. Introd. M. M. Goldsmith. London: Frank Cass.

———. 1983. *De Cive.* Ed. Howard Warrender. Oxford: Clarendon Press.

———. 1994. *Leviathan.* Ed. Edwin Curley. Indianapolis: Hackett.

Holborn, Hajo. 1959. *A History of Modern Germany: The Reformation.* Princeton: Princeton University Press.

Homer. 1990. *The Iliad.* Trans. Robert Fagles. Harmondsworth, Middlesex: Penguin Books.

Hood, F. C. 1964. *The Divine Politics of Thomas Hobbes*. Oxford: Oxford University Press.

Hooker, Richard. [1888] 1970. *Works*. 7th ed. 3 vols. Arranged by the Rev. John Keble. Introduction Isaac Walton. Rpt. New York: Burt Franklin.

Hughes, Philip. 1965. *Theology of the English Reformers*. London: Hodder and Stoughton.

Hunt, John. [1870] 1973. *Religious Thought in England From the Reformation to the End of the Last Century*. Vol. I. London: Strahan & Co. Rpt. AMS Press.

Johnson, Paul. 1974. "Hobbes's Anglican Doctrine of Salvation." In *Thomas Hobbes in His Time*. See Ross, Schneider, Waldman 1974.

Laird, John. 1934. *Hobbes*. London: Ernest Benn.

Lange, Frederick. 1881. *History of Materialism*. Vol. I. Boston: Houghton, Mifflin.

Lawson, George. 1657. *An Examination of the Political Part of Mr. Hobbs His Leviathan*. London.

Lewis, C. S. 1964. *The Discarded Image*. Cambridge: Cambridge University Press.

Lloyd, S. A. 1992. *Ideals and Interests in Hobbes's Leviathan*. Cambridge: Cambridge University Press.

Lucy, William. 1663. *Observations, Censures and Confutations of Notorious Errors in Mr. Hobbes His Leviathan*. London.

Mansfield, Harvey C., Jr. 1971. "Hobbes and the Science of Indirect Government." *APSR* 65, no. 1:97–110.

Martinich, A. P. 1992. *The Two Gods of Leviathan: Thomas Hobbes on Religion and Politics*. Cambridge: Cambridge University Press.

Maurice, F. D. 1862. "Thomas Hobbes." In *Modern Philosophy*. London: Griffen, Bohn.

———. 1872. *Moral and Political Philosophy*. New York: Scribners.

McLachlan, H. John. 1951. *Socinianism in Seventeenth Century England*. London: Oxford University Press.

Mead, Sidney E. 1963. *The Lively Experiment*. New York: Harper and Row.

———. 1977. *The Old Religion in the Brave New World: Reflections on the Relation Between Christendom and the Republic*. Berkeley: University of California Press.

Metzger, Bruce M., ed. 1965. *The Oxford Annotated Apocrypha*. New York: Oxford University Press.

Milton, John. 1931–1938. *The Works of John Milton*. Ed. Frank A. Patterson. 18 vols. New York: Columbia University Press.

Minogue, K. R. 1963. *The Liberal Mind*. New York: Random House.

———. 1974. "Parts and Wholes: Twentieth Century Interpretations of Thomas Hobbes." In *Anales de la Catedera "Francisco Suarez"* 14:77–108.

Mintz, Samuel I. 1962. *The Hunting of Leviathan: Seventeenth Century*

Reactions to the Materialism and Moral Philosophy of Thomas Hobbes. Cambridge: Cambridge University Press.

Nagel, Thomas. 1959. "Hobbes's Concept of Obligation." *Philosophical Review* 68, no. 1:68–83.

Neve, Lloyd. 1972. *The Spirit of God in the Old Testament.* Tokyo: Seibunsha.

Oakeshott, Michael. 1975. "Introduction to *Leviathan.*" In *Hobbes on Civil Association.* Oxford: Basil Blackwell.

———. 1975a. "The Moral Life in the Writings of Thomas Hobbes." In *Hobbes On Civil Association.* Oxford: Basil Blackwell.

———. 1975b. "*Leviathan:* A Myth." In *Hobbes On Civil Association.* Oxford: Basil Blackwell.

Orr, Robert. 1967. *Reason and Authority: The Thought of William Chillingworth.* Oxford: Clarendon Press.

Orwin, Clifford. 1975. "On the Sovereign Authorization." *Political Theory* 3, no. 1:26–44.

Parker, Samuel. 1681. *A Demonstration of the Divine Authority of the Laws of Nature and the Christian Religion.* London: R. Royston and R. Chriswell.

Peters, R. S., and H. Tajfel. 1957. "Hobbes and Hull—Metaphysicians of Behaviour." *British Journal for the Philosophy of Science* 8, no. 29:30–44.

Peters, Richard. 1956. *Hobbes.* Westport, Conn.: Greenwood Press.

Pieper, Josef. 1960. *Scholasticism.* New York: Pantheon Books.

Plamenatz, John. 1957. "Mr. Warrender's Hobbes." *Political Studies* 5, no. 3:295–308.

Popkin, Richard. 1982. "Hobbes and Scepticism." In *History of Philosophy in the Making: A Symposium in Honor of Professor J. D. Collins.* Ed. Linus J. Thro. Washington, D.C.: University Press of America.

Raymond, D. D. 1962. "Discussion: Obligations and Rights in Hobbes." *Philosophy* 37, no. 142:345–48.

Reedy, Gerald, S.J. 1985. *The Bible and Reason: Anglicans and Scripture in Late Seventeenth Century England.* Philadelphia: University of Pennsylvania Press.

Reventlow, Henning. 1984. *The Authority of the Bible and the Rise of the Modern World.* Philadelphia: Fortress.

Richey, Russell E., ed. 1974. *American Civil Religion.* New York: Harper and Row.

Robertson, G. C. [1886] 1971. *Hobbes.* Rpt. New York: AMS Press.

Ross, Ralph, H. W. Schneider, and T. Waldman. 1974. *Thomas Hobbes in His Time.* Minneapolis: University of Minnesota Press.

Rosse, Alexander. 1653. *Leviathan Drawn Out with a Hook or, Animadversions upon Mr. Hobbs His Leviathan.* London.

Rossiter, Clinton, ed. 1961. *The Federalist Papers.* New York: New American Library.

Schneider, Herbert. 1974. "The Piety of Hobbes." In *Thomas Hobbes In His Time*. See Ross, Schneider, and Waldman 1974.

Smith, C. U. M. 1976. *The Problem of Life*. New York: John Wiley and Sons.

Smith, R. Payne. [1882] 1954. "Genesis." In *Ellicott's Commentary on the Whole Bible: A Verse by Verse Explanation*. Vol. 1. Ed. Charles John Ellicott. Grand Rapids: Zondervan.

Steenberghen, Fernand Van. 1970. *Aristotle in the West: The Origins of Latin Aristotelianism*. Louvain: Nauwelaerts.

Strauss, Leo. [1936] 1952. *The Political Philosophy of Hobbes: Its Basis and Genesis*. Chicago: The University of Chicago Press.

———. 1953. *Natural Right in History*. Chicago: University of Chicago Press.

———. 1959. "On the Basis of Hobbes's Political Philosophy." In *What is Political Philosophy?* Westport, Conn.: Greenwood Press.

Taylor, A. E. 1908. *Thomas Hobbes*. Port Washington, N.Y.: Kennikat Press.

———. [1938] 1965. "The Ethical Doctrine of Hobbes." In *Hobbes Studies*. See K. C. Brown 1965.

Thomas Aquinas. n.d. *Treatise on Law (Summa Theologica, Questions 90–97)*. Intro. Stanley Parry. Chicago: Regnery Gateway.

Tocqueville, Alexis de. 1966. *Democracy in America*. Trans. George Lawrence. New York: Anchor Books.

Trevor-Roper, Hugh. 1988. *Catholics, Anglicans and Protestants: Seventeenth Century Essays*. Chicago: University of Chicago Press.

Troeltsch, Ernst. 1934. "Troeltsch on Natural Law and Humanity." In Appendix, *Natural Law and the Theory of Society, 1500–1800*. See Gierke 1934.

The True Effigies of the Monster of Malmesbury, or Thomas Hobbes in His Proper Colours. 1680. London.

Tulloch, John. 1874. *Rational Theology and Christian Philosophy in England in the Seventeenth Century*. 2 vols. Edinburgh: Blackwood.

Waller, C. H. [1882] 1954. "Introduction to the Book of Joshua." In *Ellicott's Commentary on the Whole Bible: A Verse by Verse Explanation*. Vol 2. Ed. Charles John Ellicott. Grand Rapids: Zondervan.

Warrender, Howard. 1957. *The Political Philosophy of Hobbes: His Theory of Obligation*. Oxford: Clarendon Press.

———. 1960. "The Place of God in Hobbes's Philosophy: A Reply to Mr. Planenatz." *Political Studies* 8, no. 1:48–57.

Watkins, J. W. N. 1965. *Hobbes's System of Ideas*. London: Hutchinson.

———. 1965a. "Philosophy and Politics in Hobbes." In *Hobbes Studies*. See K. C. Brown 1965.

White, Howard B. 1972. "Francis Bacon." In *History of Political Philosophy*. 2d ed. Eds. Leo Strauss and Joseph Cropsey. Chicago: University of Chicago Press.

Whitehall, John. 1679. *The Leviathan Found Out: Or, the Answer to Mr.*

Hobbes's Leviathan in that which my Lord of Clarendon hath past over. London: Godbid and Playford.

Whitney, Charles. 1986. *Francis Bacon and Modernity.* New Haven: Yale University Press.

Willey, Basil. 1934. *Seventeenth Century Background.* London: Chatto and Windus.

Williams, J. Paul. 1951. *What Americans Believe and How They Worship.* New York: Harper and Row.

Willms, Bernard. 1982. "Tendencies in Recent Hobbes Research." In *Thomas Hobbes: His View of Man.* Ed. J. G. van der Bend. Amsterdam: Rodopi.

Wright, George. 1991. "Introduction, 1668 Appendix to *Leviathan.*" *Interpretation* 18, no. 3:323–47.

Zagorin, Perez. 1985. "Clarendon and Hobbes." In *Journal of Modern History* 57, no. 4:593–616.

Index

abortion, 257n13
Abraham, 87
account of the whole, 205; need for, 13; slighted by Hobbes's science of natural justice, 234
Adam, 108
Allen, J. W., 123
ambiguity: allowed Hobbes to seem not to depart from the tenets of Christian faith, 63; avoidance of necessary to philosophy, 188; hides the dimunition of the biblical role of Christ, 233; and Hobbes's use of the notion of incomprehensibility in *Leviathan*, 199–200; intentionally employed in *Leviathan*, 18, 20, 76, 111, 156; likened to a diaphanous veil covering Hobbes's project, 36–38; used to invite traditional theistic interpretations, 81–83, 84
America, 257n13; in Abraham Cowley's poem, 10; Hobbes's teachings flourish in, xi; Hobbes's view of the divine manifested in, 239n1, 241n7; tension between natural rights and revealed religion not evident in, 15
American Constitution, xi
amusements, 230, 237, 257n10

ancients, 203; modern superiority over, 92, 93–94
Andrewes, Lancelot, 125
Anglican(s), 39, 127, 158; Hobbes considered as orthodox, 22, 29
Anglican Church, 17, 29, 122, 125, 130–31
Anglicanism, 132; of Archbishop Laud, 241n6; and Hobbes, 130
approval: human need for as check to self-indulgence, 230
Aquinas, Saint Thomas, 25, 102; and conscience as "the law of righteousness," 106, 111. *See also* Thomistic natural law tradition
Aristotelianism, 185–86, 189, 255n3
Aristotle, 203, 225, 232; *Ethics* of as a form of dogmatic learning and a threat to political order, 101; inveighed against by Luther, 121; metaphysics and physics of as source of diseases of commonwealth, 185, 187, 192–93; the need to free and lead people away from, 19, 23, 211; reasons for appropriation of by Christianity, 198; and substance, 186–89; "vain philosophy" of, 188
Arminianism, 122–23, 125–26
Arminius, 122, 125

267

sociation, 229–31; as chief concern of the exercise of natural rights, 7; as the foundation for politics, 208; of God, 112; Hobbes's desire to be free of, 233; multiplies with opinions about vital matters, 117; need for, and government of by Leviathan, 227-28; and obligation (*see* obligation, role of fear in); religion created out of, 18, 209; wisdom of biblical and Christian views contrasted, 5–6
fear of violent death at the hands of men, 102, 247n2; as basis for civil society, 3, 10; compared with fear of what lies beyond death, 204–5, 208, 228–29; supplants fear of God as foremost human interest, 37
Featly, Daniel, 122
freedom (liberty): as absence of obligation, 8; as bedrock upon which civil association is first generated, 113-14; as cause of war, 49; defined, 4, 5, 44–45; extent of in state of nature, 61; and liberty synonymous in *Leviathan*, 239n2; limited by self-interest and not God in state of nature, 50–52, 109–10; how limited in Hobbes's political thought, 44-61; and natural right, 244n6; not originally limited to self-defense in state of nature, 47–51; and obligation, 74–75; of sovereign, 135; in state of nature, 9, 51

Galatians, epistle to the: and Hobbes's "marks of true prophecy," 150–51
Galileo, 126
Gassendi, Pierre, 126
Genesis, book of, 106, 110; Hobbes's exegesis of "spirit of God" in,

193–95; story of Jacob, Rachel, and Laban in, 224–25
geometry, 91–100, 102, 104, 126, 131, 233
Gierke, Otto, 67
glory, 42
Glover, W. B., 39
God: as author of human autonomy for Hobbes, 257n10; Blake's picture of, 98–99; as body or matter, 194, 196, 198, 254n7, 254n9; danger of faith in biblical, 87–88; dethroned by natural rights, 2; dethroned by sovereignty of man in *Leviathan*, 37; as endower of natural rights of man, 1–2, 182, 239n1; fear of offending through obedience to civil power, 14; Hobbes's view of, 87–89, 202; how allied with civil power by Hobbes's teaching, 222; incomprehensibility of in Hobbes's teachings, 199–202; and incorporeal substance, 253n4; as invention of human anxiety, 5, 209, 240n3; and mechanistic materialism, 240n5; mysterious "otherness" contrasted with the naturalizing of, 194–95, 196, 253n5; of nature, 40, 239n1, 246n12, 252n1; necessity of to Hobbes's theory (*See* Warrender, Howard, and acceptance of Hobbes's equation, etc.); no longer man's master, 4; no knowledge of possible through reason alone for Hobbes, 85, 124, 240n3, 247n15; and obligation (*see* obligation); as portrayed in arguments of *Leviathan*, 244n4
Golden Rule, 70, 243n1
good and evil, 131
Gospel: and civil obedience, 145; and Saint Paul, 151; story of

Jeremiah, xii
Job, 244n4; not an example of Hobbesian man, 109
Job, book of, 43, 109
John, Saint, the apostle, 110, 171
1 John, epistle of, 110–11
Johnson, Paul J., 28–30, 32, 86, 122, 126–27, 248n3
Joshua: as author of last chapter of Deuteronomy, 159
Joshua, book of: and authorship of the books of Scripture, 251n5; and the meaning of the biblical phrase "unto this day," 160–62
justice, 91

"Kingdom of Darkness," 255n3
kingdom of God, 225; naturalizing of, 232; as a political issue, 212; as threat to worldly peace, and Hobbesian reinterpretation of, compared, 220–22
1 Kings, book of: two stories discussed from, 137–40
knowledge: of God not possible by means of unassisted reason, 5; true only constituted by science, 232–33

La Peyrere, Isaac, 161, 162
Lange, Frederick, 22–24, 36, 248n3
language: abuse of, and Aristotelianism, 186
Laodicea, Council of, 158, 164–65, 166
Laud, Archbishop William, 122, 125, 127
law, 44, 45, 57; and the authority of the sovereign, 156; how the Scriptures are made into, 178–80; implies a lawgiver, 65
Lawson, George, 129, 173–74, 181–82, 251n8, 253n4; criticism of Hobbes's exaltation of peace,

213–14; on Hobbes's placing Scripture interpretation in hands of sovereign, 120; on Hobbes's use of the term "spirit," 195
learning: dogmatic, 89–91, 101–2; mathematical, 89–91, 95, 96–97, 101–2, 247n1
Leviathan: chapter 1 discussed, 240n5; chapter 32, first paragraphs of analyzed, 114–20, 248n2; chapters 1–12, meaning of, 11–12; compared to the Christian story of salvation, 256n8; comprehensiveness of considered proof of Hobbes's genuine faith, 23; geometry and part 1 of, 95–96; and the goals of human existence, 169; and immortality of the soul, 214–15, 216; as the "natural word of God," 118–19; and the necessity of religion for the preservation of commonwealth, 226–29; preservation of as a kind of salvation, 223–24; Review and Conclusion of, 19; as title, 43; two gods of, 75
Leviathan, first half: summarized as "political reason," 158; summarized as "principles of natural reason," 113–14; themes of, 97–98, 247n3
Leviathan, kinds of readers: characteristics of Hobbes's principal audience, 68, 204, 207, 225; and Hobbes's intentions toward the largest part of his audience, 37, 63–64, 140–41, 176, 236–37; and the inclination to view Hobbes as a theist, 29, 30, 241n3; three general categories, 17–18, 232; the unprepared modern reader, 153
Leviathan, second half: meaning of, 14, 201; principles of natural rea-

Index

98; betrothed to Hobbes's reinterpretation of Christianity, 229;
challenged by dogmatic learning,
100–101; founded on idea that
human beings possess natural
rights, 37; implications of, 233–
38; importance of religion to,
xiii; and support of by novel biblical interpretation, 143–44, 147,
154; synonymous with "natural
word of God" or "political reasoning," 140, 247n3; and transcendence, 205
secular/secularization, 33, 47, 209,
228
self-gratification: social implications of persons whose lives are
characterized by, 229–31, 256n9
self-preservation: and anticipatory
action, 42, 49–50; as fall-back position taken by human freedom,
11; as guiding passion of science,
247n2; Hobbesian principles of in
tension with teachings of Christianity, 109–46, 178, 223–24; and
natural law, 65; not easily made
into the basis for political life, 3;
principles of veiled by Hobbes's
appropriation of the Bible, 226–
29, 237; and the sovereign, 135
sense, 189–90, 192–93
Sermon on the Mount, 243n1
Shklar, Judith, xiv
Simon, Richard, 161, 162
sin, 43, 170, 222–23; absent in state
of nature, 8; Saint Paul and
Hobbes compared concerning,
106–11
skepticism: and biblical interpretation in *Leviathan*, 217; Chillingworth and Hobbes compared concerning, 130; as crisis of Hobbes's
day, 127–29; did not blind

Hobbes to assistance religion
could give to political science,
237; discounted in Hobbes's
work by segregating matters of
faith from reason, 36; encouraged
by denial of Moses' authorship of
Pentateuch, 251n7; engendered
by quarreling over questions of
faith, 167; about human capacity
to know, 124; responsible for
Hobbes's conclusions about
Christianity, 126; and the trustworthiness of Scripture, 136,
161–62, 164, 234; underlies
Hobbes's embrace of geometry,
92
Socinianism, 125–27
soul: Aristotle's relationship to the
Christian view of, 187. *See also*
immortality of the soul
sovereign: authority of and Hobbes's
use of Epistle to the Galatians,
151; authority of and prophecy,
134, 141–54; authority of superior to that of church, 148,
165–66, 184, 200, 221–22, 255–
56n6; freedom from obligation of,
74–75, 147–48; and the frontispiece of *Leviathan*, 135; justified
by both the natural and revealed
word of God, 134; *Leviathan* as a
handbook for, 203–4; to be as
Moses, 144, 147, 148; and the
power of punishments and rewards, 218; prudence and the
limits of the power of, 134–35,
148; Scripture made authoritative by authority of, 120, 140,
155–59, 175–82, 249–50n1; as
sole legitimate interpreter of divine will and Scripture, 118–20,
134–35, 137, 144, 147, 200; as
ultimately serving natural rights,
119–20, 140, 147–48, 248n4

speech, 95, 188
Spinoza, Benedict, 161, 162
spirit of God: arguments against
naturalizing, 195–99, 252n3; criticism of Hobbes's contemporaries concerning his teaching of,
195–99; Hobbes's teaching concerning, 192–99, 253n6; and
Hobbes's use of the notion of incomprehensibility, 201; and materialism, 31; meaning of in
Scripture, 191–95
state of nature: and the Bible, 105–6;
characterized by complete freedom from law, 41; civil war as,
182; defined, 8–10; equality in,
41; extent of liberty in, 51; as
first axiom of Hobbesian political
science, 98, 100, 102–3, 113; as
foundation of Hobbes's political
thought, 12, 112; founded apparently on natural science in *Leviathan*, 11; and God, 71–72; as a
hell to be saved from, 228; hidden
from human beings by law and
custom, 10; history of, 243n7; as
Hobbes's discovery, 10; and
Hobbes's view of man, 206; and
natural, as opposed to supernatural, genesis of man, 99; and natural law, 57–58; restraints to
human passions in, 6
Strauss, Leo, 4, 24
substance, 189–90. *See also* incorporeal substance

Taylor, A. E., 24–25, 31–32, 35,
242n1, 246n11
Tertullian, 195, 198
theology: of English Reformers,
121–22; of the Enlightenment,
246n12; of Hobbes, 229, 236–37;
of Hobbes's contemporaries,
120–31; natural, 40; Reformation, 241n6

Thomistic natural law tradition: associated with Hobbes by some
modern readers, 36; transformed
and secularized by Hobbes, 47,
64–65
Tocqueville, Alexis de, 257n10
transcendence, 3, 192; addressed
only for the sake of secular security, 208; the need to address, 205,
207, 226–29; and rights, 237;
slighted by Hobbes, 169
Trevor-Roper, Hugh, 126, 127, 128,
249n8
truth: capacity of human beings to
know, 130; constituted by right
use of names, 188; generated by
consent, 103–4; and reason, 99–
100; twofold doctrine of, 23, 30,
36
Tyndale, William, 121–22, 147, 148;
and immortality of the soul, 215,
216

Unitarianism, 125
universities: danger of Aristotle's
teachings in, 189; and readers of
Leviathan, 225; training should
include *Leviathan*, 19
Urizen, 247n4

"vain philosophy," 188
virtue, 207, 208

war: and state of nature, 43, 48–49
Warrender, Howard, 38, 63, 64, 207;
and acceptance of Hobbes's equation of the word of God and the
laws of nature, 68–69, 76–80; and
failure to understand Hobbes's
project, 246–47n12; and God,
242n5, 243n3, 245n9; importance
to Hobbes studies, 40–41; mistaken assumptions of, 47, 59,
80–85, 244n7; as model for one
group of the Hobbes-as-theist

Index

About the Author

Paul D. Cooke is visiting assistant professor in the Honors College and the Department of Political Science at the University of Houston. He received his Ph.D. in 1991 from Harvard University, where he was a Jacob Javits-National Graduate Fellow.